Telling It Like It Was

Telling It Like It Was

My First Quarter Century

Lloyd Root

CROWN RESOURCES

San Francisco   California

CROWN RESOURCES
San Francisco, CA

First Edition
Book and cover design by Chloe Rounsley

ISBN-13: 978-0-615-33376-2

This Book is dedicated to

my father Lloyd
my mother Elvira

and

my grandmother
Marie Etchebarren Yparraguirre

with love and gratitude

Chapters

My First Quarter Century

Chapter 1

Coming to California
Our Family's Story

San Francisco in the 1920s was an exciting place for a young boy to grow up, especially because we were 'dual citizens' of sorts. My family lived both in the bustling City, as well as the rural ranch and farmlands of Grass Valley. My father worked nearby running a gold mine in the scenic foothills of the Sierra Mountains. This made for a unique and eventful childhood. Even at a fairly young age, it felt like the best of both worlds to me.

It was also my good fortune to have wonderful and supportive parents and relatives, many of whom had great influence – especially those on the Basque side of the family – on my beliefs and values. They led active, interesting lives and encouraged me to do the same. But of course, the family saga began long before I was born, so that's where I'll begin.

THE ROOTS
My father's great grandparents were **Jeremiah Root** and **Emiline Root**. Jeremiah was born in 1802 in Vermont, and Emiline was born in Livonia, New York. They lived in Ohio until the early days of the Gold Rush in 1849. Intrigued by the tales of "gold in those hills," they set off for California in a covered wagon to seek their fortune. Their 13-year-old son, **John F. Root**, born in Ohio on February 29, 1836, (and who would later become my great grandfather), made the trip with them, walking behind the wagon most of the way.

The Roots spent much of that spring and summer traveling. It was a challenging journey for them, no doubt, just as it was for nearly 150,000 other gold seekers ('49ers') who made the long trek West. Hardships were many and quite a few lives were lost along the way. Wagon trains traveled not only through treacherous weather conditions, but through treacherous territory as well.

When the Root family arrived in Greenwood, California on August 20, 1849, they met John Greenwood, an Indian scout and fur trader (who was the half-Indian son of the famous mountain man Caleb Greenwood). From him, they heard the story about how his Indian heritage had helped secure his family's safe passage:

When Caleb and his oldest sons, Britton and John, first came to California in 1844, their wagon train encountered Chief Truckee of the Paiute Indian tribe along the way. But rather than hinder them – or worse – the Chief and his party showed Caleb's wagon train the way over the mountains now called Donner Summit. Three years later, Caleb organized a rescue expedition to bring the surviving members of the Donner Party, who had been snowbound at Truckee Lake, to safety at Sutter's Fort. His sons John and Britton Greenwood were part of the rescue party.

Although the town of Greenwood was originally little more than a trading post near an Indian settlement called "Long Valley," by the time Jeremiah, Emiline and John Root arrived in 1849, it looked like a good place to settle down. John Greenwood was the owner of the local hotel and both Jeremiah and Emiline worked there for a time.

My great grandfather, **John F. Root**, spent the remainder of his teen years in Greenwood, however, with a new stepmother after his father married his second wife, Sophronina, in 1852.

John Root was involved in mining and prospecting in El Dorado County in California and in Nevada, mostly in ledge and placer mining (in streams and riverbeds), rather than underground. While successful during his early years in Nevada, he probably lost most of his savings – like so many miners did – when the value of silver sharply declined.

That may have been why he moved and established a home and farm in Santa Rosa, California. In any case, that was where he met and fell in love with Annie M. Culp, born on October 16, 1838 in Pennsylvania, to a family that migrated to California in 1852.

John and Annie were married in 1857 and had five children; three boys and two girls. The first son, (Samuel) Franklin Root, was born November 19, 1857, followed by John Boyce Root on September 28, 1859, and my grandfather **George Washington Root**, born on September 9, 1862, in Santa Rosa. Their first daughter, (Etta) Maud Root, was born on February 20, 1866, followed by (Ada) Mabel Root, born March 9, 1876.

My great grandfather, John Root, is the handsome man standing in the back row (on the right), and is the only one without a beard!

My grandfather George worked on his family's farm as a young man, and later had an interest in a hotel in Elvina with his partner, G. W. Culp, but sold it in early 1887.

His parents, John and Annie, lived in San Francisco for a time, where John was employed as the head wharfinger (overseeing goods delivered to the wharf) on the San Francisco docks. But by 1901, they had moved to Lafayette, California, so they missed being directly involved in the 1906 earthquake. John and Annie remained on their 7-acre farm in Lafayette[1] for the rest of their days, and were eventually buried (along with their son John Boyce) in a small cemetery on the south eastern side of town.

As for George's grandparents, Jeremiah and Sophronina, they made their home in Hollister for the rest of their lives and were laid to rest there. Sophronina died on March 18, 1888, and Jeremiah followed her ten years later in 1898. My great, great grandfather Jeremiah was the first in a long line of relatives who lived to such an old age. He lived to be 96 years old at a time when the average lifespan was several decades less.

My grandfather, George Washington Root, frequently referred to as "George Washington" (or simply "Wash"), had some information published about his life "as a pioneer" in a historical volume entitled, *History of Placer and Nevada Counties, California*. According to his biographical entries, he went to grammar school in Santa Rosa and completed his formal education there by the age of 12. It states that he left school at that point, went to work in mines in Grass Valley, and that he spent his life working in mines from age 12 on, gaining experience in every level of mining, as well as later prospecting in both Mexico and Alaska.

Since books were always an important part of my life, I read this one from time to time during my childhood. It was of particular interest since it included information about several members of my family. Because my grandfather contributed his

[1] After her parents died, Mabel, the only living child, inherited the homestead in Lafayette.

version to the book, I had no reason to doubt it. However, when I recently did research and reviewed the government census reports from that time period, something was a little odd. While there was confirmation of some of the details I had about his life, there were also some idiosyncrasies with regard to him being a miner "all his life."

The census lists George Washington Root as living in San Antonio Township, Monterey County, with his parents as a 7-year-old in 1870. The 1880 census reports him as 18 years old and working on his father's farm in San Antonio County, which later became part of San Benito County. Reports also indicate he was working in a hotel in San Benito in 1887. In fact, an article in the local newspaper, the *Hollister Free Lance,* specifically states he sold his interest in the small hotel in Elvina, California, (also in San Benito County) where his father had a farm in January, 1887, and that he intended to go into the stock business.

The records go on to state that he married his wife, Minnie Johnson, in 1888, moved to San Francisco in 1893, and was employed as a wharfinger in San Francisco. Following that, he got a job as the Clerk of the Supreme Court for several years. This coincides with the information I have about my grand-father's professional life. He obviously was a successful man and I'm sure his reputation of having a "gift for gab" didn't hurt. But so much for having "always been in the mining business."

The details about my grandmother, **Minnie Johnson,** are firsthand since she was actively involved in my life. She was born in the Santa Rosa area on July 10, 1870. Her parents came to California from the Midwest and were ranchers in the Hollister region at the time she married my grandfather, George Washington Root, in September of 1888 in San Benito, California. They had three children; two girls, Gertrude, born in 1888, and Hazel, born in 1889, followed by my father, **Lloyd Root.** He was born on April 4, 1891 near Hollister, California.

His oldest sister, Gertrude, however, died when she was 3-1/2 and Lloyd was only 1 year old. Needless to say, my grandmother Minnie was devastated. But losing Gertrude was just the first tragedy; the next came nine years later.

In 1893, two years after Lloyd's birth, my grandfather George moved the family to San Francisco and was employed by the City of San Francisco working on the wharf (as referenced in the census report). He did this for four years and then obtained a job as the Clerk of the Supreme Court of California, where he worked for another four years. However, early in 1900, George deserted his wife and children.

Left in San Francisco on her own with two young children, my grandmother Minnie took Hazel and Lloyd and moved to Berkeley in 1900 to live with her sister. This meant that in addition to caring for her children, she was forced to work as well. But at least, she was able to be near young Hazel and Lloyd since her sister ran a dressmaking business out of her home. In those days, women either made their own dresses or bought them from other individual seamstresses, so my grandmother helped her in this profession.

My grandmother Minnie filed a decree of desertion on March 31, 1900, (signed by Judge Murasky of San Francisco), but oddly, the divorce – or perhaps not so oddly given my grandfather's background in the court system – was not awarded until 1903. In fact, the *Hollister Free Lance* newspaper in San Benito County, reported on May 19th, "These records were concealed in the County Clerk's office and it did not reach the public until yesterday."

The article went on to note that George Washington Root had formerly been the Clerk of the Supreme Court at that time, which substantiates the suggestion that George may have had a hand in their mysterious 3-year-long suppression.

In conclusion, the *Hollister Free Lance* reported, "Of three generations of the Root family conspicuous in the mining industry of the far West, George W. Root of San Francisco represents a splendid example of the courage, persistence and will to succeed that made such characters memorable in history. The representative of the third generation is the present State Mineralogist of California, Lloyd L. Root, officially a resident of Sacramento, but also with offices in the Ferry Building at San Francisco." [They got this last part wrong; he was a resident of San Francisco, but with a second office in Sacramento, which he used only occasionally when he was there].

More about my grandfather George "Wash" Root follows, but in his later years, he pretty much dropped out of sight – it could be said he was conspicuous by his absence – though a 1900 census notes he was living in San Francisco without a wife or children. However, the 1910 census states that he was living in San Francisco with his wife, Emma (his second wife).

In any case, back in 1900, when George deserted his family, he left my father – who was only 9 years old at the time– without a father in his life. As time would show, this was hard on Lloyd, especially when he reached his teens. But before we move on, let's look at the Basque side of the family.

The YPARRAGUIRRES

My Basque grandfather, **Juan Francisco Yparraguirre,** on my mother's side of the family, was born on May 26, 1851, in Etxalar, Navarra, located in the northern part of Spain. (Etxalar[2], by the way, is the Basque word for "ancestral homeland.")

---

[2] TX" is a compound letter – there are seven of these compound letters in the Basque language. There is no "c" in the Basque alphabet and "tx" is pronounced like the first part (ch) of "chocolate." So Etxalar is prounounced as "Echalar," and it is also the Spanish spelling of the town.

Etxalar was a tiny town, in a small valley surrounded by hills, near the French border. Cows, sheep, and goats grazed up into the hills until winter. Most farms also had chickens, pigs, and horses as well. The animals lived in the barn, which was literally the first floor of the family home; the family lived on the second and third floors.

The houses were made of stone and wood, and there were little lean-to buildings up on the higher hillsides where the young men lived while caring for the grazing animals in the summertime. Small streams from the hills ran through the middle of town.

Etxalar was – and remains today – a very neat and charming town with a small church, a small hotel, and two bars.

Juan Francisco was the oldest of his family, and as such, he had a modest education provided by the church. When he was just 20 years old, Juan set sail for America, probably because he didn't want to get caught up in the local wars in Spain. A smart and ambitious young man, he was also eager to seek his fortune in the new "land of opportunity" he had heard so much about.

His ship sailed around the bottom of South America and up the coast, and reached San Diego in 1871. His job onboard was to care for a herd of breeding bulls destined for a major stock breeding company, Miller & Lux, in California.

After his sea voyage, Juan Francisco remained in California. He found work as a sheepherder for a successful rancher and landowner named Juan Etcheverry, driving sheep from San Diego north and inland several hundred miles to Tres Pinos (near Hollister). At that time, it was common practice for a Basque rancher to employ a Basque herder to move his sheep through the vast area from San Diego to the Central Valley.

Typically sheepherders like my grandfather were paid $25 to $30 per month, which included food, and sometimes a rather unusual fringe benefit; a share of the stock. Since additional lambs were born during the course of the year-long trip, naturally the size of the herd increased. At the end of the year, the herder could take his pay – or part of his pay – in lambs rather than money, if he so chose. This meant that by the herder's second trip (and subsequent ones) delivering sheep to the Central Valley, some of the sheep in the herd might be his own.

That was the choice Juan Francisco made. After four years of delivering sheep to Juan Etcheverry, my grandfather had enough money from the sale of his herd to go into business for himself. He and a Basque associate, Matias Jaurequi, purchased a small Basque ethnic hotel and boarding house in San Francisco called the HOTEL VASCO, (*Vasco* means Basque in Spanish), located on the west side of Powell Street near the Broadway intersection.

Juan really took to the business, made it work, and prospered. The hotel was a lively, jovial place with music and entertainment. Sometimes even Juan Francisco, himself, would sing. And by the time he proposed marriage to my grandmother, **Marie Etchebarren**, Juan Francisco had assumed full ownership of the HOTEL VASCO. Thus, in true immigrant spirit, the young Basque sheepherder from Spain became the proud proprietor of his own successful hotel.

Speaking of which, it's interesting to note, that during my grandfather's sheepherding days, even though the area was so vast, the total California population was only 560,000 people. So, much of the time he drove his sheep through largely uninhabited and undeveloped parts of the state. At one point, he and his herd camped on the same land in Pasadena where the legendary Huntington Hotel stands today.

Before picking up the tale from the time Juan Francisco married my special grandmother Marie, here's the rest of my grandfather's story. He, of all my ancestors, had a particularly profound impact on our family's legacy.

Juan Francisco was not only the oldest sibling, but also the first born son in his family, an important distinction in his culture. He had three younger brothers and three younger sisters. His first brother was Leon, the second was Pablo, and Francisco was the youngest. His sisters were Maria Agustina Juana, Maria Cruz, and Manuela Josephine.

Portrait of Juan Francisco Yparraguirre

After establishing himself in California, Juan Francisco helped each of his brothers and two of his sisters to come to the United States as well; Leon was the first in 1874 or 1875, (he worked for Juan at the HOTEL VASCO), followed by Pablo, and then Maria Cruz and Manuela Josephine, who came over between 1878 and 1880. Francisco was last to arrive. He was about 13 years old at the time and worked with Pablo in sheep ranching areas in California and Nevada. Later they joined together to run their own small spread of sheep in the Tuscarora area in Nevada.

Only Juan Francisco's oldest sister, Maria Agustina Juana, remained in Etxalar. When she got married in 1877, it was her husband, Padro Martin Sansinena, who inherited the Yparraguirre family home. According to Spanish law at that time, the oldest male child inherited everything, leaving all of the younger members without property. However, if that individual was no longer in the country, the second, third or even fourth male could be eligible to take over the property. Since all of Juan's brothers and his two younger sisters were no longer in Spain when Maria Agustina got married, the inheritance went to her husband. This is why there is no longer a home in Etxalar under the Yparraguirre family name.

Maria Cruz Yparraguirre married a Basque rancher from the Riverside area named Charles Garat. They had one child, Joseph, born September 2, 1890 in San Diego, California. Juan's youngest sister, Manuela Josephine, married Michael Sehabiaque, a baker, in Tres Pinos. They later moved to San Francisco, started a small bakery, and had one daughter named Marie.

Around 1889, Leon, who was married with three children by then, (all born in San Francisco) purchased the small Tres Pinos hotel from John Etcheverry. Then in 1901, Juan Francisco joined with his two youngest brothers, Pablo and Francisco in purchasing a 3,200-acre ranch in Nevada near the California border, known as the **Sweetwater Ranch**. The fourth partner was Juan's friend John Arambide, who owned the Arambide quick silver mine in Mendota, California. The younger brothers brought their sheep from the Tuscarora area as their contribution to the partnership, and my grandfather–along with John Arambide–contributed on the financial side. According to the title records, the purchase price was $8,000 in gold coins.

But let's get back to Juan Francisco's very first hotel, the HOTEL VASCO in San Francisco, and my grandmother Marie Etchebarren's part of the story.

My grandmother, **Marie Etchebarren**, was born on May 5, 1859, in a very small village called Urepel, in Baigorry, France. Urepel is the Basque word for "warm water," as there are warm springs in that area. She and her family lived at the end of the road on the edge of the village where the farmland began. Her mother was Marie Erreca and her father was Pierre Etchebarren. I know that she had a sister and a brother. (The sister eventually went to Argentina, and the brother came to California.)

When Marie was just 21 years old, she left the French Basque country – on foot, no less – for the first several miles. Then she traveled by boat from Bayonne to New York, where she caught a train to San Francisco, and for the last leg of the journey, she rode a bus to Tres Pinos. She was greeted there by her aunt, Mary, and John (Juan) Indart, (her aunt's husband), and their two teenage children. Marie's job was to be their housekeeper, and presumably their cook.

Juan Indart had come to California in 1851 during the Gold Rush and with his gold findings was able to purchase a share in a partnership with two other French Basques, Juan Iribarri and Juan Etcheverry. They bought one-third of a Spanish land grant that had previously been divided into several large ranches. Their new ranch, the Sentinella Ranch, (commonly known as the *Ranch of the Three John's*[3]), was located in the San Joaquin valley, between Fresno and Stockton. Juan Indart and my grandmother's aunt, Mary, were married in 1863 and lived on the Sentinella Ranch until the partnership split up in 1865.

At that point, they moved to Tres Pinos and purchased a substantial ranch there. Juan Etcheverry, who had previously moved to Tres Pinos, purchased property there, and as you will recall, employed my grandfather as a sheepherder (shortly after Juan Francisco arrived in the United States). Etcheverry also built a small hotel on his ranch, next to the Southern Pacific railroad depot, where the line ended. This depot was utilized for shipping farm produce to San Francisco. Juan Etcheverry may

[3] Name of ranch from *Home Away from Home* by Jeronima Echeverria, University of Nevada Press, 1999.

also have been instrumental in helping my grandfather Juan Francisco obtain his hotel in San Francisco.

In any case, once again Marie found that living on a ranch and the farm life was not for her; nor was it her concept of a good life. Having come from a very small village in the French Basque country, she had always wanted to live in a city environment. That had been her goal when she left France, so after working for three years for her aunt and uncle, she decided to move to San Francisco.

Marie was able to find a job in a French laundry in the heart of what was known as the French Quarter in San Francisco. There was a fairly large settlement of French people in San Francisco at that time, particularly in the downtown area near the French Catholic Church, located on Bush Street between Stockton and Grant Avenue. The church overlooked a French settlement that consisted of businesses, offices, stores, residences, and bakeries. There was a French-American bank, the City of Paris department store, as well as various restaurants, laundries, and hotels catering to the French. But the French Catholic Church was the central hub of the French Quarter.

On the other hand, this neighborhood, like most of the other ethnic neighborhoods in the city, also had its share of more "earthy" types of establishments. There were several well-known bordellos located nearby on Maiden Lane that did a brisk business. Although the charming two-block-long alley/ street named Maiden Lane still exists, (right near Union Square), the old-time activity was stopped long ago.

What didn't stop in the 1850s was the flow of people into the Golden State. There had been some immigration of French into California prior to the gold rush period, but immigration quickly accelerated when the big news of "striking gold" reached Europe and South America in 1849. Financially cooperative French groups were organized, quickly outfitted, and set sail to California. Some were successful, some were not.

After the initial river and stream gold collection fell off, large American and English companies organized hard rock mining and massive hydraulic placer mines in the Mother Lode country. However, these hydraulic methods were so destructive that the California State Legislature found it necessary to stop that type of gold collection. [To my knowledge, this was one of the first environmental laws passed.] Since all the debris was carried down from the hills, it entered into the rivers and valleys, and was utterly ruining the farmlands. Even today, over a hundred years after this type of mining was stopped, vast areas of damage are still visible in the Sierras.

Hard rock mining required a knowledgeable group of miners. Many Cornish miners were brought over from England because they had experience in underground mining. They had to know how and where to dig in order to utilize dynamite. They also had to know what working underground encompassed, including dangers of cave-ins and falling rock. They had to understand how to follow the vein that was being pursued, and if they couldn't do any of that. . . they could always get a job being a farmer.

After it was no longer profitable for some of the individual French miners to make a living, they reverted to establishing other kinds of businesses in San Francisco, just as my grandfather Juan Francisco did with the HOTEL VASCO. As it turned out, even though he and his future wife – my grandmother Marie – both lived in San Francisco during the same time period, they didn't meet until they were both back in Tres Pinos. He was there visiting Juan Etcheverry at the same time Marie was visiting her Aunt Mary Indart. The rest, as they say, is history.

Not long afterward, on July 6, 1886 to be precise, they got married in San Francisco at the French Catholic Church. They worked together running the popular HOTEL VASCO, lived across the street in a Victorian flat [where the firehouse stands today], and soon started a family.

My dear mother, **Elvira Yparraguirre**, was born on January 21, 1893. She was the third of five chidren, all born at home (as was typical at that time) and raised in that house, except for the oldest, and only, son who died in childbirth.

The first of the four daughters was Elena Marie, born in 1890, the next was my mother Elvira Lucille, followed by Catharine Cecilia in 1895, and the last was Emilie Marga-ret, born in 1897. As you can see, the first two girls were

Wedding portrait of my Basque grandparents Juan and Marie

given Spanish first names, and French middle names. However, the last two daughters both had two French names. Juan Francisco, it seems, had lost the battle on Spanish versus French names, and after four daughters, he gave up having any more children. But theirs was a close, happy family. The girls thought the world of him.

When my mother was 4 years old, she was sent to stay for the summer with a couple who lived on a ranch in Los Banos so she could learn how to speak Basque. "Every day," she told me, "they would take a nap. And I'd go to the front porch to just sit and look at the animals. I was so lonesome, I found myself talking to sheep, cows and horses, but I never did quite master Basque!"

My mother Elvira, circa 1897

Elvira with her sisters and mother

(She's the girl seated in the middle)

My mother's growing up years, although more carefree and settled than my father's, were fairly typical of youngsters raised in San Francisco during that era. Until, that is, the monumental event that rocked – and shocked – the City to its core.

It happened in 1906 when Elvira was just 13 years old. She and her family fled, like nearly half the population in San Francisco, to escape the chaos, panic and destruction that reigned down that earth-shaking day. . . and during the fiery days that followed.

My mother's first communion

Chapter 2

San Francisco – 1906

The City Built from Gold Dust is Reduced to Ashes

History was made the day the earthquake hit San Francisco, causing great damage and ripple effects throughout the region. While my father and his family, like most everyone in Northern California, was indirectly affected, my Basque relatives experienced it firsthand. But before I tell their story, let's take a broader look at the reports of what happened.[4]

It was still dark on April 18, 1906, at 5:12 a.m., when a 300-mile surface rupture on the San Andreas Fault caused a devastating earthquake that nearly leveled San Francisco. Considered one of the most significant earthquakes of all time, it was estimated to be somewhere between 7.9 to 8.3 on the Richter scale. Even though the epicenter was a few miles off the coast near San Francisco, the effects of the earthquake were felt all the way from Oregon, down to Los Angeles, and inland as far as Central Nevada.

But as bad as the damage and destruction was from the earthquake – and from more than 25 aftershocks on that day alone – it was the raging fires that burned for three days afterwards that did substantially more damage. In fact, some reports indicated that 80-90% of the damage was from the fires – and from all the buildings that the soldiers and fire department dynamited in their frantic, futile attempts to create firewalls.

---

[4] Information researched and compiled from various accounts of the disaster (see Appendix).

Some estimated that nearly half the buildings they destroyed with dynamite might have survived the fire.

The main problems were that there were so many wooden buildings, they were so densely packed, and the fire spread so quickly and burned so hot that it incinerated everything in its path. There was also a severe shortage of water since most of the water mains had ruptured. Even though there were more than twenty city water cisterns with 16,000 –100,000 gallons of water stored in each, only a few senior fire officials knew their locations. It didn't help that the Fire Chief, Dennis Sullivan, (who lived over the fire engine house on Bush Street) was one of the first victims.

The Police Captain's report stated that, "The principal water mains were shattered, leaving the fire department practically helpless" and that "fires were started by the overturning of stoves, crossing of electric wires, and the liberation of chemicals by breakage of containers."

Since the earthquake occurred in the predawn hours, most people were still asleep when they were jolted awake by the rumbling noise and rolling movements of the initial shockwave, which lasted 40 seconds. Chimneys, walls, fixtures, staircases, and entire houses tumbled down. Some people were hit by falling bricks and debris, or were trapped inside due to jammed or buckled doorframes. Many people, still in their pajamas, roused their families and grabbed whatever valuables or provisions they could carry and ran for their lives.

What they found outside was chaos. The streets and roadways were dark – there was no electricity – and many were damaged or ruined. Rubble and smoke was everywhere. People were rushing out of buildings with their loved ones, and possessions they couldn't bear to leave behind, but often ended up discarding along the way. Most people fled either by boat, or by train. On April 20, the U.S.S. *Chicago* rescued 20,000 victims. The efforts were said to be one of the largest evacuations by sea in history, almost on the same scale as getting British and Allied troops out of Dunkirk during World War II. But it was the trains that had the most impact on both evacuation and recovery efforts.

"As soon as news reached E.F. Harriman, president of the Southern Pacific Railroad, he immediately launched a remarkable rescue and recovery effort that provided free train transportation out of the City. In the days that followed, they not only evacuated more than 200,000 homeless citizens, but hauled away thousands of carloads of debris. Harriman himself went to San Francisco immediately after hearing the news and for two weeks personally directed railway-based disaster relief operations from an improvised command center. Within days of the earthquake, Southern Pacific crews laid down new tracks on Market Street in the heart of the City."[5]

Other residents escaped by carriage, or by automobile (if they had one and the roads were passable), but many more fled on foot and sought refuge wherever they could find it; at Golden Gate Park, the Presidio, at the beach, even in graveyards. Response by soldiers, police and officials was rapid. Just over an hour after the earthquake, General Funston ordered all available troops to report to the Mayor at the Hall of Justice. Less than 24 hours after the earthquake, Secretary Taft ordered 200,000 rations sent to San Francisco from Vancouver Barracks. Not long after that, he ordered that all tents the U.S. Army had in stock be sent to San Francisco. 'Tent cities' sprung up all over to provide shelter for displaced residents.

With so many people left homeless with inadequate food and supplies, the police seized the contents of 390 grocery

---

[5] From *Mr. Swan's Big Idea* by David Alan Vasquez, SoPo Press, 2009.

stores that were in danger of burning down in order to get food to the refugees. They moved nearly 200 prisoners from the downtown jail to Alcatraz, and removed patients from hospitals and transported them by ferry to Oakland. The morgue was quickly filled and an "emergency morgue" was set up in the police pistol range. Many people had to be unceremoniously buried right away because there was no more space.

To this day, no one knows the exact number of people who perished. Because of the intense heat, many victims were too badly burned to be identified and claimed by their families. Nor were records available because they were stored at City Hall, which was destroyed the first day. Shockingly, there were rumors that the Chinese victims were not counted and reported in some accounts. Then too, it was believed that the official numbers were downplayed in general because of concern over property values and anything that might hinder the prospects of rebuilding the city. So you can see why it's hard to accurately access the loss of life.

But this will give you an idea of the scope of the disaster. City Officials at the time estimated that 700 people perished, and 1906 U.S. Army relief operations reported 664 dead (498 in San Francisco, 64 in Santa Rosa, and 102 in San Jose). However, researchers in later years, especially the 1980s, report the actual death toll (of direct and indirect deaths) to have been closer to 3,000.

Whatever the exact numbers, it's been called the worst natural disaster in U.S. history. A total of 2,831 acres of the city; more than 490 blocks in downtown San Francisco, were destroyed. This included 28,188 buildings – 24,671 wood buildings and 3,168 made of brick – 30 schools, 80 churches, and 250,000 homes were lost. At a time when San Francisco was the 9th largest city in the U.S. with a population of 400,000 people, there were 225,0000 left homeless.

Troops and soldiers rallied and restored order to the extent they could, but there was still lawlessness. Eugene E. Schmitz, the Mayor of San Francisco at the time, however, didn't waste any time in letting any would-be scoundrels or criminals take advantage of the situation. (Ironically, he, himself, would later be indicted on 17 counts of graft and bribery). He immediately issued a Proclamation that was posted throughout the city in an attempt to bring about some order during the emergency.

He didn't mince any words:

PROCLAMATION
BY THE MAYOR[6]

The Federal Troops, the members of the Regular Police Force and All Special Police Officers have been authorized by me to KILL any and all persons found engaged in Looting or in the Commission of Any Other Crime.

I have directed all the Gas and Electric Lighting Co.'s not to turn on Gas or Electricity until I order them to do so.
You may therefore expect the city to remain in darkness for an indefinite time.

I request all citizens to remain at home from darkness until daylight every night until order is restored.
I WARN all citizens of the danger of fire from Damaged or Destroyed Chimneys, Broken or Leaking Gas Pipes or Fixtures or any like cause.

E. E. SCHMITZ, Mayor   Dated: April 18, 1906

He and the city officials were serious about the shoot to kill warning. Reportedly, 500 looters were shot by the police.

6 Original document can be viewed on the internet, along with other details (see Appendix).

No doubt this type of "zero tolerance" (as they would call it today) helped protect citizens and their property, during an extraordinary time when everyone had more than they could handle just getting themselves and their families to safety. California may have been considered to be the "Wild West," especially by Easterners at that time, nonetheless, it's interesting to note how rapid the response was to this unprecedented disaster.

*   *   *

By now you have a pretty good idea of the scale of the disaster, but let's pick up the story of my own family's experiences and observations during the earthquake and fires. Here's what I heard, mostly from my mother and grandmother, about what happened.

When the earthquake struck before dawn on April 18, my grandmother Marie quickly gathered her children; my mother Elvira, her older sister Elena (who was 16), and her two younger sisters, Catharine, who was 11, and Emilie, 9. They hurried to the top of the hill at Jones Street (above Taylor) where they would be able to see what was happening downtown.

"It was terrible," my mother told me. "We saw all the big buildings on Market Street burn." The fire continued to consume more and more structures and hotels. The Hearst Building at Third and Market Street caught fire at noon, and by 1:00 p.m., St. Mary's Hospital at First and Bryant Street burned. Marie could see that unless the fire was somehow, miraculously brought under control, they would have no choice but to leave.

They went back down the hill to their house – which was still standing, as was the HOTEL VASCO which backed up against a hill – to pack clothing and supplies. They held out for awhile amidst all the confusion, but by later that day, things had only gotten worse. The fire was getting closer, and entire blocks were aflame.

They headed for the Bay.

Along the way, they were forced to step not only through the rubble of smoldering remains of buildings, but also over dead bodies. "It was a nightmare, " my mother said. When they found out the last boat for Oakland was leaving, Marie and her children got onboard and went across the Bay to Emeryville, where she had friends. They stayed with them for two days, and then went on to Stockton, 83 miles east of San Francisco, to seek temporary shelter with other friends.

"In the meantime," my mother said, "my father would not leave the hotel."

Juan Francisco had stayed behind, determined to fight the fire in the area around his hotel. He was, however, thwarted in his attempts by the military. By the second day, they ordered him to leave and go to Golden Gate Park because they intended to dynamite his property. He had no choice but to comply, but not before he gave away all the food he had in the hotel.

"The Chinese were leaving Chinatown," my mother explained, "and headed toward the Marina with all their be-longings. My father kept telling them to come in and take all the food they wanted. A lot of them were talking to themselves."

Most people fleeing the downtown neighborhoods of the City were dazed and unsettled, as they tried to save whatever they could, gather food and provisions, and get their families out safely. Many were grieving or looking for lost or missing relatives; their efforts made all the more difficult because it was hard to move around safely amidst the rubble of fallen or burned-out buildings.

The entire business section of San Francisco, hotels and businesses on Market Street, Chinatown, North Beach and the huge mansions that overlooked the downtown area were substantially damaged. (The Ferry Building was an exception because fire boats on the bay were able to save it.) But the vast majority of the buildings in this northeast section were without water protection.

While the soldiers were very careful to save two Irish Catholic Churches located on Van Ness Avenue, the Italians felt that they were treated as an inferior group to the Anglo's and not very much attention was given to saving their neighborhoods.[7] Some enterprising Italians, however, were able to save isolated buildings on Telegraph Hill by pouring barrels of their homemade wine on the fire! A few other houses in the Russian Hill area also survived.

But by the time the fire was officially declared over, everything was either still smoldering, consumed by flames, or destroyed by soldiers who had dynamited buildings. It seemed strange to everyone in the neighborhood at the time that the soldiers did not make more use of the water from the bay, which circled the burning area for three miles from the Ferry Building around to Van Ness Avenue. So no one was surprised later when a *Boston Herald* news article reported: "In five years, San Francisco will be a better city than ever before. New building laws and a new auxiliary fire protection system, drawing its water from the bay, will give us security."

It was strongly felt by those in the community that the Basque area around the Spanish Catholic Church was probably given very little attention by either firemen or the army, as a result of the strong anti-Spain sentiments regarding the recent Spanish-American War in 1898. The incident which provoked the U.S. to attack Cuba was an explosion – one that claimed the

7 A recent review of areas near my current apartment, bordering Jackson Street (across the street from the Ferry Building), show there were several buildings in this area that were saved and are still in use today. It seems that it was, indeed, possible to get water to fight the fire, if you had enough money to purchase it.

lives of 260 American officers and enlisted men – aboard the U.S.S. *Maine* naval vessel, while it was in the Havana harbor.

Without the benefit of facts, much less proof, Spain was immediately blamed, despite the fact that Spanish authorities had been hospitable until then. But yellow journalism in the United States fueled the public furor and was instrumental in creating the war-hungry atmosphere that prevailed.

Eventually it was determined once and for all that the explosion was not the result of any Spanish or Cuban action, but rather an explosion within the ship itself. Despite President McKinley's desire to keep America out of war, Americans were looking for an excuse to go to war. "Remember the *Maine*, to hell with Spain!" became a battle cry for the Spanish- American War.

In Chinatown, the military apparently didn't give the Chinese much incentive to stay and fight the fires in their neighborhood. So they fled like everyone else. At one point an entire herd of longhorn steer (that had escaped from a stockyard near the wharves) stampeded right through the downtown area and into Chinatown, further terrifying the residents still there.

And what became of Juan Francisco, who stayed behind after he opened the doors of his hotel pantry to his fleeing Chinese neighbors? The soldiers blew up his hotel – along with other hotels, churches and buildings around it – in their desperate attempt to create a back fire.

Imagine how my grandfather must have felt, forced to watch the HOTEL VASCO destroyed that way. Worst of all, he had gotten separated from his family. Even knowing the children were in Marie's capable hands, he was still very concerned.

He began to search for them.

"He had no idea where we were," my mother said. "Purely by accident, he met a lady we knew and she told him where we had gone."

By this time, he had no access to the East Bay or his family, but a week later he was finally able to reunite with them in Stockton, and he took them to the **Sweetwater Ranch.** With the HOTEL VASCO forever gone, the **Sweetwater Ranch** became his primary business holding and base of operations. [Although my grandfather had insurance on his hotel, the insurance company refused to pay because the hotel was destroyed by the Army – rather than the fire.]

And poor Marie, once again, found herself living on a ranch, though not for long. She moved to Reno, to a house on 4th Street, where she lived for two years, so that her three younger daughters could go to school while Juan worked at the ranch. Elena, meanwhile, a junior at San Francisco Girl's High School, had moved back to San Francisco to live with one of her school mate's family out in the western part of the City, beyond the fire area. Aunt Elena not only completed her high school education, but was vice-president of her senior class.

In 1907, Juan Francisco's second brother, Leon, sold his hotel in Tres Pinos, and also went to work at the **Sweetwater Ranch.** Like Marie and the girls, his wife, their two boys and three girls also moved to Reno so the children could attend school there. In fact, they lived next door to my grandmother.

But for my grandparents, San Francisco was where they called home, and in 1908, they moved back to their beloved City by the Bay. Marie found them a flat in a restored building on Broadway, near Mason, across from the Spanish Catholic Church. Elena returned home to live with her family, and my mother attended school at Jean Parker Elementary School on Broadway, where she continued through the 8th grade.

Astonishing as it seems – given it had only been a little over two years since the earthquake – much of the City had already been rebuilt.

In many places, especially downtown, the City really did seem to have risen from the ashes to return to its former glory.

Chapter 3

Life in Grass Valley

My Dad's Teen Years

While my father, Lloyd, experienced some of the earthquake as a young boy, there was very little damage in the Grass Valley area, where he was living at the time. When we left him, as you recall, he was 9 years old and living in Berkeley, California, in a household of women; his mother, his aunt, and his sister. Although he was a smart boy who was fond of his family, he began having problems at school and became increasingly hard to handle.

By 1904, when he was 13 years old, he stopped going to school altogether. That's when my Grandmother Minnie got in touch with her ex-husband, George Washington Root, to enlist his help. It was decided that Lloyd would go to Grass Valley to live with his father. As it turned out, the change ended up being a good one, as was having a father figure in his life again.

My grandfather George, by that time, was no longer with the Supreme Court but was supervising a small gold mine in Grass Valley. By then, he had been elected to a two-year term in the State Legislature representing Nevada County. One of George's close political friends, George Hearst, was a State Senator. The two of them had previously campaigned together and caroused together. They established a reputation as the two mining men who drank a lot and liked women a lot.

George won his election, as did George Hearst. Hearst became extremely wealthy through a series of very successful mining ventures, including three of the largest mining discoveries ever; the Homestake Mine in the Dakotas, the Comstock Lode in Nevada, and the Anaconda Copper Mine in Montana. Some of the Hearst fortune was used by his wife Phoebe to fuel much of the early building of the University of California at Berkeley. Thus, one of the earliest university buildings was named the Hearst Mining Building. Mrs. Hearst was actively involved in a lively competition with the wife of another philanthropic couple, the Stanfords, with regard to endowing universities.

Stanford University was founded in 1885 by Leland Stanford, a former California governor (and later a U.S. senator), and his wife Jane Lathrop Stanford. After their only son, Leland, Jr., died of typhoid fever in 1884 at the age of 15 (while traveling with his mother in Europe), his parents decided to build Stanford University as a lasting memorial to their son. [Stanford University was unique for its time in that it was a coed and non-denominational university in an era when most universities were neither.]

George Hearst had one son, William Randolph Hearst, an ambitious young man who was interested in both newspapers and politics. After going to Harvard and majoring in journalism, he found out that his father had acquired the *San Francisco Examiner* in a transaction said to be related to repayment for a gambling debt. Although his father fully expected him to become involved in the lucrative family ranching and mining endeavors, William had other ideas. Newspapers were in his blood and he managed to convince his aging father to turn the *San Francisco Examiner* over to him to run.

Shortly after that, the younger Hearst went on to New York and acquired the *New York Journal* and became involved in a fierce circulation war with the *New York World*, owned by his former mentor, Joseph Pulitzer. From there he continued to acquire newspapers in a couple dozen major cities in the U.S. and then magazines as well. Needless to say, his family's substantial fortune helped him build the Hearst publishing empire.

William Hearst was recognized for aggressive investigative reporting and hiring top journalists like Ambrose Bierce and Mark Twain to work for him (even if he had to poach them from other papers). But his competitive spirit, often over zealous promotional tactics, and sensational, exaggerated banners and stories, also earned him a reputation of using yellow journalism to sell his paper, whatever the consequences. In fact, many believed the Spanish-American War was incited by just such journalism. In any case, through his newspapers and political career – he was twice elected to the U.S. House of Representatives – he did have considerable influence. When he ran for Governor of New York in 1906, however, he was defeated.

After my grandfather George Washington Root completed his term of two years in Sacramento, he also ran for a seat in the U.S. House of Representatives, but he, too, was unsuccessful in his bid for office that year. Instead, he continued to operate the two small mines that he owned in the Grass Valley area. One was the Alcalde Mine, and the other a small placer mine near Rough and Ready. He also saw to it during this time that his son (my father Lloyd) straightened out, and made sure he was attending school in Grass Valley.

During 1908, my father's older sister **Hazel** married a baseball player by the name of Charles Adrian Baum, known as 'Spider,' whose family was also from San Francisco. Spider Baum was an excellent pitcher who eventually went on to become one of the first inductees listed in the Pacific Baseball Hall of Fame, even though he gave up a shot in the major leagues in 1908 for reasons of love and family. Rather than going to Philadelphia for the majors, he decided to move back home to California and marry my **Aunt Hazel**.

They moved to Fresno where Spider played in the California State League. A talented pitcher, said to have invented the low-to-the-ground "submarine delivery," he managed and pitched for the Fresno Tigers with considerable success. He won 26 games in 1908 in the California State League. He then moved to the Pacific Coast League.

Spider and Hazel had a daughter the next year, who they named Adrienne (a variation of his middle name). When little Adrienne was just 2 years old, she attended a ball game to watch her father play, only to become more directly involved than anyone dreamed – she was hit in the head by a foul ball that Spider pitched!

John F. Root, George Washington Root, Adrienne and her mother Hazel
(photograph courtesy of Mark Morris, from the Morris Family Collection)

Although Adrienne was temporarily paralyzed, she soon recovered. The incident was later immortalized in a newspaper cartoon by the famous cartoonist, writer and explorer Robert LeRoy Ripley–who was also from San Francisco–and who became best known 20 years later for his syndicated features *Ripley's Believe It or Not* that appeared in 17 newspapers.

Anyway, after Robert Ripley moved to New York in 1909 to create cartoons for the Hearst newspaper, he became friends with my Aunt Elena, who also lived in New York at that time. Although Elena was not permitted to go to college, she was allowed to take drawing lessons in New York. She and Ripley remained close friends, and he visited her whenever he was in San Francisco. He also later included his cartoon of Adrienne being hit by the baseball in one of the two books he wrote featuring his work.

Tragically, however, just months after that ball game, Adrienne's world – and Spider's – turned upside down, and my father lost his only sibling. Hazel Baum got blood poisoning and died in October of 1911.

She was only 22 years old.

Since Spider's baseball career involved traveling, which made it difficult for him to be actively involved in raising so young a child, Adrienne moved to Oakland to live with her grandmother (and mine) **Minnie Johnson,** who raised her.

Adrienne. . . sweeping

. . . with our grandmother Minnie Johnson

Her father was traded to the San Francisco Seals for the 1914 season. In 1915, Spider won 30 games and lost 15, with a pitching average of 2.45, which helped the Seals win the PCL pennant.[8]

*   *   *

The next year, 1912, in the world of politics, Elihu Root, the United States Senator from New York (who I believe is one of my relatives) received the Nobel Peace Prize for his efforts to insure international peace. He served as Secretary of War under President William McKinley and President Roosevelt, as well as Roosevelt's Secretary of State from 1905 - 1909. In that capacity, he negotiated the 1908 Gentlemen's Agreement with Japan. An interesting note: Elihu Root was a lawyer as well as a statesmen, and he was railroad tycoon E. H. Harriman's corporate attorney at one time.

As I said, I don't have too many details about Elihu Root on a personal level, but he is said to be one of my cousins, and he certainly lived an active political life.

Around the same time, in 1909, George Washington Root returned to San Francisco to an office in the Mechanics Building on Post Street. From this location, he operated and promoted mining property, including some of his own personal properties. As mentioned earlier, according to the 1910 San Francisco census, he was living with his new wife Emma then.

At any rate, George left his son Lloyd, who was about 17 at that time, in Grass Valley in the care of his close friends and neighbors, the **Whittit family.** My father still had a couple years of high school education to finish, and he attended Grass Valley High School until he was 19 years old. The Whittit family definately influenced my father's early life. In fact, he treated them almost like his mother and father.

8 Additional details about Spider Baum's professional life, courtesy of Mark Morris.
  (Also see Appendix).

They had four children of their own; three daughters and one son, Bill, who was about two years younger than my father. Bill and my father went to high school together, then both attended the University of Nevada.

My dad returned to Berkeley to live with his mother in 1910 and gradu-ated from Berkeley High School. He then attended the University of California, Berkeley, in 1911 for one year to study mining engineering at the Hearst School of Mines.

Bill Whittit

From there, he went to Alaska in 1912 to prospect during the spring he turned 21. Later, in 1913, he transferred to the University of Nevada at Reno, where they had a more active mining environment at that time.

During the summer time, he worked in various mines in Nevada surveying and assaying to pay for his schooling. He was good at his job and was a popular man who made friends easily, but he was also a very tough man when he needed to be.

My dad was an ex-cellent athlete who competed in foot-ball, track and base-ball.

He set the school record for broad jump, 22'– 1-1/5," in 1914, his junior year; a record that was still in existence **20 years** later. During his senior year, he was captain of both his football and track teams.

My dad's the one standing in the middle holding the ball

Again, my dad is the one in the middle

Throughout my life, I've always been proud of my father for a number of reasons. One of them was his aptitude and proficiency in whatever athletic endeavor he undertook.

Like my father, I, too, loved sports, and they have always been an important part of my life, especially during my school years, and later in the Navy during WW II.

Chapter 4

When Lloyd Met Elvira
Meant to be

After my mother, Elvira, finished 8th grade at Jean Parker Elementary School in San Francisco, she started high school at a convent called Notre Dame. She hated it with a passion and it didn't get better over time. She promised her mother that if she let her drop out in her second year, that she would practice the piano three or more hours a day. She was as good as her word.

Her father hired a well-known composer, Vincent Arrillaga, as her piano teacher. She practiced 4 to 6 hours a day over the course of three or four years and became an accomplished pianist. As she told me, "I practiced hard. Then everything was calm again, and North Beach was a wonderful section of town to live in."

Elvira was well liked by her peers. Being able to play the piano during a period when there were no radios or record players enhanced her popularity. She and her sisters had a special father and mother who provided for them quite well. They were always outgoing, stylishly dressed young girls. They lived in a lively, bilingual community composed mostly of people from Spanish Basque and Mexican descent, and attended English-only speaking schools where they made friends and got a good education.

But the center of their life was the home front.

My grandparents Marie, Juan and their daughters, Catharine, Elena, Elvira and Emilie

As my mother put it, "We had a very nice home life. My parents were wonderful. There was lots of music in our home. We always had a lot of people in our home, and lots of singing." The sisters had always enjoyed performing in their father's hotel when they were young.[9] Even though they all went back to the **Sweetwater Ranch** every summer (where they were joined by their girl cousins who lived in Reno) and always had a great time, they all missed the HOTEL VASCO after it was gone. It was truly the end of an era. However, the summers at the **Sweetwater Ranch** definitely helped fill the gap.

When she turned 18, Elvira decided she wanted to be a nurse and went to train, and work at the French Hospital. She was there for a year before she decided that was not for her. ("Too many bedpans"!)

---

[9] Elena later went on to work as a dancer in New York in a well known female dance group. At one point, she went to Pasadena and danced with a male partner at the Huntington Hotel, where her father had camped long ago while he was herding sheep (before the hotel was built). He asked why her name was not on the Marque. She said because it was too long!

She got a job, instead, at an insurance company. But it was during her summer vacation of 1915, when she was at the **Sweetwater Ranch**, when her life dramatically changed.

That was the summer she met my father, Lloyd.

My father was a college student at the University of Nevada in 1915, but that summer he was working at one of the Aurora mines in Nevada. Like most everyone else in town, he attended Aurora's big 4th of July celebration. These annual celebrations were big social events in the Western part of the United States, not just in mining areas, but in all towns.

The Aurora celebration, held about 30 miles from the **Sweetwater Ranch,** was no exception. There was plenty of food and entertainment, holiday speeches from the politicians, patriotic music, sports events and races. There was also a substantial amount of betting on the races.

As you know, my father was quite the athlete, even though that was not exactly common knowledge because college sports coverage was not published in the Aurora newspaper. That was what my father and his friends had counted on. No one else knew that he was on the University of Nevada team and how good he was. So much so, both he and his friends helped finance their final days of college by betting on my father's athletic abilities.

Anyway, Lloyd and five of his college buddies had pooled their resources to bet on my father in the 100-yard dash, one of his college track events in which he excelled. They were all eager for the big event coming up later in the day, confident that he would win.

However, fate intervened and my father's athletic prowess – and charm – won him far more than a mere foot race.

Ironically, Elvira had attended with her boyfriend, Bill Conway, who was also one of my father's classmates. And it was Bill who introduced them. Conway's father's ranch was near the **Sweetwater Ranch**. His father was very prominent in the transportation of machinery and timber through the pass from Mono Lake to the mines at Bodie, Aurora, and Masonic. These mines were at considerable height above Mono Lake. Today, the pass from Mono Lake on Highway 395 is named the Conway Summit for Bill's father.

Bill Conway, my mother's boyfriend, before she met my dad, that is!.

There were many mines near the town of Aurora at that time, but much later Aurora became a deserted ghost town when the surrounding mines ran out of ore.

As you may have guessed, my father won the 4th of July race without any trouble. His friends were pleased, and my mother was also impressed. They became close friends. Elvira went to Reno to watch Lloyd play football a couple times that fall.

Since her cousins went to school and lived in Reno, she had a place to stay when she was in town. When my father visited her in San Francisco that winter, they attended the 1915 World's Fair together.

My dapper dad, how could she resist?

Talk about a magical and memorable date!

*　　　*　　　*

This grand fair took place on 635 acres (with 47 miles of connected walkways) down on the bay front of the Presidio, where the Marina district stands today. It was officially called the Panama-Pacific International Exposition, supposedly built to celebrate the opening of the Panama Canal (in August of 1914), which had taken 50 years to build. However, everyone, (especially in the City of San Francisco) recognized that it was just as much to prove to the world that San Francisco, then the largest and wealthiest city on the West Coast, had been rebuilt to its former glory after the 1906 earthquake.

More than 30 nations from around the world built exhibit halls, as did many states in the U.S. Nearly 19 million visitors came to see technological "wonders" such as airplanes, cars, telephones and movies being featured at this elaborate fair. Even Presidents William Taft and Theodore Roosevelt attended, as did inventors and luminaries such as Thomas Edison, Alexander Graham Bell, and Henry Ford.

In addition to the exhibit halls, there were skyscrapers, towers, palaces and all manner of colorful structures, buildings, cultural events and attractions. In fact, there was so much to do that it was said it would have taken a year to see everything. The reproduction of the Panama Canal alone covered five acres. To view it, visitors rode around the model on a moving platform, with running commentary provided by way of a telephone receiver.

At the Palace of Transportation, there was an actual Ford assembly line set up where people could watch the cars being produced right before their eyes; to the tune of 4,400 of them during the course of the Exhibition.

The Machinery Palace, the largest wooden and steel-building in the world (at the time) was so huge that Lincoln Beachey,[10] the famous San Franciscan aviator and stunt pilot who was dubbed "the World's Greatest Aviator"(Wilbur and Orville Wright went to observe *his* flights), was actually able to land inside.

Sadly, however, although Beachey was only 27 years old and at the height of his career, he ended up flying his final flight during the fair that year. He was trying out a new stunt – flying upside down to prove the reliability of his *Little Looper* plane – in front of an awed, but soon horrified crowd of 250,000 people. (There were 50,000 on the Fairgrounds and another 200,000 watching from the San Francisco hills.)

Something went terribly wrong and he crashed into the Bay. Even though he survived the crash, he drowned in the San Francisco Bay before rescuers could get to him, and pull him out of the plane.

The Fair prominantly showcased other forms of transportation as well. The South Pacific Railroad had exhibits featuring the *C.P. Huntington*, the first steam locomotive purchased by Southern Pacific (now on display at the California State Railroad Museum in Sacramento). And the famous Liberty Bell was transported by rail from Philadelphia for display at the 1915 World's Fair, the first and only time it was ever moved.

Apparently, Alexander Graham Bell made the first transcontinental telephone call to the Fairgrounds before the fair opened, and then a cross-country call was made every day of the fair, much to the delight of the crowds.

---

[10] It was said Lincoln Beachey sometimes made more in a day in his exhibition flying than an average person earned in a year. He was known for flying over Niagra Falls. Less well known was his stunt in 1914, when he dive bombed the White House and Congress in a "mock attack"– something he'd never get away with today – to prove his point about security risks given technological advances in aviation.

Then there was the ultimate stained glass work of art, the 40-story-high Tower of Jewels, with 102,000 small pieces of multi-colored glass "Novagems," made brilliant by the sun during the day, and illuminated at night by 50 powerful electrical searchlights. That had to be a pretty impressive sight.

No wonder so many people traveled so far to see the World's Fair in the fair city of San Francisco that year.

It was certainly memorable for my parents.

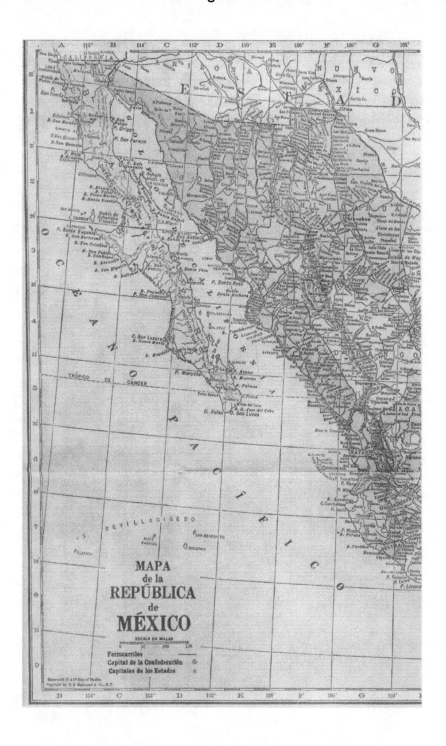

Chapter 5

Love and War

South of the Border

In early June, 1916, after Lloyd graduated as a Mining Engineer from the University of Nevada in Reno, he was offered a job in Mexico running silver mines (owned by an American company) in the state capital of Durango. He represented Col. Daniel M. Burns of the Mexican Candelaria Company (SA) mine, located in the village of Sinaloa, near the town of Dimas, as well as in the City of Durango.

Interestingly enough, Francisco de Ibarra, the Spanish Basque explorer who was the first to colonize Durango, named it after the Basque town of Durango in the Biscay province of Spain. But as it turns out, the city is also famous for its scorpions.[11]

While Lloyd was excited to "jump right in," the job offer had its negatives because the Mexican government was having trouble with rebels at that time. With the political conditions so dicey, American hostages could easily become fair game. This meant taking a wife to the mining area was temporarily out of the question. So while Lloyd joined his company in Mexico, Elvira pursued her secretarial career.

---

[11] Durango is so notorious for its scorpions that the people of Durango were sometimes referred to as *Alacran de Durango* (Scorpions from Durango).

Three months earlier, in March, PanchoVilla[12] had invaded small portions of the United States along the New Mexico and Arizona borders. Although he was subsequently thrown back by the U.S. military, he had succeeded at building a rebel group that fought the Mexican government. The rebel leader in Durango, Juan Bettencourt, was a lesser problem than Pancho Villa, but he was still a problem. My father said that the heavily armed Durango rebels would ride into the mine living area, line everybody up and ask: "What party are you for?"

My father's reply was "the peaceful party." This satisfied the rebels, who then asked for money and some food from the company canteen. They would then set off on their horses, only a day or two in front of the Federales.

A couple days later, the Federales would blaze into the mine area, also line everybody up against the wall and ask the same question: "What party are you for?" The reply again was "the peaceful party," which also satisfied the Federales. However, they too asked for money and food from the canteen before taking off on their horses to chase the rebels.

This went on several times a year over the next two years until the Federal government finally took control. Subsequently, there were no more raids by the rebels. Meanwhile, Elvira, as you will recall, had left nursing and was doing work more to her liking at the insurance company on Bush Street.

Late in November in 1918, the rebels were defeated once and for all, and my father wrote to my mother asking her to come to Mexico and marry him.

[12] Pancho Villa, born Doroteo Arango, spent most of his life in Durango. In addition to killing a man at age 16 (who reportedly raped his younger sister), he was many things to many people: Bandit, legendary hero, revolutionary, bank robber, cattle thief; he was even a miner - off and on - but opted for violence and action over manual labor. He also loved the ladies and was married 26 times, according to his last surviving widow.

Elvira agreed and she received an engagement ring in San Francisco from Lloyd's father, George Root. Early spring of 1919, Elvira arranged to take a combination cargo/passenger ship from San Francisco to Mazatlan for the wedding.

My mother's first passport

Since Mazatlan was a seaport on the western coast of Mexico, the ship made many stops loading and unloading freight, as well as passengers, along the way. This meant that even though she left San Francisco in early February, her ship took nearly a month to arrive at its destination in Mazatlan. Since there were no piers in those days, ships anchored off shore. Then both passengers and freight were transported to the shore in a small, non-powered vessel. A look at her 2nd passport picture taken just a few months apart, makes me think the trip may have been a little more tedious than she imagined!

When it was time for my father to meet my mother in Mazatlan, Lloyd had a three-day mule ride back downhill through canyons to the coast. As it happened, his mining company had its main office in Mazatlan, and they communicated with their three different mining areas by a primitive telephone system. So word got out about Elvira's imminent arrival. When she finally did arrive, she was greeted not only by her husband-to-be, but also the office personnel who threw a party for them.

My parents were married on March 11, 1919 and honey-mooned for several days before taking their long trip uphill; a four-day ride to the Durango area. This was a serious mule ride back up the hills and over canyons. Even though my mother had been used to riding horses as a young girl in Nevada, she said she felt that "her heart was in her mouth," as she put it, over half of the time on the way up the hills.

Shortly after their marriage, I was conceived, probably near the silver mine where my father worked, and they decided to come back to San Francisco before I was born.

So it was, that I also made the return trip back to Mazatlan by the same three-day bumpy mule back ride, all the way down the hill from Durango to Mazatlan, and then on to San Francisco—by ship—for my eventual birth in the City by the Bay.

I suspect I enjoyed the ride. My mother. . . not so much!

Passport photos

Elvira

Eager young bride-to-be   Bride after the mule ride

Chapter 6

Finally, the Big Event

And then there were three

I was born in San Francisco at 7:45 a.m. on the 26th day of December, 1919, at the Santa Filomena Sanatorium on Bush Street. This building (which is no longer there), was about three blocks west of the French Catholic Church, Notre Dame des Victoires, which was – and still is – located at 566 Bush Street.

My father was 28 years old at the time and my mother was 26. My birth certificate indicates that they lived and worked in Grass Valley; my father as a mining engineer, my mother as a housewife. However, my birth certificate says nothing about the type of people my father and mother were, nor their parents. But I do know this. They all had the daring and courage to face travels and conditions that not many people could handle today.

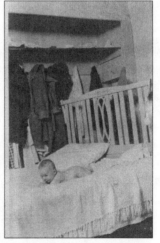

Me in my birthday suit at 3 months old (April 3, 1920)

The certificate, of course, also said nothing about California and the beauty of this part of the world. The most western state was spectacular and diverse. From its pristine coastlines, rivers and streams, to the majestic mountain ranges, rolling hills and grasslands, to its wealth of forest areas, the "Golden State" was not only geographically unique, but also offered a milder climate than most other parts of the country.

However, California at that time was nothing like the state is today, primarily because of the impact of the massive influx of people and the large-scale construction of cities, buildings, high-rises, housing developments, highways, dams and bridges that occurred as a result. Transportation, of course, played a major role in settling and building cities and towns in the West.

In just six decades, transportation advanced from the earliest sailing vessels (like the one Juan Francisco sailed over on), to the oxen-drawn wagons that crossed the country in my great great grandparent's days, to steamships, early automobiles, and eventually to cross-country trains.

California at that time, also had some extremely rough edges. The areas outside of main cities didn't even remotely resemble what exists today. Early 'highways' were only two lane roads, rarely three lanes, and then only in heavily traveled spots. Many roads were dirt, little more than well-worn horse trails or wagon tracks.

The population of the State was a mere 3,427,000 people at the time I was born. Most of the people lived in the metropolitan cities of Los Angeles and San Francisco, as well as in mining areas along the Sierras and in the Central Valley, near Sacramento, Stockton and Fresno. One of those mining areas was Grass Valley.

In December, shortly after my birth, we moved there, where I spent the first 3-1/2 years of my life. My father had started working to upgrade my grandfather's Alcalde gold mine, which was located three miles southwest of Grass Valley. They had sufficient money to drive the shaft down to the 400-foot level, installed a new and larger stamp mill with other large, heavy machinery to pound and crush the ore. They also explored the veins at the lower level.

Even though these machines were noisy, I obviously liked the mill noise, for I slept well as long as the stamp mills were active during the years that I lived at the mine. (This seemed to carry over when I was 10 to 12, as well, and lived at the Silverado silver mine outside of Calistoga; and later at other mines where I lived or worked.) Clearly these were sounds I considered to be a natural part of life.

In those early days in Grass Valley, my parents and I lived in a simple 3-room wooden miner's house. My mother washed clothes in a large galvanized washtub and I shared this same tub for my baths.

In my tub, carefully observing the nature of H2O as I transfer it over the edge

I was fat, happy and growing

My Mother
The Center of My Universe

While I was too young, of course, to have recollections of my time in Grass Valley during those first three years, there were sobering things going on in the rest of the country. Namely, the 18th Amendment, Prohibition, became the law of the land, with the Volstead Act to enforce it. This significant, if misguided, Senate bill changed the U.S. Constitution.

It provided for the prohibition against the manufacture, sale, and distribution of alcohol, and had a dramatic effect. It virtually put distillaries, brewaries, and wineries out of business, at least for a time.

With my grandfather

just returning from a spin

It also had a huge impact on the agricultural areas that supplied these industries. Surprisingly, California had over 600 wineries at that time (most of them very small and family run), but nearly all of them were forced to close their doors.

There was, however, a wine allocation that each family could use for making their own wine for "personal" use. The limit was a generous 200 gallons of wine per year. So even though commercial wine making became nearly nonexistent, the demand for and production of wine grapes remained the same as before Prohibition. All that really changed was that there was more illegal activities going on. Liquor was shipped in from Canada and other places, gin mills and "speakeasies" sprung up all over, and prescriptions for "medicinal" whiskey from neighborhood pharmacists suddenly skyrocketed.

Further complicating the situation, was the fact that it was not illegal to drink alcohol, just to make it, buy it, ship it, and sell it. And needless to say, American ingenuity rose to the challenge. Washtubs like the one I was bathed in were called into service in homemade stills, although they usually used bigger tubs. People discreetly brought their own bottles to restaurants and clubs to augment the glasses of seltzer they ordered.

Other people simply planned ahead and "stocked up" before Prohibition officially went into effect on January 16, 1920. Despite the teetotaler's determination to the contrary, Prohibition was found to be a non-workable program and after 13 years or so, it was finally repealed in 1933.

The overall effect, as mentioned, was that rather than dramatically stemming the consumption of alcohol, Prohibition simply increased bootlegging and gangster activities. Irish and Italians competed for the bootleg liquor service, with the Italians winning out in most major cities.

A second Senate bill, the 19th Amendment, was highly significant, but in a very positive way. Long overdue and driven by the Women's Suffrage movement, it gave women the right to vote and hold public office.

Me, making the rounds at the Alcalde Gold Mine

Then, of course, there was everything that was evolving in this country in the 1920s in terms of science, technology, the arts and culture – from automobiles and telephones, to radios and movies (from silent films to the first "talkies"). There was an overall optimism and emphasis on all things 'modern,' and it was a time when almost anything seemed possible. In fact, many of the mysterious, exciting and downright futuristic things that my parents had seen in Exhibition Halls at the World's Fair in 1915 in San Francisco were already becoming part of the culture. Automobiles, for instance, were becoming far more commonplace. By age 3 or so, as you can see below, I was big enough to sit on top of my grandfather's 1921 Buick all by myself.

I seem to recall thinking that things looked pretty good from up there and that I decided I might just stay with these people a little longer. They wouldn't even have to try very hard to convince me.

Three generations of Roots
George, Me, and Lloyd, Sr.

About this time, there was some serious convincing going on down at City Hall in San Francisco. A small engineer, he was just over 5 feet tall, arrived on the scene with some very big ideas.

His name was Joseph Strauss, and he was able to convince his friend and colleague, City Engineer Michael M. O'Shaughnessy that he could build the 'O'Shaughnessy Dam' in the Hetch Hetchy Valley. And he did, despite the objections of John Muir. The Tuolumne River was dammed, forming the Hetch Hetchy Reservoir. This provided water for not only San Mateo and Alameda Counties, but for San Francisco as well.

He even wrote a poem about it entitled, "The Mighty Task is Done,"after the Golden Gate Bridge was completed. Recognized the world over as an engineering marvel, perhaps he felt that after the Golden Gate Bridge, his most important work was, in fact, done. Or maybe it was just his time, because he died a year later.

But for me, I still had my whole life ahead of me. Life was good. I had great parents, interesting surroundings, and a dog named Zip, who followed me around everywhere I went from the time I learned to walk.

Me and Zip at our house near my grandfather's mine

Notice how Zip is almost as big as I am!   George Root at his Alcalde mine [13]

Zip was always the first to let us know if there was a rattlesnake nearby. Like me, he was curious about everything. He even came with us when my mother and I routinely checked the tailings pile out back near the mine for small rocks that may have contined small flecks of gold. We were, after all, a mining family.

Little did I know that I had another, very different kind of adventure in store, even though Zip – for the time being – would be out of the picture. Fortunately, there weren't many rattlesnakes where we were headed.

[13] Photograph of George Washington Root at his gold mine, the Alcalde, in Grass Valley, (Photo courtesy of Mark Morris, from the Morris Family Collection.)

Chapter 7

Back to Our Roots

Return to San Francisco

In 1923, we moved back to San Francisco because of my father's job. On the 15th of February that year, he was appointed by Governor Richardson to be the State Mineralogist. This was a State of California office, but surprisingly the main office was located in San Francisco, not in Sacramento. So my father turned his work at the Alcalde Mine over to someone else, my parents packed up our bags, we gave Zip to the Whittit's in Grass Valley to care for (knowing I could see him summer times), and off we went.

My father's office was on the second floor of the Ferry Building, about a mile away from the apartment. There were a number of other offices and a large mineral museum located there as well. My father also had a small office in Sacramento, which he used during his infrequent visits up there, but he did most of his work from the Ferry Building in San Francisco. This

Lloyd Root, Sr.

included supervision of oil well drilling in Southern California.

One of his responsibilities was making changes in the Department of the State Mineralogy Group. At that time,

San Francisco had a single stock exchange involved in mining activity, and for some reason non-technical people were using the mining bureau as part of a stock brokerage business. It was important for the Governor to have a qualified mining engineer in charge, and one of my father's changes was to eliminate non-professionals. He made sure his new staff of ten employees had the background to evaluate what they were reporting on.

In the thirteen years from the earthquake and fire until my birth, almost all of the downtown area had been rebuilt. The hotels were new, as were the office buildings and banks. All of the buildings around where I was born were also new, although there were still quite a few vacant lots. Cable cars were back in existence and new streetcar lines had replaced the old systems. But it was all new to me, of course, and I liked it a lot.

Our family's first home in the city was on the third floor of an apartment building on the southeast corner of Broadway and Jones, with a view out toward the Bay. Broadway was a restricted street from Jones east to Taylor at that time. The western part of Broadway was separated from the eastern side by a huge concrete retaining wall that stopped all traffic. (This wall is still in existence today.)

The western section of Broadway, where our apartment was located, was level for about one-third of the way facing east. But on the eastern side of this retaining wall, the street dropped precipitously down to Taylor, Mason and Powell streets at the bottom of the hill. This is the same hill where my mother and her sisters watched the fire after the earthquake, right before they evacuated the city!

But the best thing about our new home, as far as I was concerned, was that my Basque grandmother and grandfather lived just 2-1/2 blocks away on Jackson Street. Unfortunately, however, a short time after we arrived in San Francisco, my grandfather, Juan Francisco, became ill and died on May 10, 1923. Although we all knew he had lived a long and illustrious life, he was loved by our whole family and was sorely missed. He continued to provide for us, however. He left his 50 percent of the **Sweetwater Ranch** to my grandmother (he had long since bought out the other original investor, John Arambide). Juan's only surviving brother, Francisco, owned the remaining 50 percent interest in the ranch, because when the other brother Pablo, a bachelor, had died in 1920, he left his share in the **Sweetwater Ranch** to Francisco. As it turned out, Francisco, himself, was 104 years old when he died – in Reno in 1968, outliving two of his daughters.

Later that year, right around the Christmas I turned 4 years old, I began to notice some changes in the apartment that I hadn't picked up on earlier. A younger sister named Virginia – they called her **Ginger** – seemed to be getting a lot of attention, and I was not being treated quite as nice as usual.

Ginger had been born on November 11, 1923, but I had just awakened to the implications of this fact. It seemed to me that she took up an awful lot of my mother's time.

I had gotten rather used to being the center of my parents' attention. But as you can see, it's *my* hand she's holding.

Sharing my mother with my sister Ginger

Plus, since we needed more space after her arrival, it meant we would be moving to a bigger apartment on Jones and Washington Street. In those days, my mother used to take me and my little sister to the park in front of Grace Cathedral. I always had a great time playing in the sandbox while my sister, I recall, mostly just laid there and slept in her baby buggy.

More interesting to me was the fact that there was a building next to the church where groups of young children sometimes gathered to play organized games. One game I remember well – and soon excelled in – was musical chairs. We'd start off with an equal number of chairs. You know how it works. As soon as the music starts, everyone walks around the chairs in a fairly calm way. Then when the music stops, everyone races to a chair. Each time around, though, another chair is removed, and that means there's no chair left for the slowest person and they were out of the game.

Usually there were about 10 children and 10 chairs in the beginning and the game would continue until there were only 2 people left. At that point, when the music stopped there was a mad rush for the single remaining chair. I soon discovered that by using my elbows and shoulders, I had a distinct advantage. Since the slower players had already left the game, the girls would already have been eliminated because they were not as aggressive, and because there were only a few really competitive boys, I usually won.

Gee, I really enjoyed those outings with my mother to that park and playground. My mother was a happy, lovely person who encouraged me, and she didn't hold back. She was the most important person in my young life. My father and I also had a very close relationship; he was always fun whenever he was home. But since his job and responsibilities involved quite a bit of travel, I didn't get to spend as much time with him as I did my mom.

My Basque grandmother, **Marie,** however, was very much on the scene and she was a very, very important part of my life from my earliest memories. We either lived with her, or nearby, for so much of my childhood that I considered myself raised as Basque. Nana Yparraguirre lived to be 99 years old and she never forgot – or let any one else forget – that she was *French* Basque. She was always quick to make the distinction that her husband, although Basque, was Spanish Basque!

All of my mother's three sisters, Elena Marie, Catharine Cecilia, and Emilie Margaret had a definite impact on me as well, especially **Tante Elena**, who was also my godmother. She married Edward Gallagher in 1917, and my cousin **John (Jack) Gallagher** was born on June 14, 1918. Jack and I were always very close, and you'll hear about some of our shenanigans as we grew up together.

My **Tante Catharine** married Seferino Alvardo approximately two years later in 1919, and their son **George** was born on October 6, 1920. **Tante Emilie** married Walter Gloistein around 1923. We were a close family group and became even more so after the arrival of my sister Ginger, and my other cousins; **Elena** Gallagher, born on February 10, 1924, and **Barbara** Gloistein, born on September 21 of that same year. My youngest cousin, **Walter,** was born on February 12, 1931.

Yes, we were given a little latitude, but not too much. And being Basque made me feel right at home growing up in the interesting ethnic neighborhood where we lived in San Francisco. Our neighbors were mostly Italian, but in addition to inhabitants from all areas of Italy, from Sicily to the Alps, there were also families of Serbian, French, Greek, Irish, Mexican, and Jewish origins, as well as some fellow Basques.

It was a melting pot, in every sense of the word. And to me, it seemed like the most natural thing in the world.

Chapter 8

The Country Life

Summer Fun

That July, my mother took my sister Ginger and me to
the **Sweetwater Ranch.** My older cousin John Gallagher,
who went by the name of Jack when he was young – and who's
always been like an older brother to me – was there, and what a
summer it was! But before I get into that, let me tell you a little
about the Ranch itself.

The **Sweetwater** property was unique. It was a
3,200-acre spread which had been purchased, as you may
recall, by my grandfather Juan Francisco and his younger
brothers Pablo and Francisco in 1901. They bought it from an
Englishman named Williams,who had acquired it in 1876 with
a plan to build a hostelry for travelers coming from Carson
City and Lovelock southward, to the three large mines; Aurora
in Nevada, and the Masonic and Bodie[14] mines in California.

At that time, traveling by horseback or stage coach
through the road at **Sweetwater Ranch** was the easiest
method to go from Carson City to the mines. So the location
was ideal. The lumber for the house had been shipped from
Europe and hauled to the Nevada site by oxen in 1876, and the
building, which faced Mt. Patterson on the west, was completed in 1882. This mountain, a huge granite outcropping 11,673
feet high and about 5,000 feet above the valley floor, produced

---

[14] The town of Bodie still exists today, although it's uninhabited. Considered to be the best
preserved ghost town in California, this gold mining town once had 10,000 people.

a water flow which traveled southeast through the Sweetwater Valley to the south and then into the East Walker River.

The **Sweetwater Ranch** included a ranch house, a three-story, 26-room hotel (that housed travelers and equipment salesmen going to the mines), and a large, busy sheep ranch, which included a wool production business on the site.

The Sweetwater Ranch house, circa 1915
That's my Aunt Elena (the only woman) leaning against the post on the right

My grandfather Juan Francisco concentrated on running the hotel while his two younger brothers primarily worked the sheep end of the business. The sheep business, it turned out, was exceptionally good years later in 1914 – 1918, during World War I, when the demand for wool clothing, especially uniforms, was acute. During those years, the sheep population rose to 25,000 – 35,000 a year

Since there was a forest area adjacent to the ranch, my grandfather also obtained approvals from the Forest Service to utilize some of these areas for grazing. Buying extra land and entering into legal agreements was very straightforward.

Sheep, sheep and more sheep

Not only was the family well established by then, they had already become U.S. citizens. Juan gained his citizenship before he married Marie, and his two younger brothers had also completed their citizenship papers by that time.

The ranch building contained a U.S. post office for handling mail for the Sweetwater Valley. On the ground floor, there was a large living room, and a dining area. The spacious kitchen had a large pantry which contained not only a lot of food, but a lot of dishes. Next to the kitchen was an area for dishwashing.

Juan Francisco on horseback with his herd and a pair of sheepdogs on Sweetwater land circa 1900

The second floor, reached by a central staircase, had several bedrooms, while the third floor had a few more bedrooms and a large dance floor. All told there were about 26 rooms, however, the toilets in those early days were located on the outside of the building, where they remained until 1924 or 1925. The overnight visitors received not only lodging, but dinner and breakfast as well.

Horses continued to be the principal method of transportation at the time my grandfather and his partners purchased the property, and there was a substantial barn that provided shelter for the horses.

Mule team and a car in front of the Sweetwater Ranch

There were also out buildings, which included a slaughter house, an underground cold room (for storage of meat and food supplies), and pumps for generating the water supply.

The activity at the gold mines increased shortly after the property was purchased in 1901. The use of a new type of gold extraction method, using cyanide flotation, made the recovery of some of the more complex veins more feasible.

The miners were also able to rework some of their discarded tailing piles and reprocess them. The gold mines were about 25 to 30 miles south of the **Sweetwater Ranch** in an arc between Aurora to the east in Nevada, the Masonic in the middle, and Bodie on the west in California.

As you can imagine, the **Sweetwater Ranch** was an interesting place for young boys to spend time. By that summer, my cousin Jack was already living there with his mother and father, because my Tante Elena had assumed management of the property.

My grandparents Juan and Marie at the Ranch

Jack was a year and half older than me and he introduced me to all kinds of new experiences for a curious 4-1/2 year old. The dance floor of the ranch house, for example, was a delight for me. Jack had a scooter that I could peddle around the dance floor.

There was so much to see and do on the ranch. I even enjoyed watching the sheep going through large troughs to eliminate the worms and tics that could cause problems for them. The many stalls in the big barn made great places for jumping into the hay. A small sled could be used on top of the little haystacks in the field to slide down to the ground.

We could also go into storage buildings that were used for dried food items, such as the beans and garlic that my cousin and I especially enjoyed eating. There were also some particularly exciting thunderstorms from Mt. Patterson that pounded through the area during the summer months. Jack and I loved all the noise and the scary, fun feeling of observing a powerful storm firsthand.

Francisco's wife, Josephine, though, had a fear of thunderstorms. I remember being up in the ballroom once with Jack during a storm. We were not concerned about the lightning, but she was running to each corner window frantically saying prayers while we continued to play. Even after the storm had passed, it took her awhile to calm down.

Jack and I had such great times, I found myself looking forward to my next trip to the Ranch before I even left!

*   *   *

That summer, my grandmother reached an agreement on the ownership of the **Sweetwater Ranch** with her brother-in-law, Francisco. She bought him out and another partner, a man named William Dressler – who owned substantial livestock in the Bridgeport area – bought into the ranch. My Tante Elena and her husband, however, continued to operate the property.

There was less going on at the mines that summer, though, because mining had dropped off considerably by this time. In fact, work at the mines at Aurora, Bodie and Masonic was reduced to only a fraction of what it had been in the earlier part of the century. On top of that, the sheep herding people were being discriminated against by the cattle people and the government. By the early 1920s, Basque sheepherders were no longer allowed to immigrate to the United States anymore and the Forest Service refused to issue permits for grazing on government land. This meant that forest fires burned in the areas where sheep had formerly grazed and kept the brush down naturally.

The wisdom of forbidding grazing was a topic of local debate, because now somebody had to put out the fires.

Everyone was required to carry a shovel in their car so that they could immediately go to wherever there was a fire, or the Forest Service sent them. One year, Ed Gallagher, like some of his neighbors, got corralled by the Forest Service into fighting fires in the area, a task for which they were paid a dollar a day.

*   *   *

As exciting as my first vacation was at the **Sweet-water Ranch,** my next trip to the ranch in May of 1925 when I was 5-1/2 was even better. My interests had increased and my cousin Jack, now nearly 7, helped me discover much more intriguing activities.

One of our favorite routines was running through the kitchen stomping around when the Chinese cook was in the process of kneading his huge ball of yeasty dough to bake bread, or else he had already laid it out to rise. Other times it was already in the oven baking. In any event, our antics produced a lot of noise and confusion, and he would chase us around the room – chewing us out in Chinese the whole time – and out the door. Usually he'd still have the huge cleaver he used to cut up vegetables or meat in his hand as he chased us. It lent a great dramatic touch.

He'd get rid of us, but the bread would still be ruined.

Sometimes we would go riding on old horses or walk down the road about a mile and a half to where an old prospector lived in a cave. We figured he was a rather odd, interesting old character, so we hoped to catch a glimpse of him doing something either odd or interesting.

Just a little farther on the right side of the road there was a small Paiute Indian settlement and slightly beyond, on the left, there was a one-room schoolhouse where Jack went to school. Every now and then, a group of the Indians from this settlement would drive by the house on the road that went through the ranch. When they did, there was always a lot of auto backfiring. The Indians seemed to have a limited understanding of how to set the cylinders to avoid it . . . or maybe they just enjoyed all the noise it made!

The local people drove in most days to pick up their mail at the post office located on the ranch. With all the people coming and going, it gave rambunctious youngsters like us mischievous ideas. Jack showed me how to put a nail behind a tire of one of these cars to potentially produce a flat tire, either when the people backed up their car or shortly thereafter as they drove down the road. He also explained how to paint a cat with a brush. I didn't actually get to try out the cat tactic, and it was probably lucky that I didn't.

I remember that my father came up to the ranch during his vacation that summer to celebrate my Aunt Emilie's 28th birthday and Jack's 7th birthday – which were only one day apart – with us. One of the highlights, at least for Jack and me, occurred while we were all out on the porch before dinner. They were having cocktails, I believe, but what we were having was a heck of a good time teasing Emilie, who we knew couldn't stand bugs of any kind.

It was irresistible; we couldn't help ourselves. Jack dropped a grasshopper down the back of her dress! I had one, too, wriggling in readiness, but her reaction was such that I never had a chance to deposit mine. Her horror at having the jumpy little critter inside her dress resulted in lots of screaming and hopping around in her efforts to get rid of it. Somehow Jack and I must have gotten away with it, because I don't remember being punished for this deed.

What I do remember, though, is how very old we thought Emilie was, having just turned 28! But that incident was not the end of our mischief.

Jack's mother, Elena, had also invited a friend from her San Francisco high school days. This friend brought her son who was about the same age as Jack and me. Anyway, some altercation took place between my cousin and this young visitor while he was playing with one of the sleds on a hay-stack. This fellow must have been shoved off, or something, because he ran crying to his mother and my cousin Jack was punished.

Unfortunately for the visitor, however, he hadn't learned how to deal with *two* relatives because when he got back to the haystack, I gave him a whack before returning him to his mother.

Just one more successful stay at the **Sweetwater Ranch.**

Chapter 9

The City Life
School Days

That fall, just short of my 6th birthday, I started kindergarten – a relatively new concept at the time – at Pacific Heights Elementary School, the only school in San Francisco that offered it.

My mother was excited because even though the school was outside of our neighborhood, she was able to get me enrolled. What I was excited about, though, was that going to school in Pacific Heights offered me a new adventure. I got to take a cable car from Jones and Pacific Street (a block away from our apartment at Washington and Jones) every day to get to school.

My Lovely Mother

I had to learn the new routine and made three trips back and forth with my mother, and then traveled the rest of the semester by myself. My grandmother lived a half block away from our apartment and she babysat my sister while my mother was training me how to take the little cable car. It traveled one-way west on Jackson Street for about a mile, and then made a full "U" turn on to Washington, going east.

I got off on Washington in front of my school, and at the end of my half-day of school, I got back on the little cable car at Washington Street to go home. Of course, the grip man and conductor monitored me, and dropped me off at the Jones and Washington stop when I returned from school.

What a wonderful world in which to grow up. I was happily carefree and gaining a sense of independence. I had a minimum amount of automobile traffic to worry about, very watchful motormen on the little cable car, and a mother who understood her son's desire to expand his world. I loved taking the cable car to school, just as I loved going to watch people flying kites on Russian Hill after school, or on weekends. Seeing them sail high, high in the air, as free as the wind was a real treat.

All in all, it was a time of many new places, and new things to do. I even became a rather amazing musician that year, if I do say so myself, gleefully pounding away on the triangle.

In December, Jack came down from the ranch to visit and stayed at my grandmother's flat on Jackson Street. On Christmas Eve, Jack spent the night at our apartment. We set an alarm clock so we could get up and catch Santa in the act, and went to bed.

Tell me again, why do I have to stand here?

Later when we heard sounds coming from the front room, we sneaked out to take a look. It turned out that my father had picked up a Christmas tree and was decorating it. My mother was stringing bells on the tree. And since there were packages nearby – which looked suspiciously like gifts – we both came to the conclusion that Santa Claus was a fairy tale.

Family dinners were always pleasant times, especially around the holidays, although one particularly stands out in my memory. It was the time Nana's brother sat across the table from me. Mostly what I remembered about him was that he was a short, balding man. But shortly after that dinner, he was significant for a different reason. He disappeared! The whole family was upset because he just left one day and was never seen again. That, however, was not so unusual in those days.

The next spring, when I was 6 years old, I made my First Communion at the French Catholic Church, Notre Dame des Victoires, at the same church my mother did. The Mass was in Latin but the sermon was in French. In my sixth year, I didn't understand either language, but I do recall that I thought the candles were nice.

At this time, there were two other events that made a major change in my life. The first one was moving to a grammar school in my neighborhood, just 3-1/2 blocks from my apartment. This was Spring Valley Grammar School, which was the oldest public school in California. It was originally located on Broadway and Polk Street but had burned down during the 1906 fire. When it was rebuilt in 1910, it was relocated to the center of the block between Washington and Jackson with the main entrance on Jackson Street. The building was exceptionally sturdy, as all schools were in those days, and it is still in good condition today. Spring Valley's grades included first grade through the eighth grade. This school, however, differed from my experiences in Pacific Heights in a couple of ways.

At the school where I went to kindergarten, everyone had spoken English, but my new school was in an area that had a predominately Italian population and not too many of my classmates were fluent in English. However, I was used to non-English conversation since my mother and aunts conversed with my grandmother in Basque and Spanish.

Our classes began every day with the sounding of alphabet letters and although there were some strange noises coming out at the start, everybody seemed to progress efficiently. Strangely, there was something in the Italian pronunciation that made the letter "h" sound like "haitch." Nevertheless, all of us made it through the first grade, and moved to the second grade together.

Then there was my clothes. When I had gone to Pacific Heights, the way I was dressed – mostly in a Buster Brown shirt and knickers – was not so unusual. Now, where most of the boys wore jeans, or perhaps corduroy pants and a T-shirt, or a regular shirt of some kind, let's just say my clothes were considered a little *odd*.

The second big event in 1926 was that we had to move out of our apartment on Jones and Washington because our building was slated to be torn down. We relocated to the northeast corner of Broadway and Leavenworth, just one block west of our first apartment in San Francisco.

At that point, Nana moved into the same apartment building with us. We took the apartment on the corner of the third floor. Nana moved into the second floor apartment on the same corner location. My Tante Emilie, Uncle Walt and their daughter, Barbara, moved into an apartment across the hall from Nana.

Nana was very much a part of our world.

She took us to parades and various outings on a regular basis. We also played cards with her as early as when I was 6 or 7 years old. And she played for money!

It was 5 cents a game. If she won, she wanted to play the next game for 10 cents a game.

Partly because of my mother's influence and musical talents, there was always a lot of music and gaiety in the house. She was a very good pianist. Not only could she play just about any popular song – she was one of those musicians who could pick up the tempo and melody from just hearing you sing it for her.

She was also the substitute organist at the Spanish Church. Whenever the regular organist was out on vacation, or ill, my mother would step in.

My mother also tried to teach me how to play, although practicing piano didn't appeal to me. Basically I was a lot more interested in being outside playing ball than playing the piano.

She finally gave up after after a time and the world lost a great piano player! I did, however, enjoy the times, usually on Sundays and after family dinners, when we'd all gather around the piano and sing Basque songs. Sometimes there'd be dancing as well.

Since my grandmother lived in the apartment below us, we often went to dinner at her house. All we had to do was go down the back stairs, open the door and we were in Nana's kitchen!

We had all kinds of delicious Basque family-style meals there, as we all gathered around her large dining room table. Basque cooking, typically without a lot of fancy sauces, included another element in Nana's kitchen . . . just about every part of the meat was put to use. So in addition to her various soups, salads, lamb, beef dishes, and occasionally fish dishes using bakailo (salted, dried, reconstituted cod fish) to make soup, from time to time she also made things like tripe, thinly sliced tongue, and sweetbreads. In fact, one of my friends once asked me, "Does your family ever eat anything but 'innards'?"

We did. We had baratxuri (Basque garlic soup), potatoes, Basque meatballs, and various chicken dishes. On the turkey days, I was "awarded" the neck, while Jack got "the Pope's nose" (although I never did understand where the nickname for that triangular little rump flap came from). On regular days we might have lamp chops, and on holidays, there was leg of lamb. Nana would usually make separate bowls of various kinds of beans; garbanzos, kidney, and white Navy beans. For desert, she sometimes made *causeras* (as they are called in French); a deep-fried cream puff-like treat (but made without the cream). In Spanish, they are called *bunuelos* or *roskillas*. Once the dough was puffed and removed from the hot oil, Nana would sprinkle or roll them in a little bit of powdered sugar. They were so good; sometimes we didn't even wait until they got their sugar coating!

In addition, Nana always had a big black pot on the back burner of the stove that was never empty. She always had something simmering. Every day, whatever leftovers she had went right back into that pot of hers.

Our new apartment location offered some new walks and outings for me with Nana. I particularly enjoyed going downtown with her to the French Bank on Sutter Street, just west of Montgomery Street. I didn't know what the visits produced because I never saw any money change hands, but I always felt that Nana was checking to see if all of her money was still there.

Another excursion I especially enjoyed was when she took me with her to play "mus," a Basque rummy game. Her friends owned a hotel on Pacific Avenue called "Concha" (the Spanish word for a type of shell). This was a small Basque hotel with rooms, a bar, and a large handball court. The court was for a Basque type of handball and the floor stretched alongside the hotel towards the next street to the north. The handball court was okay, but my primary interest was an illegal saloon that was run by a bootlegger named Izzy Gomez.

Izzy's saloon was next door on Pacific and had some interesting young ladies who moved past a side window from time to time. So while my grandmother played cards, I was picking up a great deal of information for a youngster my age.

Speaking of information, at the time I went to school, each child was challenged to meet the requirements before continuing to the next grade each year. This is unlike the school system today that promotes people, regardless of their ability to do the work. Our school system was also quite strict on people who created problems for their teachers. Our no-nonsense grammar school also had a "three strikes and you're out" program, as did other schools in San Francisco. If you didn't obey the rules you didn't get to stay and bother others. You went to a "continuation school" and were subjected to much more pronounced discipline in the company of other problem students.

One of my classmates from the neighborhood, Joel Caselli, started out in the grade ahead of me, but later ended up in my class for a short time. He was a disruption for the teachers, and after being sent to a continuation school twice, he only had one "strike" left. His third and last strike happened when he flipped his ink pen at our teacher. (Our desks had small wells with fluid ink.) Joel targeted the teacher's back as she was walking away from him. But evidently she anticipated the event – or she really did have eyes in the back of her head – because she spun around and caught him in the act.

We never saw him in our school again, only on the city playground on the weekends.

In our own household – and in our lives – Nana was the one who always knew what was going on, and made sure that it was going on in exactly the correct way. Nana was our babysitter or nurse when we were ill. We thought her remedy was often worse than the illness. Sometimes there was a dose of cascara, milk of magnesia, or castor oil. Occasionally we got some warm water with honey and a shot of bourbon. I liked the last one best.

Nana also made sure we went to church. She took Jack and me to the Spanish Catholic Church, Nuestra Senora de Guadalupe, with her. Here the Mass was in Latin, and the sermon was in Spanish. By now I had a very slight understanding of Latin and a limited knowledge of Spanish. I did understand that whenever Father Antonio gave a sermon and used the word, "inferno, inferno," someone was in for a bad time.

I also knew this couldn't have been directed at me because I didn't speak Spanish. Later, when Jack and I became altar boys, Nana never forgot to critique us after church on the way we carried out our duties that day.

By this time, I was pretty well acclimated to city life, a good thing too, because my Grandmother eventually sold the Ranch to a Los Angeles investor who raised horses there. But to this day, summers at the **Sweetwater Ranch** hold fond memories for me, especially of the fun times my cousin Jack and I spent there.

Chapter 10

My Neighborhood

Holding My Own

Around this time, I found myself in several fights I didn't start. The Italian boys thought they were the smartest guys in the world, but of course, we Basques knew better. Nevertheless, I was frequently challenged that year since I was the new kid in the neighborhood, and because of my clothes.

Jack and I running across Crissy Field, playing football in our knickers and caps
(Still image from footage my father shot in the 1920s with his movie camera)

It seemed that some of the Italian boys wanted to 'test me out' because my clothing didn't appeal to them. But they soon found out that just because I dressed funny, it didn't mean I couldn't fight. Not only did I enjoy the challenge, I also found out that I enjoyed fighting.

That year, in the fall of 1926, I was aware that grapes made an entry into the Broadway and Leavenworth neighborhood. Almost all the Italian families who had basements got a truckload of grapes to make wine for the coming year. Each family was allowed to produce 200 gallons of wine legally under Prohibition regulations, as mentioned earlier, and each family probably made a little more. The grapes were squeezed to convert into juice, put into barrels to ferment and then transferred to large aging barrels. This was the first year I remember seeing the action, but it repeated itself each year thereafter.

Broadway was a steep cobblestone street between Leavenworth and Jones during the first two years that we lived there. (The Broadway tunnel wasn't built until after WW II.) The road was blocked by a retaining wall and Pacific Street was the nearest street running east to west. It carried the bulk of the traffic in both directions. Traffic was light in those days, though, probably less than a tenth of what we have today.

Street lighting was by gas-fired lamps that were ignited each evening by an individual who used a long pole. I recall looking out of our apartment front window and watching the "lighter man" going from lamp to lamp and starting up each light. Two years later, all of this would be gone when the gas lamps were taken down and new electric units were installed. The cobblestone street was also removed and a new cement one replaced it. This was a decided improvement, particularly for young people like myself who wanted to skate on coaster boards that we made ourselves from old roller skates. But there were mixed emotions on the lights changing. Everyone seemed to miss the man who had turned them on for so many years.

Vegetable deliveries were made by horse and wagon, and there was a "rag, bottle, sack man" who came through the neighborhood with his horse and cart to make collections. Refrigerators were scarce and the iceman delivered large blocks of ice on his back by walking up the back stairs and dropping the ice chunks into vented wooden cupboards which were accessible from both inside and out. All kitchens had them at the time; no electricity was required for keeping food and liquids chilled, courtesy of the ice and the brisk San Francisco air.

My grandmother, however, was happy to buy one of the first electric refrigerators, which was a much better system than the iceman having to trudge up the back stairs for her. And that refrigerator lasted for at least 25 years. She also had a car, a tan-colored Studebaker Sedan.

Since automobiles were a rarity, hardly anyone parked on the street unless they were delivering something. Our apartment building was new and did have a small basement for cars. The few families in the neighborhood who did have cars parked them in commercial garages or in revised basements. This enabled entire streets to be open for the important use of touch tackle football, softball, 'one foot off the gutter,' hockey on roller skates, or 'kick the can.'

Still image (from my father's movie camera footage) of me, Jack & Ginger
at Crissy Field

This neighborhood was three-quarters Italian, and was also interlaced with Serbians, Mexicans, French, Basque, Greek, Irish, Jewish and assorted other groups. The four blocks centering around Broadway and Leavenworth consisted mostly of duplex flats, three-story apartments, small mom-and-pop grocery stores, one full service grocery store (with a meat market) on Pacific Street, one cigar manufacturing operation (with six employees), and a variety of small service businesses such as barbers, laundry, cleaners, small candy stores, and French bakeries.

There were two small mom-and-pop grocery stores across from each other on the corner of Broadway and Leavenworth. They are fondly remembered by me because one of them was where I first saw sliced bread. Previously, all bread was sold as a solid loaf and you sliced your own pieces. While this may not be important to anyone else, the sliced kind certainly made my sandwiches easier to eat. My mother had many talents, but slicing bread was not one of them. What you got were wedges.

My favorite store was Rathjen's, a large German butcher shop. They would provide each of us with enough butcher paper to make book covers for our new school books. For a treat, they also gave each of us a large piece of baloney. This was a ritual each semester when the books were passed out. Stopping at Rathjen's was a must.

Italian last names permeated the area. Some of these were Lanza, Figone, Carnilia, Cirimeli, Luisetti, Silvestri, Fazio, Grillo, Dito, Pasqualetti, Addiego, Chicazolla, Sarubbi, Piava, and many others. Intermixed with them were the Serbians, such as Mikovich, Pavlich, Sheravich, Slavich, Lucich, and Begovich. There were two Greek families, Contos and Bouduros, as well as two French families, Chevalier and Cagoule. There were also three Jewish families, Latz, Harris, and Moses.

Various others included the half-breed Basques, Gallagher, Alvarado – and Root – as well as the Irish families like Kelly, Ficken, and Remminger.

Many of my friends had old country Italian first names such as Ezio, Angelo, Luigi, Elmo, while some of the Serbs had first names like Milivoy and Milan. Some had English first names, but very few. Many of us went by nicknames such as Satchel Ass, Bubble Head, Powder Puff, Bombo, Beacon, Fats and Jack. I inherited Junior. This name also led to several fights when I was young. But still, school was interesting and I enjoyed every bit of it.

Even today, after all these years, I can still recall at least 40 names of kids we played sports with in our neighborhood. So you can see, the neighborhood and its inhabitants, as well as the comradery – or competitive rivalry! – between us really left an impression on me.

Also, in those days, parents did not get involved in their children's sports activities. Back then, none of our parents went to any of our sports events. It just wasn't done. They let us be on our own and have a good time. My dad just wanted me to have fun and enjoy everything I did.

For another thing, when we were in grammar school, our games were held during the week and everyone's parents were usually out working. When we got a little older, some of us would get involved playing with a club on Saturday or Sunday, but fortunately our parents were reasonable; not like some of the idiots today who sit on the sidelines and make trouble by either pressuring or harassing their own kids – or even the coach – if they don't like the results of a decision or a play.

My parents, Ginger and I also spent time in Oakland at my grandmother Minnie's house. We'd go there for family dinners and holidays. She had a large backyard and we'd have Easter Egg hunts there. I always enjoyed the chance to see my East Bay Nana, and to spend time with my cousin, Adrienne, on those visits. She and I continued to get together over the years.

One of the fringe benefits of spending time both in San Francisco and Oakland was that I got to enjoy the funny papers on either side of the Bay. When I was in San Francisco, I had Superman serials to read in the *San Francisco Chronicle*, and when I was in Oakland, there was Buck Rogers in the *Oakland Tribune*. Just another benefit of being a 'dual citizen.'

Still, as interesting as the time I spent growing up in San Francisco and the Bay Area, I also always looked forward to the summers in mining towns such as Grass Valley. In addition to the change in locale, there were so many differences and I enjoyed seeing another side of life.

In the country, men were engaged in mining, ranching, farming and forest related operations. Almost all enterprises had some sort of boarding accommodations but entertainment was centered in their local areas. Almost all towns had a 'banana ranch' featuring attractions – or should I say distractions – for lonely, local males. There was also a variety of bars, some with their own dance halls. As you know, even though Prohibition was the law of the land from 1920 until 1933, the outlying country towns of western states paid little heed to what it prohibited. Saturday night was night to go into town to get drunk, get laid, or get into a fight. . . or to do all three.

Country living included a lot of 'outside plumbing.' Little wooden structures with small quarter moons cut out for ventilation dotted the countryside. The fragrance of an outhouse on a hot summer day needs to be experienced to be appreciated. The paper in these steaming little outhouses was not a plus, either. And of course these 'facilities' weren't lit.

Electricity was not always available even in people's homes. In some of the smaller towns, everyone got by with candles or kerosene lamps. And if there was ever a fire, volunteer fire fighters came to the rescue.

*   *   *

In Grass Valley, there were two fire departments. The main one was closer to the eastern border of town and had two trucks. The other station was south of town near the North Star Mine and had a single truck. The fire department was all volunteer but very well trained. There was a very large bell also near the North Star Mine that rang out the number of the fire alarm box near where the fire was burning. Most everyone had a list of all the alarm boxes so they could check the location of the fire. The first volunteers to get to the fire house started up the engines and went immediately toward the blaze, picking up other volunteer firemen along the way.

If the fire was somewhere in the western part of town, the trucks had a little more of a problem getting up the hills in the area. Nevertheless, as in most small towns, all the neighborhood kids ran after the trucks to watch the volunteers working.

There were not many fires, though, in Grass Valley because people were very conscientious and careful about avoiding them. Streets were kept clean; trees, bushes and shrubs were maintained, and there was general knowledge about fire safety.

Making a living off the land in the country areas was in sharp contrast to living and working in the cities. In the City, men were primarily engaged in building trades, financial businesses, manufacturing, transportation, fishing, and service and supply companies. They were likely to be married, with families and were therefore more stable. There was still, however, an ample supply of bars, dance halls and whorehouses to keep everyone happy. There was probably just as much fighting or drinking in the City, but it was spread out over the week rather than just on the weekends.

Travel, of course, was vastly different and much slower in those days. At that time, traveling by car from San Francisco to Sacramento took five hours, instead of 1-1/2 or 2 hours. It was a real production; driving to the Embarcadero waterfront to get on an auto ferry, then the boat ride to Oakland, accessing San Pablo Avenue and driving through Emeryville, Berkeley, Richmond, Hercules, Pinole, Rodeo to catch a small auto ferry, then crossing over to Vallejo, and onward to Vacaville, Fairfield, Dixon, Davis . . . and finally reaching Sacramento.

Every town along the way required a 25 mile per hour 'tour' through its downtown area. Thankfully, the towns were smaller and less congested in those days, but it still took three times longer.

I always enjoyed traveling with my father, though, because our trips were primarily through rural areas which allowed me a bird's eye view of society other than the urban ethnic one where I spent most of my time.

Chapter 11

On the Road with Dad

Business and pleasure

In April of 1927, Jack and I spent our Easter vacation traveling with my father. He was looking for viable property with a mine that could be expanded. We were looking forward to the fun and adventure of going on a trip together.

We left San Francisco by car and about halfway through the first day, my father deposited us at a soda fountain while he made a stop to visit someone. Jack had some money and he told me to get whatever I wanted and to order him a Coca-Cola while he went to the lavatory. When he returned, I was already halfway through my Banana Split Special and he did not seem too impressed with my selection and the cost of it.

Our trip involved going north to Yreka, in Siskiyou County, California. We reached our hotel in Yreka late that night and Jack and I shared a room. We were goofing around, mispronouncing "Siskiyou" on the cover of the phone book as "Sky High You," and so forth until we got to laughing so hard that we couldn't stop. By ll:00 p.m., my father stepped in to help us do so. I believe he threatened to throw us out the window if we didn't settle down so we could all get some sleep.

The next morning, we traveled about 75 miles going north and west along the Klamath River on a very windy, narrow and only partially paved road to a very small town called Happy Camp. After checking into the hotel, we drove west about 15 miles along the river. The mine was located on the other side of the river, and there was no way to cross over to get to it by road. So we parked the car and got into a small wooden transportation device that was suspended over the river with a pulley on top (which could be controlled from either side of the river).

After our crossing, my father examined the property and began taking samples. Meanwhile Jack and I explored the hills near the mine. As we did so, we noticed large bear tracks in the snow. We immediately took off, slipping and sliding down the hill at such a rapid pace that our Levi's left a trail of blue streaks in the snow behind us!

After my father completed that afternoon's work, we returned to Happy Camp in the evening. The next morning, after cracking the ice that had formed overnight in the ceramic washing bowl, we brushed our teeth and cleaned our faces before eating breakfast. Then off we went to the mine again.

My father continued his work while Jack and I tried to make bows and arrows. However, before completing this project, we began swinging the willow branches at each other like swords instead. Until, that is, our fun was interrupted by my father's shouts as he started toward us . . . worried, no doubt, that we would poke each other's eyes out.

Jack and I split, running in different directions up the hill. My father came after us, and Jack got a whack in back of the head before my father came after me. I thought I had enough of a lead, but he changed directions and caught me too. This ended our playing with branches. Soon after that, my father completed his work and we returned to Yreka to spend the night. The following day, we began the drive back to San Francisco.

*   *   *

It was around this time, that I recall becoming really fascinated by airplanes. So naturally I was very interested when aviation pioneers began making their historic flights. Charles Lindbergh, especially, really captured my attention.

In 1924, Charles Lindbergh had graduated first in his class at the U.S. Army flying school and became the first air mail pilot to fly between Chicago and St. Louis. He was also a member of the exclusive Caterpillar Club for those people who were able to save their lives by parachuting out of a plane. Lindbergh did this three times.

On May 20 to 21, 1927, Lindbergh flew his solo, 3,600 mile flight across the Atlantic Ocean – the first nonstop flight ever made – from New York to Paris. Almost overnight, he went from being a dedicated, but virtually unknown U.S. air mail pilot, to a highly famed international hero.

My dad had a movie camera that he used for inspecting property and the mines, so he had all the equipment to project movies against a wall. We had a copy of the professional Lindbergh film and we watched it about 30 times. I have it to this day.

Like most young people, the event left a major impression on me and I enjoyed seeing pictures of him and his plane in the newspapers. I became an avid aviation enthusiast and have remained one throughout my life; from the time I tried to join the military aviation branch prior to WW II, through Naval aviation training during the war, to flying gliders in St. Helena and Nevada during the 1970s and 1980s.

At that time, however, Lindbergh's activity really opened up peoples' minds to flying. All of a sudden there were a whole series of events that reflected both changes in the aircraft, as well as the government's attitude about the importance of transportation. For instance, on Crissy Field in San Francisco, the old biplanes from WW I were replaced by mono-wing fighter planes. The Navy developed two lighter-than-air rigid dirigibles, but with duraluminum hulls.

One of them, the *Akron*, was flown in the East but was totally destroyed in a very severe storm. The *Macon*, the largest of these air ships, was stationed at a new base, south of San Francisco in a huge hangar at Moffett Field, located between Mountain View and Sunnyvale. This dirigible was so large, it carried its own airplanes inside; up to five *Sparrowhawk* planes could be stored in the aircraft.

Later, on February 12, 1935, the *Macon* ran into severe weather conditions and crashed into the Pacific Ocean, off the coast of Point Sur. Two men died, but 81 survived. However, these two Navy aircraft crashes ended up sealing the fate of the Navy's use of dirigibles for fleet activities.

On the same day that Lindbergh landed in Paris – on May 21st, 1927– the Carquinez Bridge was completed. This was very exciting because it made traveling to Sacramento, and to Grass Valley so much easier. We no longer had to wait for a slow ferry in order to cross the strait in either direction.

There were some changes in my own life as well. After the Lindbergh incident, I skipped a half grade in school. This moved me up to the third grade. More significantly, it also allowed me to leave the lower playground for younger students and I could now mix with the older students.

By this time I was becoming an avid reader – I especially liked Tom Swift books – and not surprisingly, added aviation to my list of books to read. I also had fun making crude model airplanes out of cigar boxes. Sometimes my father helped me.

In the spring of 1927, my father left his job as State Mineralogist and joined up with a financial partner and developer named Sig Janis. Their goal was to find a reasonable mine for them to develop and operate as a corporation. They decided that a silver mine just outside of Calistoga had the most promise.

The mine was located about two miles northeast of town. The backdrop for the mine area was the Palisades, a strong vertical ridge that ran north towards Mount St. Helena. The road that led into the mine site was relatively flat with a small creek running along one side. There were two main houses on the property and an old mine shaft that needed repairs. The shaft was on the south side of a hill about a half mile from the mill. The mill, on the north side of the property, also needed improvements.

My father had diamond drilled the area before purchasing the mine. This particular mine had shown great potential and depth. The corporation they formed gave my father the responsibility of re-establishing the mine shaft, providing a new cyanide flotation mill, and gathering a crew to operate the mine. His partner, Sig Janis, was responsible for developing the financing for the mine.

My father also contributed to the search for investors by contacting people he knew from his previous work as head of the State Mining Bureau. One Sunday, I recall visiting a very palatial home in Atherton[15] with my father, mother and sister. The man we visited was William Bourn, who was the owner of the Filoli Estate, as well as the Empire Gold Mine in Grass Valley, which you may recall I visited with my father years earlier. I remembered our trip to the mine well even though I had been quite young at the time. Mr. Bourn, as it happened, had inherited the mine from his father when he was

[15] Although located in San Mateo county, Atherton is still considered part of the San Francisco metropolitan area. It is one of the wealthiest cities in the United States.

about 18 years old, and it certainly prospered over the years. When the mine closed in 1956, it had produced 5.8 million ounces of gold. Later, in 1975, the State of California bought the land – over 770 acres – and formed the Empire Mine State Park.

In any case, while my father was making his presentation to Mr. Bourn, my 4-year-old sister Ginger and I amused ourselves by taking a walk through the vast, impressive Filoli gardens.

Even though I usually held her hand when we were walking together, I must have let go for a minute, because when we went over to check out a very large swimming pool along the way, my sister ventured too close and fell into the pool!

She was rescued by a young college student who was nearby, probably a relative of Mr. Bourn, but it was a very startling incident to me, so I can only imagine how Ginger felt.

I didn't receive any information about whether Mr. Bourn agreed to finance part of the Calistoga mine, but I did get my sister back, even though she was all wet!

Shortly after that, I also remember going on a visit with my father at the office of a gentleman in San Leandro who had started the Caterpillar Tractor Company. He had developed the tractor while he was working on Mare Island during WW I and located his manufacturing plant in San Leandro in the early 1920s. (He later moved this plant to a much larger operation in the Midwest sometime after WW II.)

Apparently my father and Sig did receive enough financing to get the mine started again. But I don't think my sister went with us on the latter trip, probably because there was no swimming pool there for her to repeat her Filoli act.

Chapter 12

Grass Valley Days

. . . and the living is easy

Summer came and I was off to Grass Valley with my mother and sister. We stayed with the Whittit's at their home on South Church Street. When my father was still with the Mining Bureau, he worked out of his Sacramento office during the week and joined us on weekends. Those were good times. One of the things I loved about spending summer time at Grass Valley was that everything was so different.

We really enjoyed being with the Whittit family and, of course, Zip. The weather was warmer, we could run barefoot, and we could go swimming every day if we wanted. Then there was the food. Mrs. Whittit was a great cook who did all her cooking on a large wood burning stove. To this day, I have fond memories of waking up in the morning to the fragrant aroma of pies, cookies and bread baking that floated up to where I was sleeping.

This was because I got to sleep in the attic, which really appealed to me. The only way to access it was by climbing up a small staircase that was pulled up or down by a rope. Also, this upstairs area provided extra cooling and ventilation to the rest of the house during the hot summer months, and it was the coolest place in the house to sleep.

Mr. Whittit was short and stocky, and Mrs. Whittit was taller than he was. He was very hard of hearing. However, he was able to listen to the baseball games on the radio by using a small metal horn. So when Mrs. Whittit asked him a question when he had his horn turned to the radio, she really had to shout at him several times before she got him to look up.

Mr. Whittit worked at the North Star Mine. I remember going to the mine and watching him lift fairly large pieces of steel – he was short but he was really strong – to cut out sections to fit some sort of mechanism.

Over the years, we had many great 4th of July celebrations in Grass Valley. My father would stop in Sacramento to buy firecrackers. He'd bring Roman candles, spinners and sparklers. The whole town enjoyed celebrating the holiday, just like when my parents were growing up.

The 4th of July parades, of course, were always part of the fun. Each year Grass Valley and Nevada City would rotate the parade and the floats between them since the towns were just six miles apart. Being a mining community, most of the floats were in that vein. There was usually someone panning for gold on one of the floats, displays of early types of gold recovery systems, and typically a float with a Pelton wheel. (However, the use of the Pelton wheel was so destructive – farms in the valleys were being inundated with the debris – that the State of California legislated against its use.)

Along with the floats, fire engines from both cities usually rolled by. A small collection of Indians walking with their family members usually brought up the tail end of the parade.

Picnics were another great treat. We went to Lake Olympia, halfway between Nevada City and Grass Valley, and also to Bridgeport on the Yuba River. I could paddle around a bit, but was not yet an accomplished swimmer. My mom and Mrs. Whittit would pack huge picnic baskets and hampers filled with an assortment of good things to eat. Food was definitely part of the Grass Valley experience. Other wonderful memories include making homemade ice cream and licking the mixers, or walking two blocks up Church Street to get some clotted cream, often referred to as "Cousin Jack" cream. We enjoyed helping make and bottle our own root beer, as well.

I also liked to help haul in the firewood to stow in the basement. Then there was chasing after a de-headed chicken in the back yard, on the days when chicken was on the menu for dinner. Some young people today think chickens come in small segregated plastic wrapped packages, with maybe six thighs, or ten legs or some other combination of parts. That's about as close as they get to a chicken, but it wasn't that way then. We knew there was only one head and two legs per bird, and that having their head loped off didn't stop the chicken from continuing to run around. It's a sight you don't forget.

Going to the library located only three blocks away was a quieter but also enjoyable way to spend my days. The Tom Swift books about Tom's college experiences of playing baseball, soccer, and football especially stirred my imagination, and were still among my favorites.

The winter I was 8 years old, my mother and father bought a big two-story house in Grass Valley.

The house was located at the top of Main Street and had a very large yard that extended all the way through to the street behind the house. It also had a big basement and huge cherry trees good for climbing, swinging, hiding, and various other forms of fun and mischief. But no, I cannot tell a lie, I never chopped one down! And they say our nation's young founding father George Washington didn't either; it was something thought up by one of his biographers to make his biography more interesting.

That spring, my second grandfather, George Washington Root, died in San Francisco. Strangely, he not only died *in the same hospital* as my Basque grandfather, Juan Francisco, but *in the very same room.* He even died *on the same day* – May 10 – only five years later.

What are the odds of that?

A few days later, the funeral was held and many of George's friends attended. My recollection was that my father cried during most of the service. He loved his father, despite his relative absence in his life. For me, it was the first time that I had ever seen my father cry, and that made an impression on me.

I was too young to notice, but something that left an impression on the other attendees that day (according to my mother, a very observant person) was that even though George Root wasn't married at the time, there were 4 or 5 of his girlfriends at the funeral. That was my grandfather George, all the way. Highly social and successful, yes, but he was definitely one of a kind.

Throughout that year, my father and Sig continued to organize the mine at Calistoga. The Calistoga area was primarily a farming valley and the local workers had no knowledge of mining operations. So the mine was soon populated with a large number of "cousin Jack" miners from Grass Valley, many of whom had been my father's high school classmates. The term "cousin Jack" (mentioned earlier as part of the lingo) was traced to Grass Valley where a mine owner who wanted to find extra workers would ask some of his existing workers if they knew of anyone they could recommend. The standard reply was "my cousin Jack." There seemed to be a lot of Welshmen available with the first name of "Jack."

Bill Whittit was in charge of the cyanide flotation mill and finishing areas. Guy Folke, another Grass Valley high school associate, was in charge of the mining operation. All in all, it was an efficient, well-run operation with a loyal crew who got along well both at work and outside of work.

Meanwhile, however, we had some changing dynamics going on in the family circle involving Jack's parents. As I mentioned earlier, Jack was basically my big brother when I was young. His mother Elena was my godmother, and in my family a godmother was a very special person.

When Jack's mother and father separated after their time at the **Sweetwater Ranch,** Jack came to San Francisco and lived in my grandmother's apartment. Tante Catharine lived there also. I recall from time to time she would holler upstairs to my father to "get this kid (Jack) out of the bathroom!" Sometimes he would gather up the Sunday newspaper to read in the bathroom while he was in the tub.

What was a little unusual about the situation was that his father Ed Gallagher, who was a very bright but very structured Irishman, refused to get a divorce because of his religion. So he and my aunt had a "separation" for life. But Jack and my times together did not change all that much. Jack continued to go on trips with me and my father on vacations and during summers. Cousin George, however, was living in Fresno, where the weather was warmer, because of some medical problems. So he was not involved much in the early life I shared with Jack.

During the summer of '28, Jack and I again had a great time climbing the cherry trees and eating as many cherries as we could. We went to the Memorial Stadium swimming pool and wandered westward to the farm where an aviation pioneer kept a plane he had built in the early days of flying machines. Lyman Gilmore was his name and he had a long beard, was reasonably tall, and very much of a recluse. A couple of times when he walked to town, we would sneak into his barn to take a peek at his unique plane; the wings had scallops on their trailing edges. Lyman Gilmore had theoretically been in competition with the Wright brothers, but the Wright brothers flew first.

But for us, it was a thrill just to be so close to his plane. Although he was looked upon as the town 'character, ' Gilmore was eventually recognized for his past experience of building early planes and the Grass Valley airport was named after him. A small model of his plane is on display in the Transportation Museum near Grass Valley.

Jack and I would also go to afternoon movies that starred cowboy heroes, who always seemed to be shooting up bad guys or Indians. After the movies, we walked up Main Street to my house, but often stopped along the way to talk with Judge Mulroy who was a friend of both my father and my grandfather. He and his friends took life easy on the porch in front of the judge's office on Main Street after the sun went down. They would tell us many tall tales, but the one I remember most was about the longest baseball ever hit.

The game took place on a Grass Valley baseball diamond and one of the players hit a long fly ball which cleared the baseball field. The ball landed in a creek that eventually carried it to the Sacramento River, then down to the San Pablo Bay, and into the San Francisco Bay. . . out the Golden Gate to the Pacific Ocean. The judge and his friends had a whole assortment of such stories that they loved to tell impressionable kids like us.

By fall of that year, the mine in Calistoga, which was called the Silverado Mine, was becoming quite successful and I spent my weekends there with my family. In those days, mules were used to haul the ore from the mine to the mill location, pulling the heavy ore cars. There was a short tunnel between the mine and mill, which were about a half mile apart. The mules were reliable, and in this case, one mule towed a load of three heavy ore cars about every half hour.

But three was the magic number. They had a great, innate gift for understanding that a three-car load was acceptable, but a fourth car was not. They would lean into the load and if they sensed the load was too much they would just stop. And they would not move until the fourth car had been removed. It seemed like the mules had a union!

I spent a lot of time wandering around the mine area sticking my nose in everybody's business and asking questions. One of the benefits of being the boss's son was that people would talk to me about what they were doing and why they were doing it.

The assayer showed me how he made evaluations of the ore. I could also go to the blacksmith and help him make wedges for the picks. The first time I helped him, though, I made a painful mistake. He was cutting off forged pieces of iron that fell on the ground. I thought I could visualize when the iron was hot by the color. But when I attempted to pick up one that I thought was cool, it turned out to be exceptionally hot. The blisters on my thumb and forefinger were substantial, and I never tried that one again.

My father frequently took me underground to witness the operation and explained what the miners were doing. I had a light and I could observe and understand the functions of what was going on in the mine.

It was fun to follow a mule on his trip through the tunnel and beyond to the front of the mill processing line. The ore cars dumped the rocks into a huge rectangular container where several large round steel balls ground up all the ore, creating quite a racket. I could then follow along and watch the flow of pulverized rock as it emptied down a chute into the cyanide flotation units.

Next, this pulverized material was subjected to a circulating unit that allowed the cyanide to separate the silver and gold from the other residue. This mine was definitely a silver mine, but the ore did contain a modest amount of gold. Eventually a type of foam spilled out onto a drying area containing both the silver and gold.

Here, there was a big rotating canvas that slowly circled in a counter clockwise direction. It also functioned as a method of separating the cyanide from the gold and silver; recycling the cyanide back to the cells, while the gold and silver remained behind on the canvas. Finally the canvas was subjected to a large brush which removed the metals to another drying area for a short time, until they were then trucked to a smelter near Vallejo.

This smelter had a main stack 250 feet high and the unwanted debris was distributed by the wind, which blew it toward the eastern farm areas. Much later, in the 1950s, the smelter and the stack were torn down because this method of separation caused too much pollution.

There were a variety of things I remember about living in Calistoga in those days. In town, there were two fairly large hot water swimming pools. Going for a swim in them, however, was not my idea of fun. I guess they may have been great for little old ladies, but not for a young boy. I couldn't wait until we got to Grass Valley to go swimming in a cool, natural pool.

Then there were the 4th of July festivities 'country style.' As an engineer, my father was always good at making things and fire crackers were no exception. He'd fashion them with very short wicks and throw them high up into the air and the dynamite would go off, leaving a bright shower of 'stars' as they fell to the ground.

But it was the Calistoga countryside, however, that often inspired more quiet, reflective moments for me. Sometimes I used to lie down on a hillside near the mine, look up at the clouds and tried to imagine what kind of man I would become.

Me, Dad, and Ginger

Another memory was my excitement when my family bought a radio. The first broadcast we listened to came all the way from Salt Lake City, a thousand miles away, and introduced us to the Mormon Tabernacle Choir. We were all truly amazed by the sound quality and volume of the choir.

The radio made a great entry that year, and became a lively, enjoyable part of our lifestyle. We'd gather around in the evenings after dinner and listen to music programs.

In those early days of radio, most of the shows were music and entertainment-oriented. Later, during WW II, however, that would change when it became a primary vehicle for news about what was happening on the war front at the other end of the world.

`   But from the beginning, everyone in our family, even young Ginger, liked listening to the radio.

But that was a leisure time activity. I also had certain 'responsibilities' around the house. My father had great love for my sister Ginger, but I was proud of the fact that it was *me* who got to help him clean out our bathtub so he could make gin during the Prohibition years.

Just like in many cities and communities across the country, the small town of Calistoga never went 'dry,' and I was pleased to play my own small part.

Chapter 13

San Francisco

The Formative Years

Later that fall, my cousin George returned to San Francisco from Fresno to live with his mother and Nana on Broadway Street. After spending most of his eight years in a much warmer climate for medical reasons, George's doctor finally pronounced that he was well enough to handle the colder San Francisco weather.

I found out that George was quite generous. He shared his chicken pox with me shortly after he arrived. This required that we spend a lot of our time on the large fold-down Murphy bed in Nana's living room. We also got a little of Nana's nursing, which you may recall, included a glass of warm water, sugar and a half shot of bourbon.

Jack, on the other hand, helped me get something I really did want – my first job, and I certainly enjoyed earning money. Jack sold *Call Bulletin* newspapers on the lucrative corner of California and Polk. My post was at the less busy corner of Polk and Clay.

On the weekends, he and I often went to the Saturday serial movies at the Royal Theater on Polk Street. "Officer 444" was one of our all time favorites. Sometimes we'd visit the Red Poppy candy store next door, after we'd enjoyed Officer 444 being rescued—again. We must have seen him escape sure death at least 100 times before the theater closed down.

As I mentioned, I was very interested in aviation and there were a lot of weekly magazines that I used to read, which cost about 10 cents. They were written about pilots from WW I, and one of the more noted men was a German pilot, Manfred von Richthofen, better known by his nickname of "The Red Baron" because he flew a bright red plane.

The Red Baron shot down a lot of beginner pilots. The Germans had a game of letting the French and English come across their lines, and once there, made the Allied forces a target. One of the Red Baron's tricks was to sit on his side of the line and nail many of these younger and newer Allied pilots. He ran up a fairly long list of conquests as the war continued.

Whenever he shot down a pilot, he marked where the plane crashed and had someone collect a "momento," which von Richthofen hung in his living quarters. By the time he, himself, was shot down, he had achieved a record of at least 80 "kills."

In the end, the Baron was killed by a senior Canadian pilot because von Richthofen was focusing all of his attention on chasing a junior Canadian pilot. The more I read about the Red Baron, the more I disliked him. The fact that he shot as many people down was a war situation, but putting up "souvenirs" on a wall was beyond reason to me. Even at that stage of my life, I realized it made me feel like I wanted to kill Germans. So I found I was happier when I stopped reading about him altogether. I started reading about other ace pilots like Max Immelmann instead.

A much decorated German fighter pilot, Max Immelmann was the first pilot to be awarded the country's highest military medal, known as the "Blue Max" in his honor. He was also closely associated with Germany's first fighter plane, the *Fokker Eindecker.*

But what particularly interested me, both as a youngster and later when I became a pilot myself, was his aerobatic manuevers like the "Immelmann turn."

Scouting was also one of the ways I spent my time. I was a Cub Scout at age 8 and 9. We had meetings once a week on Friday nights in a large basement room in a church on Larkin and Pine. Sometimes we drilled there, but I noticed that we had a smaller space in the basement than the Boy Scouts did.

We marched around a lot and learned how to display and salute the flag with our two-finger salute. Our uniforms consisted of matching shirts and pants, with a distinctive neck scarf. The project that impressed and interested me the most was a display of roughly 20 different knotted ropes. We were taught how to tie these various knots, and I must have excelled in the procedure because I still remember them today.

When I was 10, I was able to join the Boy Scouts, which put me in that larger section of the basement. Our uniform was usually short pants and long socks, and a different colored neck scarf from the one I wore as a Cub Scout. Our Troop was Number 27, and a patch with our troop number was sewn onto our shirt's left sleeve.

We took the Scout oath and followed the Scout law. Basically the "law" indicated that a Scout was "trustworthy, loyal, friendly, courteous, kind, obedient, cheerful, thrifty, brave, clean, and reverent."

This was a major task to live up to!

As a Scout, you could increase your knowledge by getting involved in their merit badge program. There were books in our meeting room that described what was required to earn each badge, and there was training available in many areas.

   Our Scout Master helped us contact the proper adults in businesses or the fire department, for example, who would help us review everything we had to learn, and then critique us. Since I was interested in fire safety, I studied the subject and then worked with the Fire Chief in my local fire station until he thought I had learned enough to earn the merit badge. He contacted the Scout Master to confirm I had completed the requirements for that particular badge, and then I could move on to another one. In the end, I recall they all got sewn onto a sash type of cloth, which I wore at scouting events.

   This seemed to be a good challenge and I continued to earn the following badges: Fire Safety, First Aid, Swimming, Lifesaving, Geology, Astronomy, Athletics, Camping, Cooking, Safety, Plumbing, Woodwork, and two others that I can't recall. In all, I earned 14 merit badges. (I was one badge short of the 15 required to become an Eagle Scout.)

   One year we were involved in a three-day demonstration and presentation of our skills in Golden Gate Park with a lot of other troops. We lived there for the duration of that time and we had visitors who came to the Park to view our exhibits.

Boy Scout Camp in Golden Gate Park in 1933. I'm the one in the middle (at the table on the left), displaying our troop #27

The Boy Scouts had a location in the hills above Fairfax that was used as a summer camp. There were about 10 large tents that housed about 10 boys each. We explored, played games, and cooked our own meals for a one-week period.

Other troops used the camp throughout the summer. Out of the four years as a Scout, besides the Golden Gate Park experience, I went to this camp for three summers. Jack came one year, and George another; but neither of them stayed with scouting as long as I did. For one thing, I did learn – much later – that George didn't like my cooking!

However, let's not get ahead of the story. Good Scout that I was, I still had a very busy schedule to keep, and a reputation to maintain on the playground.

*   *   *

By the 4th grade or so, I was starting to really come into my own, and I'll admit – chalk it up to youthful exuberance, I suppose – that I began to think I was "Mr. Wonderful." (Although it was less about feeling that I was wonderful, and more that my life was.) I liked school, and my teachers and parents were happy with my work and grades.

Life was good.

Plus I was good at sports and was willing to trade punches whenever necessary. Some people, however, took a little convincing. Bobby Jones was a frequent challenger and he and I fought several times. Problem was, he was not improving and I was. The first time was a draw, I won the second time, the third time, and the fourth. . . at which point he finally gave up.

Other sporting encounters were just as enjoyable, but less combative. There was a Japanese family who lived on an alleyway off Broadway Street in our neighborhood. They were very nice people, and the father owned a dry cleaning business on the western side of Hyde Street. Their son and I used to enjoy playing together. I remember they had some sort of Japanese swords that we used to spar with. But we didn't get together too often because his school in Japan Town was in session after our school let out in the afternoon.

On a sad note, one very unhappy event that made a huge impression on me happened the year I was in 4th grade at Spring Valley Elementary School. We had a classmate who was having problems. He just didn't seem to fit in socially and he had difficulty with his school work. He definitely seemed to withdraw from the rest of us.

One day our teacher announced to the class that he had tried to commit suicide by eating poison. He did survive, but he did not come back to our school. I was sorry I never tried to include him in anything. It bothered me for a long, long time. It must have hurt him terribly not to have the comradeship that most of us had together. For one thing, sports was largely what drew many of us together, and he just didn't seem interested, or inclined to participate.

It took me a long time to get over the fact that I had not tried to be his friend. I promised myself that I would never forget him, and I would try to help any classmate who might be having any kind of social problems, or needed a friend.

*   *   *

By the time I was 9 years old, I had another half-year promotion into the 5th grade. About this time, I got involved with a new newspaper route where I delivered the papers to homes and apartments. When I had been selling newspapers on the corner of Polk and Clay Streets, I sometimes hopped aboard an afternoon street car and sold the *Call Bulletin* to

workers going home from work. For this I was paid the prince-
ly sum of 1 cent per paper. But when you consider that the
cost of each newspaper was 3 cents, it was a pretty good deal.

For my second newspaper job, I picked up my papers
on Leavenworth between Clay and Sacramento, across the
street from the Fire Department. The new route provided me
with more money than the previous street corner location, but it
did have its negative side. I not only had to deliver the newspapers, but I also had to collect the amount owed for them on a
monthly basis.

An important aspect of my new route was that it would
soon include a major 18-floor apartment building that was
under construction at the southeast corner of Clay and Jones.
It was almost completed and after it went up, so would my
salary. I was eagerly looking forward to it, not yet fully appre-
ciating how much easier it was to deliver papers than to collect
for them.

That was my work routine. Then there were several
places in my immediate neighborhood that I remember vividly
in terms of sheer fun and outdoor recreation.

One was a large vacant lot about a block and a half from
where we lived. It was about 100 feet wide at the street level,
but what made it so appealing to us was that it went straight
up another 100 feet or so into an abrupt cliff that leveled off at
the top. This provided an excellent place to play 'King of the
Mountain.' One group would be stationed on top of the hill
with access to grass and dirt clods, which could be used to pelt
the lower group as they climbed up the the hill to try and take
over possession of the top.

Early in life I found it wise to start out on top of the hill
to avoid getting hit on the head with a large grass and dirt clod.

The neighborhood had a great group of male sports enthusiasts who were eager to compete either at our playground or on the streets. In addition to the streets being a major place for us to play, there was also the Helen Wells Playground, located two blocks west of our apartment on Larkin and Broadway. It was named after a great Bay Area tennis player. When they decided to bestow her with this honor, they also changed the floor surface from redwood bark to asphalt. God, what a great change.

During the next 14 years growing up with Jack and George, I obtained a large number of black eyes, won several fist fights and rematches, and was smart enough not to take on anyone who would make me lose this record. Some of the boys I was careful to avoid were those who had older brothers who were professional boxers and trained their younger brothers.

Early on, I could run faster than most of my classmates and generally was chosen first or second when somebody was selecting a team. Whenever our class played another school, I was always selected for the baseball or basketball team. In the fifth grade, I competed at the City track meet in the 50-yard dash and the broad jump. I took second in the broad jump but was caught lacing my shoe in the 50-yard dash when the starting gun was fired. Needless to say, I was pissed.

The Helen Wells Playground consisted of a full-size basketball court with a second half basketball court, two tennis courts, and a small area where very young children played in the sand box or on swings. There was also a small office with equipment storage. It opened at 8:00 a.m. on Saturday and Sunday, and was open every day when school was out.

There was always a group of eager beavers waiting for the gates to be opened and the basketballs to be handed out. I was one of them. I was an especially active kid. But back then, most of us were, so we were all pretty fit. This was probably because there was not the steady stream of sedentary distractions like televisions, computers, video games and electronic gadgets to get in the way of our sports!

Unfortunately, there is hardly ever a soul at this wonderful playground anymore.

On Saturdays we usually played basketball all morning and went home for lunch, returning for the balance of the afternoon. Most of the time we played half-court ball with three people to a side. After one side scored 22 points, the next team replaced the losing side. On the days no tennis players showed up, we could play softball or touch-tackle football on those courts by taking down the nets. The sport we played depended upon the season.

Sunday we gambled by shooting baskets from center court as individual shooters. Generally we played for 25 cents per game, although when we got a little older and had a little more cash, sometimes games could be as much as $1 per person contests.

I must point out that we did not play basketball at a slow speed. Our brand was played at a different pace than in colleges, high schools or grammar schools. Our game involved both close defensive guarding and shooting one-hand shots . . . done much of the time on the run.

Later, when I was a teenager, our neighborhood had a football team. Our team, including Jack at that time, went down to the Marina Green to play with a Japanese football team. They were not only good, the were "properly" dressed in full uniforms, including helmets, cleats, and other things. We, however, showed up in our usual uniforms of jeans and tennis shoes. We played a good game, but they still beat us.

In one series, we stopped the Japanese team on our 5 yard line. Frank Cagoule, our kicker, punted from behind our goal line and had the wind with him. He got off a tremendous punt, which landed on their 20 yard line, rolling out beyond their end zone. It was a kick Frank was never able to duplicate again.

Ezio Lanza, another classmate, lived across the street from our apartment on the other corner of Broadway and Leavenworth. We went to school together, played baseball and basketball together – either for or against each other – as well as games like 'kick the can' in the street. Later, when we had enough money, we both bought tennis rackets and enjoyed playing against each other.

Ezio's mother looked out for all the kids in the neighborhood. Some of the empty lots had debris from new buildings, and if one of us got injured, she would come out with her magic 'mend it' box and patch us up with her own Italian goo cream, definitely not a store-bought item, and cloth bandages. She also looked out for us when the Irish policemen occasionally attempted to disrupt our street games of football or hockey on roller skates.

The police would cruise up the street in their car, roll down their windows, prepared to challenge us. Instead they would be on the receiving end of a barrage of Italian from Ezio's mom, who was always quick to open her window and shout at them. They couldn't get a word in edgewise, even if they could understand what she was saying. Finally, they'd just close their windows and drive away.

One reason Ezio's mother was so effective was because she had a great voice with huge volume. On a calm day, she could be heard within a three or four block radius, all the way from our street corner to the playground. She would holler

"EZIO" and he would answer, "Che Cosa, Mama," no matter where he was.

Mrs. Lanza was also a great cook and I had meals at their home many times on Sundays. The dishes were numerous and humongous and the time spent at the dinner table was at least three hours. There was always an assortment, including meat dishes and vegetables, big bowls of soups, and platters of different pastas and desserts, all accompanied by lots of talking.

Like all the Italian families I knew, the Lanzas invested time and money in their children by making sure they had voice or music lessons. Ezio didn't have it going on for him vocally, but he did learn to play the trumpet, and like it or not, the whole neighborhood was privy to his progress. Every morning promptly at 7:00 a.m., the neighborhood was subjected to Ezio playing the Stanford March "Come Join the Band" with his bedroom window wide open.

He gave a whole new meaning to the word 'practice.' Thing is, he was determined to play it the whole way through without any mistakes. So every day, without fail, he would get into the piece, continuing along just fine until he hit a bad note. When he did, he'd immediately start all over again from the top. Everyone knew that he was going to play it over and over again until he could finish the whole song perfectly before he left for school.

So we all either groaned, prayed, or held our breath, hoping that Ezio would get it right, for once, the first time so we wouldn't all have to suffer. There was always a collective sigh of relief in the neighborhood on days when he did.

But that doesn't mean we didn't like music or that we didn't appreciate a well-played trumpet. About that time, Louis

Armstrong – one of the most celebrated singers and trumpet players in jazz history – released "Ain't Misbehavin," which became his signature tune.

Boy, could he blow that horn.

Other songs like "Happy Days Are Here Again"[16] came out just a few months before that and reflected the optimistic, upbeat mood of the country in early 1929. Then there was the clever "Puttin' on the Ritz" by the legendary composer Irving Berlin. "Singin' in the Rain" (by Arthur Freed) came out that year, as well as Michael Cleary's "Singin' in the Bathtub," which spoofed Fred Astaire's dancin' feet version.

As you can see, there was an abundance of riches – musically speaking – for us to listen to that spring, so none of us really minded Ezio's musical meanderings.

Of course, none of us knew – nor did the rest of the country – that we would soon have much bigger things to worry about in the days ahead.

---

[16]This song by Milton Ager later became the theme song for Franklin Roosevelt's presidential campaign in 1932, as well as the unofficial theme song of the Democratic party.

Chapter 14

Then Came the Crash

The Depression

That year started out pretty much like most years. I was busy with school and sports, and Jack and I had our newspaper routes. He and I did things together outside of school and work, just like we always had. I remember one time his father, Ed Gallagher, took us to meet one of his friends, a Chinese butcher who had a shop in Chinatown, not far from old St. Mary's Church on California Street.

Inside his shop, he had whole chickens and various cuts of meat hanging, as any standard butcher did in those days. But below the street level was an entirely other world of underground tunnels. Jack and I were curious about this. Although some people assumed there were things going on below the street levels – likely having to do with opium dens, gambling and prostitution – Jack and I had never had a chance to see the tunnels firsthand.

So when the butcher took us downstairs below street level to show us the basement studio he used for writing and drawing (as well as storage), we caught a glimpse of the long dark tunnel where he hung some of his extra cuts of meat. The additional space, as well as the cooler air temperature, provided him with his own cold storage area. He had strung a string of lights to illuminate the tunnel.

In his studio, he proceeded to show us all kinds of things, but what was especially interesting to me was when he pulled out a large sheaf of paper and illustrated how Chinese characters were made. We'd never seen anyone use a brush with black ink to write. I was also impressed with the idea of having an underground room like his.

My family – not just my parents, sister and I – but other family members as well, were still living in the 3-story apartment building at Broadway and Leavenworth that was our home for several years. As mentioned, we lived on the third floor, and Tante Emilie, Uncle Walt and my cousin Barbara, lived across the hall from Nana on the second floor. This arrangement made it easy for us all to spend time together.

Frequently, the family played poker on Saturday nights in the large dining room in my parent's apartment. Sometimes my mother and father's friends would come, and other times they changed locations and went to my Aunt Mabel's house. On those occasions, my parents often stopped at Mayes Oyster House on Polk Street to get food on their way out to her house in the Panhandle near Golden Gate Park.

If our apartment was used for the card games, my sister Ginger would be in my mother and father's room – usually napping – and Jack and I would go down to Nana's apartment. We'd amuse ourselves by playing games, eating snacks, and drinking juice or punch (or even a little wine when we could sneak it). One of the adults would come by occasionally to check on us and make sure we were okay. For the most part, we behaved ourselves, although a couple times, Jack and I would manage a little mischief or game of our own; like pelting eggs down at the people who were walking down the street across from our building.

Around 11:00, the grown-ups would stop playing cards and they'd have a meal of whatever food people had prepared or brought over. Then early the next morning while everyone was still asleep, Jack and I would get up and eat whatever food was left over.

Ah, those were the days.

My father and I also spent time together on weekends, on occasion, building things or doing other projects around the house, which was always fun. He was extremely patient every step of the way when showing me something new. He not only had a good sense of humor, but he always took care to not just tell me what to do, but to teach me things at the same time. He also liked to surprise me.

I remember when he brought home a baseball that one of his friends gave him to give to me. This was a very special ball because it had been signed by Babe Ruth. But I played catch with that ball over the years as if it was just a regular baseball. In fact, it eventually got so beat up, I put friction tape on it to hold it together!

But my dad did not oject at all. It was mine to do with as I wished. I had a wonderful upbringing and supportive relationship with both my parents and Nana, as well as all my cousins. They were always there, loving and accepting of me, but also encouraging me be active, have fun, be independent, and fully enjoy being a boy – and then later a young man.

A couple of years later, another friend, my father's gin supplier from in the '30s, gave me a football for Christmas. So whenever we played football, we used my ball. Needless to say, the neighborhood got a lot of good use out of that ball. Whenever we went down to the Marina to play other teams, whether from our school or other schools, we had our own ball to use.

Speaking of school, I must confess that what I remember most about school that year was my 6th grade teacher. She was a young, good-looking Italian woman and she was an excellent teacher. But what really left a big impression on me at the time was that she had big 'jugs,' as they so indelicately put it in those days. All the guys noticed that. How could we not? But for me, this may have been my first awakening of my being attracted to the opposite sex.

Life seemed to be moving along, just like usual, not only in my small world, but in the world in general. Herbert Hoover took office on March 4th, 1929, and the mood of the public seemed to be mostly upbeat. Although there had been a gradual economic downhill slump that seemed to be gaining momentum – and making some people nervous – that was mostly the experts and long-term investors. After all, the market had soared the year before. So after nearly a decade of prosperity, most people seemed to think that it would all turn around.

But it didn't. And a big change had evolved.

The stock market, previously considered a calculated risk, primarily the domain of knowledgeable investors and financial big shots, had become more of an open playing field. People talked about 'making a killing' in the stock market, and 'get rich quick' schemes suddenly sounded plausible. More people than ever wanted to 'play the stock market' and amass great wealth.

But on Tuesday, October 29th, 1929, it all came tumbling down. They called it "Black Tuesday," and it was the day Wall Street Stock Market crashed, taking many, many people with it. Then came "Black Thursday." It was like a line of dominoes, when each one fell, it set off a chain reaction. As stock market prices plunged, people frantically sold their stock – at one point, as many as 16 million shares on the same day. Everyone was trying to dump their stock before it was too late.

But it already was.

Banks closed down because they had invested their customers' money in the market. This, of course, caused widespread panic and everyone rushed to the bank to withdraw their savings. And for every bank that went bankrupt, so did all their customers who weren't able to get their money out in time. It was a disaster, and it was just the beginning of the downhill spiral that became the Great Depression.

At a time when California's population was 5-1/2 million, there were millions of Americans out of work. Not only did they lose their jobs when the companies they worked for cut back, or closed down altogether, there weren't many new jobs to be found. Even rumors of jobs, even in another state, brought literally thousands of applicants. This meant that unscrupulous employers could get away with paying practically next to nothing in wages. And they did.

Between 1929 and 1933, wages dropped nearly 40%, and the unemployment rate soared to 25-35% at the height of the Depression.

Farmers also had to contend with severe drought conditions in the Great Plains and devastating dust storms. This triggered a mass exodus of people heading to California. They had to leave everything behind, except what they could tie on the roof of their cars, in their search to start a new life out West.

It was definitely one of the darkest chapters in American history. As my mother, Elvira, said. "It was terrible . . . it was one of the two worst things that ever happened to me in my life. " (The second came 10 years later.)

And for me, as a young boy during that time, even though most of the families in my neighborhood were getting by, I saw firsthand the level of despair it caused, and how that drove some people to desperate acts.

One incident, in particular, stands out in my memory, even after all these years.

As the Depression grew more severe, I started having problems collecting money owed to me for the newspapers I delivered. The 18-story Clay/Jones building had been completed by that time, but with the financial situation, only a few people had moved in. One of them was my customer on the top floor.

When I went to pick up my newspapers for delivery one day, I happened to glance down and notice the photograph on the front page of the newspaper. The picture showed the Clay/ Jones Street building. There were a series of dots from the 18th floor to the ground level. That's how I found out that my subscriber had jumped. Many other people were doing the same thing in the San Francisco financial district.

But this one really hit home, and not just because I felt bad for the guy. I was a practical kid, and the jumper owed me for one and a half months of deliveries when he went out that window. Then I learned of my father's troubles and realized just how widespread the disaster really was.

My father's silver mine in Calistoga was in jeopardy. Although silver and gold were of equal value during 1861 to 1865 – the Civil War years – gold was selected as the dominant currency. The price of gold was protected by the government, however, silver was not. In 1929, silver had a value of $18.35 per ounce. But it kept declining so that by 1931 it was $8.37 per ounce and $5.79 by 1932.

Ironically, if the Silverado Mine had been a gold mine instead, it would have been protected. The price of gold was set at $22 per ounce, but in 1933, Roosevelt boosted the price of gold to $35 an ounce, an increase of more than 65%. In addition, people could no longer exchange their paper money for gold.

During the Depression, the price of silver continued to drop lower and lower. My father's Silverado mine that had started off so nicely just a couple years ago had to be shut down. So that was the end of that. He simply couldn't afford to operate it any longer and pay wages when the price of silver fell so much. The mine and equipment had to be sold. To make matters worse, his partner stiffed him on some of the proceeds from the equipment. So it was an unhappy ending to what had been a profitable enterprise.

Our house in Grass Valley was also sold.

My father had a difficult time getting a job. He took small jobs, and whatever consulting jobs he could find during this time. One of these projects involved finding the proper source of soil to build Treasure Island for the Exposition. He took me with him to Marin County to visit a farmer who had property that fronted on the Bay. The best part of the trip for me was watching this man's two huge horses – similar in size to Clydesdales working the fields.

I also recall his driveway was lined with glass "float balls" from Japanese fishing nets that had slipped away as a result of heavy seas, and made their way all the way from Japan and washed ashore in California. Evidently this farmer eventually decided not to get involved with the Treasure Island project because I don't remember hearing anything more about it. I do remember the trip with my dad, though, and those huge horses.

My father also went to Alaska acquiring contract work to research potential mines for individual investors. My mother was able to land a job with the Park and Recreation Department playing piano on the city playgrounds for young children, a job she continued to do for many years. Jack's mother, my Tante Elena, was remodeling houses.

Tante Catharine had a job working for an automobile parts company doing clerical work. Tante Emilie worked as a bookkeeper for Del Monte (using a comptometer, an early kind of computer), and Walt's father was a policeman, while his two uncles were firemen. So my family was less affected than some people were in other parts of the country, particularly in the Midwest. Still, it was definitely a more somber time than the earlier decade.

Starting over was what many had to do.

Many people were desperate. They were doing whatever they could do to get by. In downtown areas of the City, people stood in line trying to get something to eat, while others were selling fruit and vegetables out of their yard. Some people had to give up their homes when they could no longer afford to pay their rent or make their mortgage.

Times were uncertain, for sure. Even the music of the day reflected the mood of the times. Duke Ellington's beautiful, but melancholy, "Mood Indigo,"[17] was recorded not once, but three times in 1930. The song went on to become a jazz standard. Then there was "Gloomy Sunday,"[18] written and composed in Hungary (but which was also popular here), which was later recorded by Billie Holiday. Some went so far as to call "Gloomy Sunday" the saddest song of the decade.

[17] "Mood Indigo," music by Duke Ellington and Barney Bigard, with lyrics by Irving Mills, was recorded by many artists over the years, including Ella Fitzgerald, Nat "King" Cole, Frank Sinatra, Nina Simone and Louis Armstrong.

[18] "Gloomy Sunday" by pianist/composer Rezso Seres in 1933 (to a poem written by Laszlo Javor).

Even one of the best-known folk songs of all time, "I've been Working on the Railroad,"[19] captured some of the sentiments of the day, with increasing numbers of men 'riding the rails' during the Depression, as they traveled from town to town looking for work, or at least the next meal.

But perhaps of all of the music in 1931, it was "Brother Can You Spare a Dime?"[20] that best spoke to the times, so much so that it was referred to as "the anthem of the Great Depression."

*   *   *

One of the things I read in the newspaper had to do with veterans and their concern over their benefits. Back in 1924, Congress had approved a bonus payment for veterans who had served their country during WW I. This payment was to be calculated at the rate of $1.25 for each day of service overseas, and $1.00 per day for time served in the U.S. This decision, however, included one serious drawback: The bonus payments would not be disbursed until 1945.

By 1932, in the midst of the Great Depression, many of the veterans were unemployed and getting desperate. In May of 1932, a huge army of WW I veterans – between 15,000 to 20,000 strong – descended on Washington, D.C., marching and rallying to demand immediate payment of their bonuses. Some brought their families along. They set up camps in the city, marched through the streets to protest, and became known as the "Bonus Army."

While the rallies, marches and protests started out peacefully enough with a degree of military-like precision and order, as time went by, inevitably tempers rose. When fighting broke

---

[19] Classic American folk song, believed to originally been written in 1890, and recorded later.

[20] Lyrics to "Brother Can You Spare A Dime," by Yip Harburgh and music by Jay Gorney.

out between the vets and local law enforcement, President Herbert Hoover – in a move of great irony– brought in U.S. Army forces to clear the former military forces out of the capitol.

Two months before the Bonus Army marched into Washington, D.C., another event captured the nation's attention in a very dramatic, heartbreaking way – the Lindbergh kidnapping, which was called "The Crime of the Century."

On March 1st, 1932, the Lindbergh baby, Charles, who was only 1-1/2 years old, was kidnapped; abducted from his home in Hopewell, New Jersey. His parents, the famous aviator Charles Lindbergh, whose exploits had so captured my attention (as well as the rest of the country) and his wife, Anne Morrow Lindbergh, were devastated.

Law enforcement personnel pulled out all the stops in their attempts to solve this high profile crime. Every detail of the kidnapping was closely followed and published in newspapers across the country. It was, as far as I remember, the first time a major crime became a national news event, closely followed by so many people.

Everyone hoped for the best, but the outcome, as everyone knows, was the very worst possible scenario. The baby was found dead on May 12th, 1932.

Four years later in 1936, a man named Bruno Hauptmann was arrested and ultimately executed for the crime. But people were still discouraged and concerned.

Not only was this the son of a person who so many felt they "knew" firsthand because of having read so much about him, it was the fact that the baby was kidnapped right out of his own bedroom in the family home that struck a note of fear and sadness in the hearts of the nation.

* * *

My own family, however, despite what was going on both in this country and abroad during the Depression years, fared pretty well. We not only had each other and a place to call home, but we always had food on the table. Nana and my family always made the most of what they had.

That was a period when Nana's Basque cooking (utilizing the less expensive parts), became especially useful. Beans and stews were the order of the day during the Depression, and that's what Nana's big black pot at the back of the stove usually contained.

Although I'd always known from a young age how fortunate I was to have the loving, Basque family and upbringing I had – a good life, defined by school, sports, family and friends – I also don't recall that many people that we knew personally being out of work during this time.

Although some people had to take jobs they didn't necessarily want, I don't remember a lot of families in the neighborhood suffering. In those days, people weren't picky about jobs, or concerned that some job or other was beneath them. They wanted to work, to succeed, and were willing to take whatever they could find.

So in our neighborhood, at least, things weren't as bad as they were in some parts of the nation.

Chapter 15

Prospecting with My Dad

The End of an Era

Of the many trips I took with my father, two of them, in particular, stand out in my mind. The trip to Empire Gold Mine in Grass Valley when I was quite young was the first. Everything about the mine was of interest to me. As we walked around, my father explained what was going on. He said this extraction method was old fashioned and not as effective as newer methods because about 20% of the fine specks of gold could be lost.

I was particularly fascinated by the large wooden 'skips' as they were called, that the men climbed on and rode down into the mine shaft. About 20 miners would ride sideways on each skip to get down to their workplace. They would SING on the way down. This really surprised and delighted me as a youngster.

My father told me that the mine was American owned, but that the miners were from Cornwall, England, and were brought over to work in the mine. Later I learned there was also a large settlement of Serbian miners who lived in the nearby town of Jackson, who worked in the large gold mines there.

Then there were the stamp mills. These were used as a secondary refining method of the ore. There were 50 or so of these big machines pounding, pounding away 24 hours a day! They were lined up together for a distance of about two blocks long. It was quite an amazing sight and sound.

The second trip that I remember best, probably more because of the companionship than the mining aspects of it, was during one summer several years later. My father was looking for potential gold mines at that time and he took me with him to Foresthill where we stayed overnight, and then took a one-lane dirt road into the El Dorado National Forest. Some of the land had been uplifted during an earlier geological period of time and there were visible deposits of gold in an old vein. In fact, this whole area revealed remnants of much earlier river activity.

The gold mine was about 200 feet above the river, near the North Fork of the American River at an elevation of about 4,200 feet. The owners of the small mine were attempting to develop it but were having problems. The State of California had passed a law long ago against using river streams for mining because of the impact of the residue on farming interests in the valleys below.

We were there for three days while my father reviewed what the owners had been doing. Since they were trying to come up with a method whereby they could still operate the mine, they wanted my dad to tell them how to work on the vein and remain within the letter of the law.

One way was to dig out the dirt and take it somewhere else to sort, instead of dumping it into the river, but that was quite difficult. The roads were poor and the cost of hauling the dirt somewhere else and then sorting through it made extractions very expensive. Another problem was that the old river bed was above ground for a relatively short distance and would not sustain a long term mine.

While we were there, I stayed outside of the mine most of the time, wandering around through the surrounding areas and exploring along the natural path of the river, accompanied by a 2-year-old German Shepherd. I found one place where the river was peaceful and calm. I also found out that whenever I would start running from time to time, the dog would immediately seize the cuff of my pants and trip me. Whenever I was walking, he was happy, but the moment I broke into a run, he would go right for my cuff again.

After about a day and a half of this, I decided to make use of the calm place in the river which I had previously scouted. I figured if I was to run and jump into the water, he would follow. Sure enough, as I began running, he was right behind me. Just as he was about to catch me, both of us made a 6-foot dive into the river. We both climbed out of the water and walked back to camp together. But I noticed that when I ran after that, he had decided it was not such a good idea to chase me anymore. But we still remained friends and continued to play after that. I thought he was a great dog.

Another activity I recall doing at this mine was using my pen knife to see what I could find in the way of gold around the entrance to the mine. I had picked out five or six small nuggets and when my father asked me what I had been doing, I mentioned my nugget findings. He told me that these nuggets belonged to the owners, not to me, and that just because I could spot something on someone else's property, I was not allowed to take it.

He did, however, buy two of the nuggets and gave them to me at the end of our trip. I never found out, though, what the final results were with this mine.

Also on this same trip, we visited another fellow that had some property he wanted my father to look at. This mine didn't have very much potential and was definitely in a period of decline. However, the interesting part of this particular visit was that this man had a brother named

Lawrence Tibbett,[21] who was an opera singer in New York (with the New York Metropolitan Opera). So while my father and I were out in the boonies to meet with this man about his mine, we found ourselves sitting in a little room in the back of his small house listening to his brother's records.

The fact that Lawrence Tibbett was from Bakersfield, an old cow town, and had achieved major success as a fine opera singer only made it all the more unusual. My father and I got a real kick out of that.

Those trips and experiences with my father were high points on the *family* front. Plus our family celebrations and events were always joyous occasions. When my Tante Catharine married Alberto Scott, our family had a big wedding party for them. After the wedding, Catharine and George moved into Alberto's home, nearby on Franklin Street between Pacific and Broadway.

But there were also some very exciting things continuing to develop in the larger world picture, especially in the field of aviation. As you can imagine, these never failed to capture the imagination of a young man like me, who dreamed about what it would be like to learn how to fly a plane someday.

What an adventurous time it was to be alive.

For all the progress made in aviation – from the earliest 'flying machines' and gliders, to the primitive airplanes and fighter planes of my boyhood, to the advent of sophisticated airplanes when I was a young man – I always considered myself lucky to have been there in the early days.

---

21 Lawrence Tibbett, renown for his affinity with Verdi's works, has long been considered one of the finest baritones to perform at the Metropolitan Opera. In fact, his records made during the 1920s and '30s are considered to be among the finest of that era.

It was exciting to witness Lindbergh making aeronautic history. Then there was Amelia Earhart. She was a very dedicated, determined young woman, more savvy than most of her generation. Her flying records, accomplishments and aeronautic feats were of interest to everyone. I remember reading about her endeavors in newspapers and magazines.

In May of 1932, Amelia Earhart made her first transatlantic solo flight; 5 years after Charles Lindberg. Only rather than departing from New York, she flew out of Newfoundland for Paris, but ended up landing in Northern Ireland (near Derby) instead. She was a pilot who frequently took chances, but she was lucky that time.

But that year, as a curious young man, not yet 13 years old, I must admit most of my ambitions were down to earth, centered on the 49-square miles of land that was my home in San francisco. I was primarily looking forward to graduating from 8th grade from Spring Valley Grammar School that year in December. That, and anticipating what my life would be like when I started high school at Lowell, a college prep school nearby, the following year.

Surprisingly enough, even though I was fascinated with aviation, my career plan at the time was to become a doctor, a choice much encouraged by Nana and my mother, of course.

Chapter 16

Playground Politics

Keeping the bullies at bay

My most satisfying fight occurred when I was in the 8th grade. We were playing baseball against Redding, another nearby grade school at the Funston Playground. By the way, while it's currently called Moscone Playground in honor of former San Francisco mayor, George Moscone, the original name of this playground was Funston, named after Army General Funston.

So since this neighborhood playground was called Funston when it opened; it was Funston when the DiMaggio brothers played there; it was Funston when I played there, and it was Funston after WW II...I still call it Funston, instead of Moscone.

In any case, this playground was large and had two full-size hardball diamonds. It also had two basketball courts, three tennis courts, an indoor basketball court, a large area for storing the equipment, plus offices for supervisors. But need-less to say, that day like any other day, all of our attention was on our game, and we were determined to win it.

Home plate for diamond #1 was on the northeast cor-ner of the playground. I was playing first base when our game was interrupted by three Italians from North Beach. The leader of this walking 'trio of trouble' was a mean guy who thought he was a big shot, instead of the bully he really was. His nickname was 'Half Man,' and he was anywhere from 5 – 8 years older than me, but was about the same size. He and his buddies came on the field and pushed our third baseman, trying to start a fight. When they got no reaction, they moved to bullying the shortstop, and then on to the second baseman. I watched all of this from first base, beginning to get more than a little upset at Half Man. Soon it became my turn.

I had carefully observed Half Man's tactics, which he started by putting both of his fists on the chest of the other ball players. So when he came over towards me with his two side-kicks and started to reach out to push me in the chest – he got my best right-hand fist on his large Italian nose instead. Half Man went down to the ground, and while one of his companions was trying to get him up, I was fighting with the other guy. I saw Half Man starting to get to his feet, so I nailed him one more time.

All of a sudden the playground supervisor, who had seen the trouble coming from about a block and a half away, ran over to our area and took over. He told Half Man and his friends that they were barred from ever coming into this playground again, and that he would call the police if they ever came back.

This was a much more serious statement in those days. Police could apply some serious consequences, and were not subjected to unbelievable hands-off restrictions like they are today. A few days after my incident at Funston, I noticed a change of attitude amongst my school friends.

There were not too many people challenging me to fight after that.

Chapter 17

San Francisco in the '30s

Music to my ears

Like for most young people, music was something that made much more of an impression on me as I became a teenager. While music had always been a big part of my home life, especially because my mother was so musically talented, it wasn't until I was 13 or so that I first started really 'hearing' music in a new way. Suddenly, it became more than just a background sound track to whatever else I was doing at the time.

Besides reaching the age when I began to notice songs that had a good melody or catchy lyrics, I think there was an increased emphasis on music in general during that decade. For one thing, people really embraced the new medium of radio. It brought the world into our living rooms in much the same way the internet does today.

Undoubtedly radio's popularity was a response, and even a refuge of sorts, from the pressing – and depressing – events going on in the world at the time. And in a sense, it was the only entertainment game in town since the film industry was still very much in its infancy. Then, when movies did become part of the culture, the songs and musical scores were a big part of the overall attraction.

Here are some of the popular songs in the early '30s that were memorable enough to have etched a small groove in my memory bank:

"Body and Soul, "Chloe" (also known as the Prisoner Song), and George Gershwin's catchy classic, "I Got Rhythm."

Then there was Ruth Etting singing "Ten Cents a Dance," and other romantically oriented numbers like "I Wonder Who's Kissing Her Now," "As Time Goes By," and Bing Crosby's "Where the Blue of the Night (Meets the Gold of the Day)." Many of you may recall "Dream A Little Dream of Me," for its evocative melody and lyrics.

So many of the songs of that decade became classics. "Night and Day," "Sophisticated Lady" and "It Don't Mean A Thing If It Ain't Got that Swing," by Duke Ellington, as well as Vernon Duke's "April in Paris," are still enjoyed by nostalgic listeners today.

Many of these songs can be heard on the internet now, where you can also find complete information about who wrote, composed, and performed these songs over the years. (See Appendix).

[22]"Body and Soul," a #1 song of 1930s was written by lyricist and composer Robert Sour, and performed by Paul Whiteman and his orchestra.

[23] "Chloe "(The Prisoner Song), was a popular song and jazz standard; music by Charles Daniels and lyrics by Gus Kahn.

[24] "I Got Rhythm," was composed by George Gershwin with lyrics by Ira Gershwin; this was probably Gershwin's most widely heard song. It was recorded in 1930 by Red Nichols (and His Five Pennies). Louis Armstrong and his orchestra, as well as Ethel Waters recorded chart-topping versions in 1931.

25 "Ten Cents a Dance," Ruth Etting's hit song, was written and published
   by Richard Rodgers and Lorenz Hart in 1930.

26 "I Wonder Who's Kissing Her Now," Music by Joseph E. Howard, lyrics
   by Will M. Hough and Frank R. Adams.

27 "As Time Goes By" was written by Herman Hupfeld in 1931. This
   classic song was recorded that year by several artists, including
   Rudy Vallee and Jacques Renard. It was featured in the film *Casablanca*
   in 1942, sung by Dooley Wilson.

28 "Where the Blue of the Night (Meets the Gold of the Day)" was a
   popular song that was also Bing Crosby's theme for his radio show.
   It was recorded in 1931, backed by Bennie Krueger's band. Writers
   were Roy Turk and Fred E. Ahlert, and Crosby contributed to their lyrics.

29 "Dream A Little Dream of Me" by Wayne King is usually credited to
   Fabian Andre and Wilbur Schwandt, and the lyrics were written by
   Gus Kahn. It was recorded by Wayne King and his Orchestra in 1931,
   and Louis Armstrong recorded it in 1932. The 1968 version by the
   Mamas and the Papas sold 7 million copies worldwide.

30 "Night and Day" was by American Tin Pan Alley composer and songwriter
   Cole Porter.

31 "Sophisticated Lady," is the Jazz standard composed as an instrumental
   in 1932 by Duke Ellington and Irving Mills. Lyrics are by Mitchell Parish.

32 "It Don't Mean A Thing If It Ain't Got that Swing" was a 1931 composi-
   tion by Duke Ellington, with lyrics by Irving Mills.

33 "April in Paris" was composed by Vernon Duke in 1932, with lyrics by
   E.Y. Harburg. Many artists have recorded it, including Louis Armstrong,
   Count Basie, Frank Sinatra, Billie Holiday, Ella Fitzgerald, but the 1933
   hit was by Freddy Martin.

Chapter 18

All Under One Roof

And becoming a teenager

In January of 1933, our family moved to a large flat on Filbert Street, between Hyde and Leavenworth.

There were three bedrooms, a full bathroom, and another half-bath (with only a sink and toilet), the kitchen, and a large dining room, which led out to a good - sized garden. The financial effects of the Great Depression required families to double up, and that' s what we did.

Tante Elena moved in with us. I now shared a room with my cousin Jack and his little sister, Elena. Tante Elena and Nana shared one bedroom, while my father, mother and sister shared another one.

Ginger, Mother and me in front of Filbert St. house

I started attending Lowell High School that year and took the usual courses in History, English, Math and Science (mostly animals, birds and insects that year, if memory serves). I also took Latin. As for Jack, who had completed his Oakland boarding school requirements by then, he went to Galileo High School. My cousin George still attended Spring Valley, but we all saw each other on the playground on the weekends.

Since Jack and I lived in the same household, we got to see each other every evening as well. I also knew his secrets; one was that he smoked. I knew this because he put his cigarette butts on the window ledge in the bathroom.

George and I also saw each other on Sundays, since we were both altar boys at the Spanish Catholic Church. Even after starting classes in Latin, I still didn't understand most of what was said in that language. What I did notice very clearly, though, was how competitive George tended to be as he went about his 'duties.' As a result, he was involved in some of the more spectacular collisions at the altar site.

There was a specific order for moving two religious items from one side to the other. When it was the other altar boy's duty to move his item to the other side first, he was always beaten to that cross-over point by George. This did not go over well, and Father Antonio was not happy about these collisions.

At the conclusion of the Mass, the altar boys were supposed to put out the candles. Although it was a nice church, it was a rather poor one. Most of the people who attended did not have as much money to contribute as the congregations in some of the wealthier neighborhoods. Anyway, for that reason, the instrument that we used to put out the candles was basically a curtain rod, and a hollow and flimsy one at that.

The idea was to blow from the bottom of the pole to extinguish the flame at the top. I discovered it was difficult to blow out the flame with most of the curtain rods because they were so holey – and I don't mean 'holy' in the religious sense. So I picked out the best pole and marked it, and then made sure I always got that one. That way I was always able to very quickly extinguish the candles in my area and then watch the other boys struggle with theirs.

I guess it was sneaky, but I didn't tell any of the other altar boys. Even George was not privy to my secret, nor was Nana, of course. She saw me as a good Catholic boy and I saw no reason to convince her otherwise. In fact, since I was 13 years old by this time, Nana felt she could trust me enough to enlist me in a most delicate and crucial task – cutting her corns! This was a slow process because I didn't want to create a problem for my grandmother. But I did keep saying to her, "Why don't you get some medicated pads from the drug store that would help you get rid of these corns?"

She didn't pay any attention to my words of advice, however, and always said, "Just cut the corns, Mr. Root." This chore lasted from that time until when I started college. And it was always the same. We would have long discussions every time about whether I was cutting too close or not, and I don't remember ever getting any salary for my special "surgical" services.

*   *   *

That year Tante Elena gave Jack and me a Christmas gift that allowed us to use 'The Plunge,' which was the swimming pool at the Fairmont Hotel for about 6 months. I remember beginning to learn how to dive. I went up on the diving board, the 10 foot board, as I recall, trying to get my act together.

It didn't work. I made my approach to do a back jackknife, and started my procedure just fine, but when I came off the board I suddenly knew I was in deep trouble. I had misjudged my jump and was not far enough out from the end of the board. Unfortunately, I recognized this fact when I was already coming down. My head hit the top of the board and I went over backwards into the water.

The people around me immediately called out, "Do it over again." Basically, they were believers in the concept of

'Don't worry about what happened the first time.' I, however, knew I was not that stupid. I thought I might hit my head again, so I swam to the end of the pool and got out. There are some things you learn early in your life – you don't do dumb things twice – even at the advice of others.

We rented our flat on Filbert Street from a nice Italian couple, Mr. and Mrs. Bargini, who lived on the top floor of the building.

Nana in front of the house

Ginger and me in the back yard

One year they gave Nana a Christmas present of home-made grappa. Of course, Jack and I sampled it, he first and me second. We knew we were both in trouble and spit it out – more because of the bitter taste than the fact it was off limits – and never tried it again.

Later we tried my father's bourbon whiskey, which went down a whole lot easier. Then we would refill the bottle with water to keep the level constant. We did this several times over the course of a month and for some reason didn't think we would get caught. But of course that day came. My father tried to serve a guest, only to discover that the bourbon had been diluted. He immediately knew it was us.

Prohibition was over by then and beer was for sale. I recall one weekend when my father purchased some for our household dinner. That was when I got to taste beer for the first time, but I was not impressed. In fact, I couldn't fathom why they even bothered to restart producing beer again at all because it tasted so bad.

Around this time, Tante Elena was fixing up a small house she owned on Filbert Street between Polk and Van Ness. After that project was completed, she and Jack moved from Filbert to a small house on Hyde Street. They had no sooner gotten settled in the new house when Jack managed to break his leg, and was shipped right back over to Nana's on Filbert Street again to get more care.

Dad and Jack

Of course, I would pop in to visit him. I especially remember one day when he was sitting there shelling pine nuts for himself, and I swiped a handful from his bowl as I walked by. I wasn't worried, though, because I knew that it was one time when he couldn't get up and chase me.

We still had Sunday dinners at Filbert Street with Tante Elena, Jack and his sister since they were only a half block away from our house. George's family, as well as Walt's, would come over to those dinners. They were always fun affairs except on Sunday nights when Tante Elena drove me nuts with her crummy choice of music. She always wanted to listen to some character named Harry Owens and his Hawaiian music.

His broadcasts were from Honolulu, where he and his orchestra performed regularly at the Royal Hawaiian Hotel. [This was the same hotel where my Tante Elena, who was a professional dancer in her early 20s, danced when she went to the Hawaiian Islands. It is also where she met and became friends with the English novelist and writer Somerset Maugham, who was writing a book about the Hawaiian Islands at the time. After that trip, Elena returned to San Francisco and married Ed Gallagher].

In any case, whether a royal hotel or not, I still thought his music was the worst. But I guess not everyone shared my opinion because apparently he had quite a following. True, the size of our music box was not one of those magnificent Magnavox machines – it was more like the size of a large dictionary – so the sound was not the best, but it never bothered me at all when *my* music was playing.

Many of the popular songs from 1933 were basically romantic songs about love, or at least the hope or promise of it; like "Don't Blame Me" or "It's Only a Paper Moon," and "Did You Ever See a Dream Walking." Then there were classics like "Smoke Gets in Your Eyes."

And me, I only had to endure a few more Hawaiian tunes because shortly after that, Tante Elena and Jack moved to another house she purchased down on Bay Street. She worked really hard at her profession and was very good at it. Her new structure had two floors. There were three bedrooms and two shower bathrooms, and a big living room with a fireplace on the

---

34 "Don't Blame Me" is by Jimmy McHugh, lyrics by Dorothy Fields.

35 "It's Only A Paper Moon" music is by Harold Arlen, lyrics by Yip Harburg.

36 "Did You Ever See a Dream Walking," a Harry Revel song, with lyrics by Mack Gordon.

37 "Smoke Gets in Your Eyes" is a show tune by composer Jerome Kern, lyrics by Otto Harbach. It was recorded by several artists including Paul Whiteman, Ruth Etting, Artie Shaw, Harry Belefonte, and was later a #1 hit for The Platters.

upper floor. Downstairs, there were three separate apartments, which she rented out individually. There was always work to do on one or more of these apartments, or outside in the yard. And there were three of us to do it; Jack, myself, and a teenager named Dante Santora, who lived nearby. The garden alone kept us pretty busy.

We moved bricks to section off areas in a more decorative fashion, replanted shrubs and flowers, and trimmed the trees and grass around the flower beds. Weeds were an ongoing problem because the yard ran all the way down the back to North Point Street. The projects never seemed to end.

As payment for our labor, Jack and I got a salami sandwich and a beer (which I didn't really like, but I didn't turn it down). Dante got paid in money since he was a little older than Jack . . . and because he wasn't a relative! The good news was that I got to go home to Filbert Street at 5 o'clock, as did Dante who lived with his brother in an alley near Hyde and Union Street. But Jack lived there so he got the jobs like painting the units at night.

Sometimes Jack and I hung around with Dante after hours in the neighborhood as well. In fact, one of the more spectacular automobile accidents I was involved in happened right around the corner of Union and Larkin Streets. Jack, Dante and his friend Max were adjusting the carburetor on their car to get it ready for a trip up to Reno and back, traveling through Sonora. So they were using the flat part of Larkin Street to go back and forth, making a U-turn each time at Union.

The accident happened when Max Sarbor was driving. He didn't quite make the complete U-turn the last time around at Union Street and crashed into a pole. I was sitting in the back of the car, but being nimble and quick, I managed to bail out just before Max hit the pole.

Jack and Dante also jumped out and the three of us took off running. Max was left sitting in the car holding the steering wheel, stunned, but unhurt. The car, however, had to be taken to a nearby garage for repairs, and Max had to pay for it since he was the one who hit the pole. That left him with no money to go on vacation, so Jack and Dante went on the trip without him.

The following year, I was still working at Elena's. One of her tenants, a man named Snoble, had a collection of small, delicate china dogs that I dusted once a week, for which I got paid a little money. This was just a small job that I did in the morning before I had my afternoon classes at Galileo, but I was not one to turn down work. I think this man worked in the financial business in some capacity. I never knew exactly what, but he was very particular about his glass animals. I had to always make sure they got put back in the exact same spot after dusting.

My Tante Emilie and Uncle Walt were living nearby on Broadway when he became a policeman. After that, they moved with their daughter, Barbara, out to the Sunset neighborhood into a new housing area at Irving and 18th Street. My cousin, Walt, was born in a hospital near there on February 12th. He was the last of Nana's grandchildren.

The streets were in at that time, but all the rest was sand dunes that ran all the way out to the Pacific Ocean. That was where I saw a glider for the first time. It was being manually towed by a car to launch into the oncoming winds. I was enthralled, and knew I wanted to do that someday. Even though it didn't travel very far, it did fly.

*   *   *

During this time, while I was caught up with everything going on in my own life and with my family, I was also aware of serious things going on in the larger world arena. There was a lot of political unrest overseas and troubling developments that I read about in the newspapers, heard about at school, and heard discussed at home with my family.

I knew, for instance, that there were serious political and economic problems in Europe as a result of the Great Depression. One development that was on many peoples' minds was the outrageously outspoken, unconventional right-wing politician who had become Chancellor of Germany in 1933 – Adolf Hitler.

He had an eerie and disturbing ability to rally masses of military force – apparently mostly under the guise of extreme Nationalistic rhetoric – amongst a population who were desperate for change. That they were as desperate for jobs, food, and economic relief as they were for political change only served to accelerate the chain of events that was to come.

Although he was perceived by many insiders as self-serving, volatile and unpredictable, the government in Germany was, in fact, deadlocked and had been for more than a decade. People wanted change – a turnaround – and that's what the new Chancellor seemed to represent. At least at first. Perhaps there was a mood of naïve optimism combined with an overwhelming sense that things would have to get better, because they couldn't get any worse.

Within a very short period of time, Hitler became absolute dictator of Germany. By the end of the year, the Nazi party won 200 seats in the German Reichstag.

Wheels were in motion and we all know where it ended.

It's hard to imagine that anyone – the government, industrialists, or even the military, much less the citizenry –

anticipated the full scope of this one mans' obsession for world domination; nor the horrendous role that he and the Nazi party would play in provoking a war, murdering millions of people, and forever changing world history.

Chapter 19

High School Sports

And a Coach Named Neff

During my first two years at Lowell, I played lightweight basketball at 110 exponents. Exponents were arrived at by factoring a student's age, weight and height. At 13 years old, I actually had only a total of only 99 exponents because I had skipped a year in grade school and was slow to start growing.

There were four basketball teams, 110, 120, 130 exponents and a varsity team. In my freshman year, I got to play on the 110 team and by my sophomore year, I had blossomed to a full 108 exponent and again played with the 110 team. Since four teams playing during the same semester were too much for one coach to handle, the high school approach was to schedule the varsity and the 130 exponent teams to play in the spring semester, while the two smaller teams played in the fall. However, we didn't have a good place to practice, so we played at the full-sized basketball court at the east side of Kezar Stadium for a few weeks prior to competition.

Early during the spring semester our coach, Ben Neff, analyzed the new freshmen, making a point of organizing a basketball team as well as teaching the sport. He took some of us and drilled us in dribbling and passing, while evaluating our ability to defend against likely opponents.

Ben was a great coach, even though a little noisy. One of his methods of teaching was to engage me and another potential member of the 110 exponent team, Al Baer, in two-on-two games during our gym period. Ben played with El-mer Harris, the track coach. Both of them were short men. Ben had played only 145 pound basketball in college. By the time our semester was over, we were able to use their own tactics – right back on them.

Al and I had a great time during the second part of the year playing other high school teams. The next year when we both played on the 110 team, Al and I created havoc for some of the other teams with our newfound approaches to guard-ing and maiming opponents. I often won wonderful accolades from the sidelines from Ben. As I said, he was not a silent coach by any means, and I recall hearing him shout to me from time to time during a game.

I remember the time we were playing Mission High, and I was stunned when the flake I was supposed to be guarding had just made a shot from the center of the court – for the first time ever – and it went in. He probably never made another one like that again in his life. I couldn't believe it. And as I watched the ball drop through the net, I could hear Neff's voice loud and clear above the din of the crowd: "Root, you god damn IRON HEAD, guard your man!"

That was par for the game. One way or another, you heard about your moves. You never had to wonder where he stood. There were three incidents that did not endear me to Coach Neff, one in my freshman year and the other two were in my sophomore year. The first was before our season started, while we were still practicing. I was on the first team but I broke my arm playing tackle football on a Saturday. I remember that my dad was away prospecting in Alaska at the time.

Anyway, Coach was furious. He just couldn't fathom how I could have been so dumb and he kept repeating that sentiment all through my recovery. I was on the second team for the season's opening game, but back on the first team for the second game.

The second event took place while we were at Kezar practicing for our upcoming basketball game. The coach was late that day so I arranged a game of touch tackle football on the basketball court, using the basketball for a football. I was right in the middle of passing when coach Neff arrived. He saw what I was doing and proceeded to throw basketballs at me as I ran around the court. After that, we all settled down and continued the basketball practice. I gathered he was not overly happy with me. However, I did start out the season as a first string.

The third incident occurred during half-time of a game were playing against Galileo. We were leading, but not by as much as the coach felt we should. So he gathered us together in a room in the Galileo gym and vigorously launched into a pep talk. For some reason, I started to giggle, like young kids sometimes do, and the more I tried to control it, the worse it got. Soon other players started laughing too, and by then I was rolling on the floor. Coach Neff didn't think it was funny.

Well, guess who was back on the second team and didn't play for a couple of games . . . I did finish up on the first team, however. Ben was nothing, if not fair. He always let you know what he expected of you, and was quick and direct about letting you know if you weren't up to speed.

Ben Neff had a phenomenal memory for names and faces. Many years later, when I was about 40 and had occasion to be at Lowell one morning, I decided to look up my old basketball coach. I knew he was nearing retirement and wanted to pop in and say hello. I expected to find him in the gym and went down there, but was told that he was monitoring a study class, so back upstairs I went to the study room.

When I entered the room and advanced towards him, he raised his hand (like a stop sign) and said, "Don't tell me!" and then immediately pointed at me and said, "Lloyd Root!"

I was pleased he remembered me. . . and that he didn't say "Iron Head."

We had a long talk about what I had been doing and how I was getting along. We talked about our gym period basketball games against one another. He said he was happy that I was small back then and couldn't do as much damage as I had wanted to do.

It amazed me that a man who had coached thousands of kids – including future All Americans and All Pros – would remember one small 110 exponent player for that many years.

That's the kind of man Coach Neff was.

Chapter 20

Building Bridges

Linking San Francisco to the rest of the State

For decades, people had dreamed of having a bridge across the Golden Gate strait to connect San Francisco to Marin County. By the early 1920s, given the growing population in San Francisco and increased traffic on the roadways and waterfront, the proposal really began to gain momentum.

But while everyone liked the idea of such a bridge, many people – including engineers – said it would be impossible to build. They questioned how feasible it would be to build a bridge so long, and one that was structurally sound enough to weather everything from relentless winds, high tides, dense fog, and earthquakes. Perhaps most formidable of all, was the challenge of anchoring the towers in the unstable soil.

Then there was the question of money. How many millions of dollars would it cost, and where would it come from, since funds had already been allocated to build the Bay Bridge. Others were opposed to the idea for aesthetic reasons; that it would be an eyesore and ruin the natural beauty of the area.

However, after nine years of controversy and red tape, proposals were taken from the top engineering firms in the country and Joseph Strauss, who was mentioned earlier, was chosen as Chief Engineer for the project. On January 5th, 1933, with great fanfare, they began construction on the Golden Gate Bridge.

It was a huge project and took many, many workers, although exact numbers are not available since so many contractors were involved and records were not accurately kept. But they labored long and hard – it took 4 years to build the Bridge – and often in bitter cold, heavy winds, and foggy weather conditions.

The Golden Gate Bridge, the longest suspension bridge in the world (at the time) was completed on May 24th, 1937. The Bridge is 1.7 miles long (with a .8 mile long suspension span). The roadway is 90 feet wide and 220 feet above the water. The bridge has two main towers that are 746 feet tall that support the two massive cables, made of galvanized steel wire.

While Joseph Strauss was the chief engineer and project advocate, the architect of the bridge was Irving Morrow, and the senior engineer was Charles Ellis.

The toll was 50 cents initially, and was supposed to be paid off fairly quickly. Then the politicians decided that the State could get the money for monitoring it, so they just kept increasing the bridge toll. Now, of course, it's up to $6 per car – until the next hike.

The Bridge was built to 'move' and it has stood the test of time. Forty- five years after it was built, the main span bowed approximately 6 to 7 feet during the harsh winter storms of 1982. Then on May 24th of 1987, during the big 50th anniversary event to celebrate the opening of the Bridge, at one point the bridge moved several feet lower and began swaying from side to side under the weight of 300,000+ people.

This went on for nearly an hour, causing some people to get seasick. Still, despite the chill, the winds, and the massive crowds, it was a triumphant, joyous celebration.

Many of the crowd in '87 called it a "once in a lifetime" experience. A few people, however, were also there when the Golden Gate Bridge originally opened 50 years earlier. According to those who had walked across when the Bridge when it first opened, the sentiment was that although the crowd had been very excited, they had also been far more serious and subdued back then.

The Great Depression had that effect.

I must admit that I did not walk across the Golden Gate Bridge when it opened May 27th, 1937, but my mother and my sister Ginger – who was a pretty young teenager at that time – did. To me, what had been most interesting was watching the work in progress from the hills on either side of the City.

Ginger

Three three months before the Golden Gate Bridge was completed, Amelia Earhart decided to fly around the world from East to West. On March 17th, St. Patrick's Day, she and her navigator, Fred Noonan, departed on the first leg of the journey from Oakland to Honolulu.

I remember watching her fly out that Sunday morning over the nearly completed Bridge, flying toward Hawaii. I was living on Filbert Street at that time and could easily watch her plane from the street.

After experiencing mechanical problems en route to Hawaii, she landed there for three days of repair. Then, upon take-off from Hawaii, something happened – perhaps a blown tire or ground loop – that forced her to have the plane shipped back to Burbank, California, by ship for repairs.

After this delay, she changed her route to fly West to East, covering a route from Oakland to Miami, and beyond.

Then there was the experience of watching the Bay Bridge being built, which was actually an even more ambitious project. Designed by Charles Purchell and built by the American Bridge Company, when completed, it was the longest, heaviest, deepest, and most expensive bridge ever built. It was also considered an essential transportation link in the state economy.

Although construction of the Bay Bridge was started on July 7th, 1933, more than five months later than work began on the Golden Gate Bridge, it didn't take as long to complete. Workmen on this bridge received an average of $1.36 an hour.

The Bay Bridge opened for traffic on November 12,1936.

Jack's father, Ed Gallagher, picked up Nana, Jack and I and drove us across the bridge for the first time. The price, if I recall correctly, was about 75 cents. It was three lanes one way and three more in the opposite direction on the upper deck. The lower deck had two lanes for trucks only, one going each direction. Additionally there was a train and two tracks; one going each way. (This is the train I later took with Adrienne when we would go to visit my grandmother Minnie in Oakland.) But that first day, I don't think we were even trying to get to the East Bay. We just went over and back to check it out.

I suppose we watched the Bay Bridge construction more often because the work progressed more quickly, although boring the tunnel through Yerba Buena Island seemed to take a long time. The Golden Gate had its own unique problems and was much more sophisticated. The work on the land part on each side was much more dramatic than for the Bay Bridge. But it was interesting to watch the construction on both bridges and to see the changes as they were each going up.

As for my father, a frequent traveler and an engineer, I believe he was less enthralled with what engineering marvels they were considered to be – especially the Golden Gate Bridge – and far more excited about how much time he'd save when he was on the road!

But as newsworthy as the Golden Gate Bridge and the Bay Bridge were during these years, there was another, quite controversial "Bridges" frequently in the news. This one, however, was a man by the name of Harry Bridges. Known as a respected union leader to some; but considered to be a notorious Communist by others, he was front and center in a violent confrontation on the waterfront in 1934 that came to be known as "Bloody Thursday."

The trouble didn't start overnight. San Francisco was a manufacturing town as well as a major port. The waterfront had always been a hub of activity, with ships sailing in and out from all over the world, and numerous men working on the docks. However, since the workers wanted better wages and working conditions, tensions had been building for years. Labor and union workers led by Harry Bridges were on one side, and management and law enforcement on the other. Noisy crowds, confrontations and strikes were not uncommon.

So from my earliest memories, it was common knowledge that it was a good idea to stay away from the waterfront and the Ferry Building. And I, for one, always made sure I did. Yet, nobody was prepared for what happened when riots broke out on the waterfront between the striking labor unions and the local police.

On Thursday, July 5th, 1934, National Guard troops were called in to assist local police in patrolling the waterfront during this strike. When angry shouts, rocks and bricks were thrown by strikers, the police fired on the huge crowd on the

Embarcadero, near the Ferry Building. Two men were killed and 109 people were injured. The City was in an uproar, and this marked the beginning of a major strike, as well as a turning point in the history of working people on the West Coast. The strike and Harry Bridge's efforts led to the creation of the International Longshore and Warehouse Union.

And within five years time, San Francisco became known as a union town, the impact of which is still felt today.

Chapter 21

Nome, Alaska

A whole other world

Over the years, my father made a number of trips up to Alaska, prospecting and looking for viable mines. The territory around Nome was frequently his destination. Located on the Seward Peninsula on Norton Sound of the Bering Sea, Nome, founded in 1901, was once the most populous city in Alaska.

People who are familiar with the annual tradition of the Iditarod Dog Sled Races, know that the popular 1,100 mile race begins in Anchorage, Alaska, and ends in Nome. What is less well known, is that the very first Iditarod race in 1925 was far more than sport; it was a race against time. An urgent delivery of serum was needed to treat a diphtheria epidemic among the Inuit (Arctic Eskimos), but blizzard conditions throughout the state prevented airplanes from getting through. So a relay of dog sled teams was quickly assembled, and they made the historic run from Anchorage to Nome to save the day.

To give a more precise sense of its location, Nome is located 539 air miles northwest of Anchorage, 102 miles south of the Arctic Circle, and 161 miles east of Russia. While Nome claims to be the 'commercial hub' of northwestern Alaska these days, in my father's day, Nome was all about its gold.

In 1898, after three men – Norwegian Jafet Lindeberg, and two naturalized American citizens of Swedish birth, Erik Lindblom and John Brynteson – discovered gold in Nome, it quickly became a thriving mining town. The population grew to 10,000. When gold was discovered in the sand of its beaches the following year, it was estimated the population doubled.

But on September 17, 1934, disaster struck Nome by way of a huge fire. This fire, which started in a hotel and spread rapidly because of the wind, destroyed 20 blocks of the downtown area. My father was prospecting near Nome at the time, and I remember he told me that immediately after the fire started, the Eskimos started to drink, which left a bunch of drunken Eskimos and didn't leave many people to fight the fire.

It was finally stopped about a day and a half later. But the main street and business section of town on Front Street was completely destroyed – 65 businesses – as well as 90 of the nearby residential homes. Many of them had been built during the Gold Rush with reminders of the Victorian architecture that was popular then.

Since so much damage was done, that area of Nome had to be surveyed before it could be rebuilt. My father was given the job. He surveyed the area and prepared the official plot map that was ordered by the Common Council on October 3, 1934. His name can be seen upon close inspection near the end of this insert.[38]

He said it was quite a job. With so many records burned, he had to use various transit fixes and any kind of old records he could find.

The streets, alleys, blocks and lots in the City of Nome, Alaska, established by the Common Council in Ordinance № 287, dated October 3, 1934, in their relation to those that existed in the same area prior to the fire of September 17, 1934.
Map prepared under auspices of the Federal Emergency Relief Administration, by D.D. Stewart, Senior Engineer, assisted by Lloyd Root, Surveyor and William Manley draftsmen.

SCALE
80 ft. = 1 inch

An interesting side note:
Nearly 20 years after my father surveyed Nome, when I first started working at Crown Zellerbach, the sales manager, Shell

38 See Appendix to find out where to view this entire plot map on the internet

Taylor, asked me if I was related to "the Lloyd Root who was in Nome, Alaska in 1935." I told him Lloyd Root was my father. Shell said he had known him, and then went on to tell me this great story about how my father had been so nice to him and his friend.

The two younger men had been working in New York and they decided to quit their jobs and travel by canoe from New York to the Yukon River in Alaska. This turned out to be a two year "adventure." Leaving the river, the closest way back to the States was via a road to Nome. Once they got there, they met my father. He gave them shelter and a home and took care of them for about 3 weeks. Then he helped them get a ship out of Nome to Seattle on their way back to New York.

I remember reading the book that Shell later wrote about their trip.[39] One experience that stuck in my mind occurred after they were about at the halfway point of their journey. It was winter and they had to 'camp' in the canoe. The 'fun' of the trip began to wane and their arguing continued, as there was no one else around to criticize. They finally pulled over to a sand bar, got out of the canoe and had a huge first fight to get rid of their pent up anger. From then on, they continued as friends, and traveled on the river to a small village where they spent the rest of that winter.

Needless to say, it was such an incredible coincidence to have an opportunity to meet someone who had known my father back then, especially given what impact he had on these two young mens' lives during that 3 week period so many years ago. The fact that it even came up in conversation is amazing.

Life is full of surprises.

[39] *New York to Nome: The Northwest Passage by Canoe: From the Recollections of Shell Taylor,* North River Press, 1987

Chapter 22

Chinese Camp

Gaining Experience

In 1935 and 1936, Lowell High School was shut down because of earthquake considerations. They needed to reinforce (what they call 'retrofit' these days) the building so that it could withstand another earthquake, or two, or three. The job was scheduled to take slightly longer than three years. The plan was that instead of everyone going to school for a full day, we had to share the City's other various school buildings.

Initially, my Lowell class went to Poly Tech High School in the afternoons for one semester. Then during the next two years of this repair work, Galileo High was a split session school. The Galileo students went in the morning at 7:30 until 11:30. The Lowell people started school at 12:00 and went until 4:00. So when I was on my way to school, my neighborhood friends were already going home and liked to give me a bad time about it. They'd wave to me with big smiles as I went by; I would give them a proper one-finger salute in return.

During the summer months, I had an opportunity to go work with my father, which I really enjoyed. He knew a very wealthy man, who was a top executive for an oil company in Southern California. (My father had met him while he was State Mineralogist).

This man had leased a piece of property outside of Chinese Camp, located about 10 miles south of Sonora. Since it was located in a valley that had previously been involved in placer mining, he wanted my father to do a survey on the property to determine its potential value. By digging core sampling holes on a programmed basis on the original plot, my father would be able to provide him with reasonable information on the property.

I accompanied my father to Chinese Camp. He had selected an area just outside of the small town that had a potential for gold. This was not a hard rock mining operation, but rather an old riverbed operation and required diggers, most of whom came from Jamestown, about five miles from our operation. The area had to be plotted as to where the river had once run, and holes had to be dug down about 12 to 15 feet deep to the hard rock to obtain the core samples.

My job, working with one of the diggers down in the hole, was to turn the winch to get the sample, and mark it with a relating number onto the original plot. There were about four or five holes being sampled at one time. Different levels were checked for the amount of gold down to the bed rock. I was there the whole summer and had some interesting experiences.

There was a Chinese cook who made our breakfasts and lunches. He was more than a little strange. He was not fond of our "open air toilet" practices, and he often yelled at me in Chinese. My father was checking his invoices one time and noticed there seemed to be a lot of tea being used. It turned out the Chinaman had some sort of fetish about tea and my father finally discovered that he had been ordering enough extra tea so that he could line his sleeping area with about three feet of tea leaves.

He was replaced with another Chinese man who didn't order massive quantities of tea leaves or anything else, except food, and didn't mind if you urinated a mere mile away from the cooking area.

Then there was the executive's two nephews who worked at Chinese Camp, and the youngest one, Bill, was a real character. He had a hot rod car and ran – I should say *raced* – the recovered gold to the Mint in San Francisco on a weekly basis to exchange it for dollars. I went with him on one of these trips. We drove from Chinese Camp to Oakdale at a high rate of speed. Bill looked for the city cop who usually parked in the center of town and we could easily see which way the car was facing. Bill would then take the opposite direction, as there were two slightly different ways out of town. Since the police couldn't ticket you when you were out of city limits, Bill never had to slow down, and the cop never caught him.

I really didn't know the oldest nephew, Hart, very well. But I remember riding in the car with my dad, another fellow, and Hart one afternoon when we were returning to our living quarters. Just as we arrived, I jumped out the back. I happened to look down by the front side of the car and saw a large coiled rattlesnake. Before Hart could jump out, I yelled "Hold it!"

Then I slowly reached down and picked up a large rock that I threw at the snake. A direct hit. After playing baseball so many years, I hit him right where I wanted; it took his head right off. It also didn't hurt that I had grown up with snakes my whole life and was well aware of how to handle them.

I enjoyed working in the area. After the sampling was finished, the mining started by the time I went back to high school. However, it turned out that there was not a viable amount of gold to support the necessary equipment and personnel. Since there was a lease on the property, it continued into the fall. There were restrictions with placer mining because you couldn't use a dredge as there was no water, just dry land.

Anyway, the whole Chinese Camp experience was a positive one for me and included some rather unusual and interesting people. For instance, I worked for a miner who was married to a woman who was rumored to have been working in a bordello when he married her. In this period of the Depression, there were quite a few young girls who took that route as the only one open to them to earn their livelihood. I do recall that the miner was a very tough man, and of course, nobody made any comments about his wife having once been a "professional."

But speaking of places of that sort, that was the year when I had my first experience with a woman. Though they often referred to them as places where men went for "relaxation," as an eager young man of 15, I must say, that was not the word that came to mind!

The "House" was on Bush Street, between Polk and Van Ness, on the south side of the street. I went there early, probably around 5:00 p.m., and was greeted by two young ladies. I seemed to be the only other person there at the time. The pros were not there yet and I had the feeling the two girls were relatively new to the business. Both girls took me into one of the rooms.

They asked me, "Is this your first time?" and I said, "Yes." The next thing I knew . . . well, let's just say everything happened very quickly. Although the young ladies of the house were very friendly and solicitous, they were not above teasing me a bit.

I can't speak for my friends, of course, but the manner of my 'initiation' was fairly typical for the day. And did I go back another day? Yes, I did go back . . . several times.

Chapter 23

The Wonderful World of Sports

. . . the local angle

In the mid 1930s, colleges with basketball teams began to recognize that the game was being slowed down by the need to go to center court and have a jump ball after each field goal. They also felt it gave the team with a taller center an advantage in getting the ball for his team. So it was that the college coaches across the nation selected the Pacific Coast colleges to try out a new concept; basketball without the numerous jump balls. They did this for a full season.

The new game only allowed center court jumps at the beginning of the game and at the start of the second half. The team that was scored upon got to take the ball out at their end of the court, became the offense, and advanced up the court toward their opponent's basket. Very quickly everyone was using one-hand and two-hand shots. Old static defenses were modified to compete against this faster game.

This Pacific Coast trial was such a success that the whole country changed to playing this open style of game.

Hank Lusetti from our neighborhood was a basketball star at Stanford. When the colleges changed the basketball rules, Hank helped revolutionize the offense by converting stationary two-hand shots to a method of using running one-hand shots. On one trip to the East Coast, he scored 50 points in a game playing against a good basketball team at Duquesne!

This was unheard of in the old days when a team typically scored 25 to 30 total points per game.

Lusetti, one of our own, single-handedly changed the way basketball was played.

Both my cousins did well in basketball. Jack went to Davis and was on the Cal Aggies first string. George was All City four years in a row during high school, got a scholarship for USF, but joined the Army just prior to WW II. He ended up being first string on the 4th Air Force All Star team during the war.

Football at that time was essentially an amateur game but a very demanding one. Needless to say, it was a very different game than the one played today in a number of ways. • Players were required to play offense and defense, and substitutions were infrequent. • If you had to come out of the game for any reason in one quarter, you were not allowed to go back into the game until the following quarter. • Players called their own plays. • Managers were not allowed to signal as to what play to call. • Kicking and conversions were done by the players on the field, and there were no substitutions for any of the kickers, either.

College teams basically played in their own area. California would play Stanford, USC, UCLA, and occasionally Saint Mary's College or Santa Clara University. Sometimes the colleges would schedule games with an Army team from the Presidio or even with the Olympic Club who used graduate players.

Professional boxing was followed very closely in the neighborhood. We had one welterweight world's champion, Fred Apostoli. Al Citrino, who lived a few blocks away, fought Henry Armstrong for the world lightweight title. I went to see the fight and poor Al was knocked down 11 times before they called the fight in the 6th round. This immediately aroused Al's brother, who jumped into the ring and proceeded to go after Henry Armstrong. Everybody seemed to be getting a few punches in before the police put a stop to the brawl.

Al lost this fight, but he was a good main-event fighter for some time after that. And as you can imagine, this fight was also the talk of the neighborhood for quite some time.

There were several other fighters who were in main-event fights but did not progress into the higher levels of boxing. Some could have made it, but four years of military service during WW II ruled that out for most people our age. Vic Grupico was a good, fast lightweight, but by the time he got out of the Service and started fighting again, he was not as fast as he had been. He became partially punch drunk within a few years.

One year, we had two title winners in amateur boxing. Melvin Chicazola was the winner in the light heavyweight division in San Francisco, and Manual Sotomayor won the second title in the heavyweight division. Both lived on our street. Remember how I mentioned I was careful never to get in a fight with a boy whose older brother was a boxer?

That's why!

There was an Italian shoe repair man on Vallejo Street, next door to the hill where we used to play 'King of the Mountain.' This fellow ran a good repair shop, saved his money, and liked to bet on fights. Primo Carnera was the heavyweight champion of the world at that time and was about to fight Max Baer, the "Livermore Larruper." Primo's great claim to fame was his size as he probably weighed 260 or more pounds and stood about 6'7" tall.

Our shoe repairman had met Primo and told us with complete confidence, "I feela his muscle, nobody canna beat him." Well, Primo lasted 6 rounds, the shoe man lost his money, and Max Baer became champion.

There was a great deal of interest in baseball, both on the professional side, as well as in college and high school teams. In San Francisco, amateur and semi-pro baseball were well supported. Companies fielded teams as did clubs, bars, hardware stores and others. The Monday morning *Chronicle* would devote two full pages to box scores from hardball games played over the weekend in the many public diamonds in the city. Funston Playground, in our part of the city, as mentioned earlier, had two hardball diamonds.

None of the neighborhood baseball players got to play in the majors, but Frank Tartaro, who pitched for the Hollywood Stars made it to the Pacific Coast League before WW II. This league was just a half step below the Eastern major leagues. San Francisco had two teams; the SF Seals and the Mission Reds. Oakland's team was called the Oaks. A whole host of San Francisco players made their way to the big leagues, with the three DiMaggio brothers probably being the most famous. Ted Williams played for the San Diego Padres and advanced to the majors from San Diego.

In football, there were a large number of high school athletes but the most memorable of the college group was the All American from Santa Clara, 'Hands' Slavich. Not many from our neighborhood went on to football in college. "Turk" Terzian, played for USC, and eventually became an umpire for the National Football League. He received a gold and diamond ring for umpiring a Super Bowl game.

Our neighborhood, as you can see, took sports very seriously.

Chapter 24

Becoming a Young Man

and Working toward College

During my last two years of high school and while I was attending Galileo part time, the country was still in a major depression. The effects were evident even on Sundays at church. From age 7 to 15, I had attended Father Antonio's parish at the Spanish Catholic Church. He was a first rate priest, however, his parish had a tough time during those years. People without money started to put buttons into the collection box as it was passed down the aisle. I remember Father Antonio's words.

"No more buttons," he said. "God understands that when people don't have money they cannot contribute, but they are still equal to others that can contribute. But there is no reason for buttons. It is my job to see that this church gets money and I will contribute my own money for the people who cannot pay."

By that time, I had pretty much given up my plan to try and become a doctor. For the time being, it seemed to make more sense to just continue working toward college and see how things developed. I had a job subsidized by the Federal Government that consisted of cleaning up the physics and chemistry labs after school. I believe I got paid $20 a month, but it meant my illustrious high school basketball career was now kaput.

I went to my Lowell coach, Ben Neff, and told him I was sorry I couldn't play basketball any more because of my job. Coach was very sympathetic and said that my schooling and helping my family was much more important than playing basketball.

That didn't mean I didn't enjoy listening to games, though. One particular evening when I was about 16, my cousin George, Ezio and I were listening to a Stanford–USC basketball game in Ezio's front room. His mother had gone to bed and his father had come home from his job as a waiter. The game was thrilling, but all of sudden there was a whole lot of familiar shouting in Italian going on in the Lanza hallway. It was Ezio's mother, now wide awake, lamenting the fact that her husband was in trouble in the kitchen. It was definitely not helping that she was running up and down the hall shouting.

But she sure got our attention.

Ezio, George and I jumped up and ran out into the kitchen. I immediately guessed what had happened; we had the same kind of windows at home. Apparently Mr. Lanza had tried to get the upper window down to get a little fresh air, and the cord had snapped and the top window had crashed down on his hands. To make matters worse, Mr. Lanza was short, and now he was standing on his tip-toes with his fingers caught between the window frames and upper and lower panes of glass. Meanwhile, Ezio's mother was still running up and down the hall hollering.

Ezio ran to the nearest drawer and pulled out a handful of wooden spoons, generally used for salads, and was attempting to use them to pry his father out. He was busting off spoons at a rapid pace when I finally found a large screwdriver in the back cabinet that enabled me to pry Mr. Lanza loose. After I got him out, George and I went on home, and left the family to console their father; the ball game pretty much forgotten by all.

As the holidays approached, my 17th birthday was coming up (the day after Christmas), and I would be graduating from high school in a few weeks. I needed to start looking for work. A family friend suggested I should contact Bethlehem Ship Building Company.

They were building two new Navy destroyers to replace the four-stack ones. I found the proper area for an employment interview and everything happened very quickly after that. I passed the review for the job and the intelligence test, and was told to report for work the following Monday. My job was to check on eight welders, measure their output, and report it on their daily time sheet.

High school graduation photo

Most of the two destroyer's fabrication elements were welded sheet metal parts. The metal thickness varied depending on where it was being used. Gun mounts, for example, had a thicker weld than a light wall panel, and adjustments were made to compensate the welder for making heavier welds. The men doing the welding were paid on a piece-rate basis, and I was required to measure the amount of welding they did, and also record the thickness of the material on which they were working.

My salary was about $81 per month, which allowed me to give my mother $40 per month, and still have the same amount to save for college or to spend on myself. I was in hog heaven; completely happy with my job measuring the amount of welds of my 8 employees.

Most of the welding was in open areas, although some places required me to crawl under flooring which was a little dirty. However, showering took care of that problem.

In May, Nana bought a house on 2544 Franklin, which became known simply as '2544.' It was set back from the street with a large lawn in the front. Tante Elena helped Nana with remodeling plans to add the whole front entrance and increase the size of the living room. Shortly after the remodeling was finished, probably in July, my family moved into Nana's house. I had a small Murphy bed in the living room, Nana shared her room with Ginger, and my parents had the second bedroom.

My father, who was extremely good at building things, offered to improve the downstairs room just off the garage and my grandmother agreed to help fund it. I was really excited about this project. I helped him turn the storage room into a playroom and social lounge type area. We selected the lumber, laid out the plans, and put in the flooring and wall paneling. I helped him do all the carpentry work. We finished the project after a few weeks and everyone agreed it was a fine addition. The final touch was a ping pong table. We went on to spend many happy hours downstairs.

During the time my grandmother lived in the Franklin Street house, she loved to negotiate with the Chinese grocery man who stopped by two days a week. They both spoke broken English, but with different accents, and neither fully understood the other. The purchase of a couple of melons, some carrots or potatoes and fruit could take at least a half hour or maybe more, depending on how often the grocery man had to go down that long driveway back to his truck for better specimens.

That was about the time I started dating Dorothy Beckworth, a high school senior about ready to graduate from Galileo. She lived about two blocks from 2544 Franklin. We started going to movies together. She was a good looking young lady and I thought she was a really nice person. However, even though I wasn't going out with anyone else, I didn't think of her as my girlfriend. I guess you could say it was a friendship but it was not a romantic relationship.

Anyway, she used to visit with my mother and the two of them often talked about me. It made my mother feel better because she frequently asked me, "Don't you know any nice girls?" When she met Dorothy, she understood that I did know at least one nice girl. Our acquaintance faded away, however, later on after I went to college.

Around the house, I also had the job of helping Nana fill her empty wine bottles. Nana bought wine in five gallon containers for the family consumption at Sunday dinners.

My responsibility was to begin the siphoning action which brought the wine into a wine bottle. From time to time, Nana suggested that I was taking a little extra sip while I was on this job. I must admit that I did find a way to sample the wine before starting to transfer from container to the bottle.

Me in my white suade shoes

What teenager could resist?

I had been working in the shipyard on the destroyers for about five
months when my Tante Elena and my
mother told me about a "fine opportunity" they heard about that I could
have at an advertising agency.

My aunt had a tenant renting
from her who said he could get me into
McCann Erickson, a major San Francisco advertising firm. I interviewed for
the job and was accepted as an office
boy.

Me and Ginger at 2544

Now I had to wear a suit every day and my salary was
only $60 per month, not the $81 that I was used to earning. I
was clean when I came home, but I lost money in the process.
That's when I made a promise to myself in the future to only
make job changes that I carefully reviewed and agreed with.

The job was a "no brainer." I opened the mail, separated
it by individual recipients, and delivered it to the man's secretary, picked up her letters, put on stamps and dropped them
down the mail chute. Occasionally one of the three office boys
would carry artwork across the street to Standard Oil, or pick
up artwork to bring it back.

Dull, dull and triple dull.

While the job provided some money for my future
college tuition, I felt that all these endless conversations about
advertising were a major bore, and I dreaded the idea of
having to do something as stupid as this for the rest of my
life.

Not only was that a grim proposition, but I also had to buy my suit to work there! The only good thing about the job was that I could go to the Sherman and Clay music emporium at lunchtime, select two or three records and listen to recordings, like Ella Fitzgerald singing "A-tiskit A-tasket "or "Where or When," Rodgers and Hart's song from the *Babes in Arms* musical. George Gerswin's "Summertime" was also one of my favorites. From time to time, I even bought a record.

When Tante Elena and her tenants in the other three apartments went out of town on the 4th of July, Jack jumped at a chance to throw a big party at the house over the holiday weekend. He invited a bunch of fellows from the neighborhood over to Elena's house.

We had plenty of drinks, food and great music, like Bing Crosby, Ella Fitzgerald, and the big bands of the day. I recall when we ran out of booze, we

Jack and me

called one of our friends who was a delivery guy at a nearby drug store on the corner of Hyde and Union. He lifted a couple of bottles and came to join us at the party. Some of us spent the night and had breakfast together the next morning.

We made sure, of course, that everything was cleaned up in the yard, as well as the apartments. Very shortly after that, someone said, "Why don't we invite some gals over" and that started the party up again.

Let's just say that some of these women were a little "looser" than those we normally dated. The next morning we were back at cleaning up the place again before anyone who lived there returned from their weekend.

After the move to Nana's new house at 2544 Franklin Street, I made three tries at going to mass at the Irish Catholic Church on Broadway and Van Ness, but it just wasn't the same as Father Antonio's church. For one thing, this was a wealthy church compared to his church, and the sermon was in English. My previous church experience was mostly in Spanish, so I did not have a great understanding about what was actually being said.

I guess I liked it better that way.

Like my father, I had my individual belief of religion and suddenly I was hearing things and attitudes at this Irish Catholic Church that I didn't appreciate. Then, on the fourth time attending Mass, I was about one minute late and as I was about to go in, I heard a loud voice, coming from one of the priests outside the church entrance, say: "You are late for church."

"I'm not late for church," I said. " I am not going to church." That was my final day at a Catholic Church, except for family funerals, baptismal affairs or weddings.

Chapter 25

College Life

Academics, Sports, and First Love

In the Fall of 1938, a year and a half after graduating from high school, I started my freshman year at the University of California, Berkeley. By this time, regarding my future, I had come to the conclusion that I would never have the money to afford the cost, nor have the time to take the necessary classes to become a doctor. So I decided that a mining engineer degree would be a good choice, particularly with all my previous experience in that field with my father.

It was not easy for freshmen to gain admission to UC Berkeley. A student had to have very good grades, period. The basic cost at that time was around $30 a semester, plus $15 a semester for laboratory courses such as chemistry or physics.

A student body card for $5 covered all sports activities. This meant that with two labs, my cost was less than $75. This was a lot cheaper than the cost of attending Stanford University or USC.

Since fraternities seemed to be a natural part of college life, I decided to check them out. After interviewing four of them, I decided to join Alpha Tau Omega (ATO). For one thing, ATO had been my father's fraternity at the University of Nevada, in Reno. I also liked the people in ATO because they were not as stuffy as some of the others.

My father's and my fraternity house at Berkeley (photo circa 1916)

After I moved into my fraternity house in Berkeley, I was assigned a senior student, Morris Bergh, as a mentor because he was an engineering major. He was on the California rowing crew and occupied the power position, Number 5, in the shell. Morris was about 225 pounds with probably 5% body fat. They practiced every day on the Alameda Estuary and the crew at that time rowed against Washington University, and later in November against a couple of Eastern colleges, as well.

I enrolled in all the necessary classes, but discovered two immediate problems. The first was my lack of mechanical drawing experience. This course was normally taken by students in high school, but with my college prep curriculum, I hadn't previously needed mechanical drawing. So I enrolled in a night course at Berkeley High School for the first two semesters to take care of that requirement. The cost was $2 a semester.

The second problem was that I needed two math courses – plain trigonometry and spherical trigonometry – before I could take the standard freshman calculus courses. This also put me a little behind, but since I previously passed the English A entrance examination and was an engineering major, I was not required to take any more English courses, a definite plus.

Despite my busy academic schedule and night classes, shortly after the freshman semester began, another pledge from my fraternity and I went to a dance at the Delta Delta Delta sorority house. (ATO and the Tri Delts had a mutual social arrangement at that time.)

Harry Leib, an upperclassman of mine at ATO, had arranged for a blind date at his girlfriend's sorority. Harry played football at Cal and he had the notoriety of attending high school with Esther Williams. (She was going to be swimming at the Exposition on Treasure Island.) Anyway, that night when the freshmen girls came down the stairs to meet us, I said to myself, "I hope I get the one on the left."

And I did!

She was Elizabeth Ralph, a very good looking young lady from San Bernardino. We had a great time together at the dance and saw each other again the next week when our fraternity and her sorority had a picnic together at Mt. Diablo Park. By the time the picnic was over, I was in love.

Elizabeth and I had marvelous times being together. She was bright, intelligent and had a good sense of humor. She was truly my first romantic love, and I was as deeply in love with her as she was with me.

*   *   *

The Cal freshmen professors were exceptionally good, especially in chemistry and physics. Our first year chemistry Professor, Joel Hildebran, was the head of the Chemistry Department and Dean of the College of Chemistry. He felt that freshmen needed the best possible indoctrination and he made sure that we got it. He lectured Monday, Wednesday, and Friday. The other days, we spent in 2-hour labs with other instructors.

The physics professor was also exceptionally good. He was ill for a short period of time and another professor took his place. His name was Professor Ernest Lawrence, and even though he had won a Nobel Prize in physics, he didn't seem to mind teaching freshmen. We were fortunate to have him.

At the beginning of my first year of civil engineering courses, I got into measuring. These were simple exercises that were used to define distances and space between buildings or the library by measuring from two separate locations to pinpoint a spot. Next we got into using transits and chains to measure between points. It made me think of some of the surveying jobs my father had done.

About this time, I was beginning to make some good friends at ATO. Bruce Jacques was the best ever. We also took the same ROTC route.

ROTC was a required course for every male student at Cal because it was a land grant college, but we had our choice about whether to do it for two years or four. (If you stayed for four years, you could get a commission in the Army or Navy.) I was not enamored about doing it at all, and Bruce felt the same way. We both decided to take the two year course.

We were required to wear Army uniforms which were probably left over from WW I, and old rifles which were stored in the University Armory. Since I was an engineering major, I was involved with the ROTC section that dealt with building a lot of wooden bridges, as well as the endless parade drills.

For fun, on the weekends Bruce and I would often take our dates to movies and afterwards the four of us would go out to get something to eat or drink. Elizabeth took it easy on my bank account, but Bruce's dates sometimes ordered enough food to exhaust his wallet. Frequently he ended up being able to buy only a small coke for himself.

I had difficulty going out for football as a freshman. In those days freshmen were not allowed to play varsity football or basketball, but even so, at 150 pounds, I was too light for the freshman team. However, they gave me a uniform and the worst pair of football shoes I have ever seen.

The freshman coach had his team pretty well organized. I got to practice with them and played end on the defensive line. The coach's backfield was not too good. Frequently, I could beat the ball carrier to the other side of the line and make the tackle, too frequently, I guess. It finally got to the point where the coach asked me not to charge against the line. He said I was 'disrupting' the first string's practice plays. I thought to myself, 'What does he think any competitor team is going to do?'

I did suit up for the first freshman game which was against the San Francisco Junior College. Melvin Chicazolla, a San Francisco neighbor, was on that team. Neither he nor I got to play that day. We ran into each other in the middle of the field after the game and I said, "Nice game, Melvin" and he said "Nice game, Lloyd." He also said, "I'm not going to spend any more time with these guys." I agreed with him and decided I was not going to play for the freshman football team and turned in my crummy shoes and uniform.

The University had excellent intramural sports programs, however, and we could play against other fraternities in basketball, touch tackle football, six-man football, and soccer, all of which occupied my athletic interests. Bruce had played basketball in high school and we made a good pair. When we played touch tackle football, I usually picked Bruce to throw to because of his skills and height.

Six-man football was a small high school game played by schools that could not field a full football team. The playing field was about 2/3 the size of a standard field and the players consisted of two ends and a center, with a backfield of two backs and a quarterback. The quarterback got the ball but could not run with it. He passed it or threw a lateral. Each team had four downs to make a first down, the four quarters were the same length of time, and penalties were the same as for regular football.

During the next semester, I made the initial cut for the freshman basketball team but found out they were switching their practice schedule to nights. Unfortunately, I was still taking drafting classes at night and could not participate.

*   *   *

Meanwhile, back at the fraternity house, the sleeping conditions were set up so that the freshmen were on the second floor and the upperclassmen were on the top floor. As is typical in fraternities, there were lots of different competitions between the guys. Someone – not me – suggested that we have a contest and it would be recorded every morning. I joined and was soon named 'Omar-the-Tentmaker,' and easily won the contest.

Enough said.

Of course, the ATO freshmen got banged around and paddled like all the other new fraternity members did. As a freshman class, we organized an event to make life difficult for our upper classmen. I set up two large batteries and a large bell attached to an alarm clock which would go off at 2:00 a.m. This apparatus was placed in the attic above the senior sleeping area. The freshmen arranged for all the lights, including the toilet room on the third floor, to be turned off when the alarm clock went off. We also laid down brown kraft paper, which we'd coated with honey, throughout the halls. Then we eagerly awaited the chance to witness the results of our handiwork.

When the alarm went off, the upper classmen didn't jump out of bed immediately because they thought the prank would be over very quickly. However, the bell kept ringing and they finally had to do something. Trying to find the clock was not easy in the dark, and now we had a bunch of uptight upper classmen slipping and sliding in the dark. They wanted to kill us but they couldn't get to us quickly enough.

The whole affair turned into a free-for-all on the first floor. It was like a madcap tackle football game without any rules. A good time was had by all.

Late at night, sometimes Bruce and I would sneak downstairs and raid the kitchen for snacks if we were hungry. Even though the kitchen was locked, we had our 'methods,' which I will not disclose for fear of getting Bruce into trouble, even at this late date.

Then one time, when he was away, 'someone' got into *his* room and filled it almost to the ceiling with wadded up newspapers. I think he was pretty upset about that.

During the two years we lived at the fraternity house, Bruce often came to Sunday dinner at my family's house at 2544 Franklin Street. I also went with him to visit his family down in the Hollywood area in Los Angeles. Sometimes our friend and fraternity brother Bob Molch would join us.

During the two years of the Treasure Island Exposition, one of my other fraternity brothers worked at the Ford Pavillion, and Elizabeth and I visited a few of the exhibits there on dates. We had fun together and had a good relationship. Even though it was my first serious one, I had a different relationship with her than a lot of my friends did with women.

For one thing, I never downgraded any woman; I never wanted to put anyone down. To me, women were precious. I respected them, just as I respected myself. I thought I was as good as any woman, but not any better. I wanted any woman I loved to be equal. However, that was not always the case with other men, at least at that time.

In addition to our social activities and dates, Elizabeth would also come join me for some of my engineering surveying projects, which we were expected to do in our own spare time. Not only was she good company, but Elizabeth would help me with my surveys. As you can imagine, this was a lot more fun than having a male engineering student as my partner.

It was a romantic time, something new for me, consequently much of the music took on a rather new meaning. We often tuned in to KRE (Radio "Cream"), a station located on the other side of the Bay Bridge, that was very popular around the fraternity house. They played all the music we wanted to hear: Glenn Miller songs like "Tuxedo Junction" and "Fools Rush In." Benny Goodman was very popular and he had three songs out during my freshman year. "Don't Be That Way" was one, and "Sing, Sing, Sing." Then there was his hit, "I've Got It Bad and That Ain't Good." But that last title definitely did not ring true for me regarding Elizabeth, my first real love affair.

I had it good and I knew it. That's why the song that best describes my feelings at that time was Tommy Dorsey's hit, "I'm Getting Sentimental Over You."

Chapter 26

Sheep Ranch

Tall Tales, Gold Mining, and a little Romance

At the beginning of 1939, a new arrival appeared at our fraternity. His name was Henry Silvera and he had just transferred to Cal from another university. He was taking a graduate course and was also a Reserve Army pilot. Every Friday, he put on his military uniform and went to Hamilton Field for his patrol duty. The Japanese were under scrutiny for spying on our coastal defense systems and he bragged about flying a search plane on the weekends to look for them.

Silvera also proudly wore a Golden Glove pin which was awarded to amateur boxers who won championships. He told us that he had won his medal in Los Angeles and was quite gabby about both his boxing and flying capabilities.

A few weeks later at our ATO lunch, Silvera began to expand on his flying career. He told the group that he had once flown in the Andes to deliver liquid nitroglycerin to a mining camp. He also told us how dangerous this had been. I began to spot some errors in his story. For one thing, I noticed he seemed to be repeating parts of a movie that I had seen several years before.

The second thing that seemed strange were his comments about liquid nitroglycerin. This was not an item that a standard mining operation would use. They used dynamite sticks that were 10 inches in length and 1-1/2 inches in diameter. Six or more of these sticks could go into a drilled hole, plus a fuse for the ignition to make a whole section of a vein shatter. This was information I knew firsthand from past experience in mining at Calistoga and other areas that I had visited with my father.

In the neighborhood where I was raised, there had been a fair number of Italians who were not above telling a person some things that were not true for any one of a number of reasons. One learned this quickly when you were young and you didn't fall for false stories. I felt that most of my fraternity brothers seemed to take Henry at face value and didn't seem to be aware that they were being conned. I kept my suspicions to myself, but it did make me wonder whether I should check on the authenticity of some of Silvera's stories.

As it turned out, an easy way for me to do so came about at our fraternity lunch the following day. Sometimes before lunch, a few of the guys would start shadow boxing. This involved not physically hitting somebody, but stopping your swing just before a hit.

I talked Henry into shadow boxing with me, and just as I suspected, found out that his coordination was not too good. I could fake him out of his jock and decided that he probably bought his Golden Glove pin at some pawn shop. His excuse to me was that he was out of condition and we stopped sparring. Henry and I didn't mingle too much after the sparring was over, but I still felt that he was conning the whole group with his Golden Glove pin and Army uniform. Since I was a nice guy, and because I didn't feel it was my responsibility to accuse him of anything, I didn't tell anyone about his being a phony.

During Easter vacation, freshmen engineering students were required to go to a camp that the University operated in the hills above Fairfax. Other freshman students got to take a vacation at Easter, but not freshmen engineers.

Now we were doing much more complicated surveys, even learning to understand how to use our transits in making railroad curves. We lived in tents, with four students to each tent who formed a team. Each of us was supposed to alternate using the transit and moving the stakes and rods for surveys. I was assigned to a team with three companions who were from South America.

I came to the conclusion after the first week that I was with three goof-offs who spoke English but didn't want to do much work. We were falling behind and I could see that we may not be able to pass the course. At the start of the second week, I had a discussion with all three, and I believe it went something like this, "We probably will not pass the course at the speed we are doing our work. I am going change the organization of our group and I will be doing all the transit work while you three run as fast as you can to the places with the stakes." It worked. In that last week we completed all of our requirements.

                    *   *   *

During this time, Elizabeth and I were having a very good time being together. I was very happy. We could sit on the stairs near my fraternity and watch the fireworks display at the Fair Grounds on Treasure Island in the middle of the Bay. She continued to help me with my surveys. It was a delight to have her come along.

My father returned to Alaska that spring. He was searching to see if there was any potential property that he could recommend to people for an investment. I, too, would be heading off soon to work in mining.

Near the end of May, between my freshman and sophomore years, I got a job working at a mining operation in Sheep Ranch, California (deep in the heart of Northern California

in Calaveras County). The mine was located about 15 miles
east of San Andreas. I took a bus the first day to San Andreas
and then the next day, took a smaller bus on to Sheep Ranch.
On the way, I thought about what my father had always told
me about mine safety. "If you work somewhere, always station
yourself where the new machines are, because they're not going
to bury the new machines, that's for sure." I wondered what the
conditions would be like at Sheep Ranch.

When I arrived, I reported to the appropriate people at
the mine, was given a physical examination, cleared for work,
and I bought myself a hard hat and a lamp.

Sheep Ranch was a very, very small town consisting of
just 2 or 3 buildings. Even the post office was in a combination
small grocery store and bar. The original mine was formerly
owned by George Hearst, who had sold it many years before. My
housing accommodations were in a large building probably left
over from the Hearst era that had been converted into a boarding house. The lobby had a magnificent collection of *Saturday
Evening Post* magazines with automobile ads where you could
trace the history of automobile development from 1910 to 1939.

The mine was now owned by the St. Louis Lead Company and they improved the mine after President Roosevelt
increased the price of gold from $22 an ounce to $35 an ounce.
This price change did much to improve gold mining in California and in many of the western states. It certainly improved the
labor situation for college students.

The Sheep Ranch Mine was a high grade gold mine
with a substantial security system. We were required to remove
our street clothes, put them in an outside locker, go through
an inspection gate in the buff with someone checking us out,
and finally getting into our work clothes which were housed
inside the mine area. After work, we hung up our work clothes,

showered, and came out naked through an inspection door where we walked over a small step, holding our hands up and talking to the inspector while going through the doorway. He was now reasonably sure none of us had any pieces of gold in our mouth, under our arm pits or between our legs. We then went to the ouside lockers and put on our street clothing.

As a mucker, my salary was 75 cents an hour for shoveling and transporting gold ore. The boarding house cost me 1 dollar a day, which included all of my meals. Although my pay was not high, my living expenses were low.

The Sheep Ranch Mine had a 1,000 foot shaft with a large winch to take the ore to the top of the mine as well as moving miners up and down the shaft for work. I got off on the 600 foot level with the miner I worked for. We worked the vein upwards to the 500 foot level.

My miner was about 30 years of age and owned a relatively new LaSalle automobile. I'm sure a lot of people questioned how he got the money to buy it, but I never saw him grab anything or hide anything during the time I worked with him. He was good to me and gave me lots of tips about the people I could trust, and also those I should avoid. I was lucky to be teamed up with him. Some of the supervisors were not necessarily easy-going people and some didn't like students coming in for summer work.

My first assignment was to shovel ore that was the residue from the previous shift's dynamite work, down a chute to the 600 foot level. I then climbed down a ladder to that level, filled a one-and-a-quarter ton ore car and pushed the car to the shaft area, about 200 yards away. These ore car contents were dumped into a holding area adjacent to the shaft where they would be picked up by the hoist and finally dumped into the processing area of the mine.

There were no mules to haul ore in this mine, like in my father's mine in Calistoga. I pushed between 15 to 20 ore cars myself, or about 18 to 25 tons during each of my 8 hour shifts. Unlike those mules I saw in his mine, I had no union!

After my shoveling and car unloading was finished, I helped my miner lay heavy planks underneath the area where he had finished his drilling. Previously he had selected the location of all his drill holes, drilled them, and inserted several dynamite sticks and a fuse into each hole.

When he completed this work, our foreman came by and inspected the drilled areas and the dynamite charges. The foreman lit each charge with a different length of fuse and all three of us went to the shaft area to wait as the separate explosions took place. Then we counted each explosion to be sure that all the holes had gone off. If one didn't, the next crew would have to make a very careful search of the rocks to determine the location of the dynamite that didn't explode. It was imperative to find any sticks and fuses that still existed. People could get killed in this kind of activity.

My miner also taught me how to operate his drill and how he determined the spacing of his dynamite holes. He even took time during the lunch hour to show me how to prepare the dynamite sticks with the fuses.

While I started on the day shift, we went to the swing shift after two weeks, and then two weeks later, worked the grave-yard shift. Among other things, this change of schedule sometimes made it hard to figure out when to go to the lavatory.

About one month after I had started, my miner asked me if I would be interested in doing some contract work in the mine. Our section of the vein was getting close to the 500 foot level and would soon be exhausted. The contract work included working in conjunction with the other two shifts to increase the tunneling we used for removing ore.

This required shooting and dynamiting a 200-yard distance on the 600 foot level, hauling all of that material out, laying track and installing several chute entry ladders extending up to the new location of the stope (where the ore was being extracted). Contractor work paid a lot more. I would be getting $2 an hour as compared to 75 cents an hour and would be able to do this for about two weeks. This was hard work, but it paid well. After this project was completed, we returned to our previous jobs and salaries.

I was happy to have this opportunity because it gave me more money for school.

Jack's father died suddenly at the age of 40 while I was working here. I couldn't come back to the Bay area and Jack had to do everything concerning the funeral without a lot of help from his mother or sister. His uncle, a Sea Captain, helped Jack by telling him to not be concerned with his Irish relatives and to do whatever Jack thought was best. If I could have, I would have gone to San Francisco for him because Jack means so much to me (then, and now).

In early August, a fire started close to the Sheep Ranch Mine. The fire was heading our way and the Forestry Department was about to make their involuntary selection of individuals to fight it. Miners were a prime target for fire duty and the Forest Service could pick up people and make them work for a dollar a day. This was the law at that time. Fires were fought with disgruntled "volunteers" as there were no forest fire fighting groups in those days.

As I was due back at Berkeley in the middle of August, I resigned from the mine before the Forest Service could get me, collected my final salary, and thanked everybody. I left for San Andreas, and went on to Berkeley looking forward to seeing Elizabeth after our long vacation apart.

At the start of my sophomore semester, Elizabeth and I often met at her sorority. By taking public transportation we

revisited the Exposition on Treasure Island, skipping a couple of classes to do so. We were happy being back in Berkeley together and found a nice quiet place on the campus to spend

Ginger

Ginger and I at Treasure Island

time together. I also went to Treasure Island with my sister Ginger, during my visits to see her, my mother, and Nana. We went by boat in the afternoon. I remember many of the exhibits, such as the impressive one from Japan.

But what I remember most was the fellow who had a zylophone, with which he could make sounds like a trumpet, or even a violin. He was exceptionally good, no one else sounded like him. To see him cost about 25 cents and he was cleaning up.

There were also Pan American sea-planes that flew off Treasure Island for their Pacific flights to Hawaii, Midway, Philippines, and Japan. They would come back that route to Treasure Island. The crew, the stewardesses especially, were very well dressed, and at that time had to have nursing experience.

*   *   *

But of course, the vast majority of my time was devoted to attending school. By now I had finished my drawing classes at night as well as my trigonometry classes. So most of my time was spent in the George Hearst Mining Engineering building, using their underground drift to do surveys. I gave Elizabeth a hard hat that had a light attached to the front of it, and asked her to come along.

I showed her how to cope with the overhead rocks that we would be using as places for surveyor positions. Underground surveying was a little more difficult than standard above ground surveys. The light was not as good as sunlight, and you couldn't use any ground positions for survey-ing because of people walking, or wandering back and forth in the area.

Sometimes the ground level could also be covered up and obliterated after several ore cars had traversed the dirt. There were not too many people using the underground area, however, and after my surveys were completed, Elizabeth and I started taking advantage of the privacy to escalate our romance.

During this time, Henry Silvera, the Reserve Army pilot in my fraternity was still putting on his act – but not for long. About two months after the semester started, I returned from one of my early morning classes, to find there was a lot of commotion and talk about Mr. Silvera. It seems that the FBI had picked him up for impersonating an Army officer! Just like that, Henry, his uniform, and his tall tales were gone. We didn't see or hear from him again.

Meanwhile, there were a lot of things on the political front that we did hear about. In August of that year, Albert Einstein wrote a letter to President Franklin Roosevelt suggest-ing that we should try to develop an atomic bomb. Einstein felt that the Germans were already experimenting.

In September, 1939, Germany invaded Poland and proceeded to beat the Poles. They also secured an agreement with the Russians to not compete with one another over the territory, but instead would split up the Polish country into two areas; Germany got the part of Poland on its border, and the other side of Poland was given to Russia. The two countries made a secret pact not to interfere with one another.

The French and English were supposed to have gone to war in defense of Poland, but neither did. Eventually they both realized that Hitler had other plans than just splitting off Poland, and they declared war against Germany.

I began to understand trouble was ahead because I was the wrong age and could be drawn into a war that I was not particularly interested in joining. It was on my cousin Jack's mind as well, and rightfully so. One year later, in September of 1940, the draft went into effect when President Roosevelt signed the Selective Training and Service Act, stipulating service of 12 months.

By the following year, however, the length of mandatory service was extended to 18 months. With all this going on, I was glad to have a girlfriend, and Elizabeth and I spent as much time together as possible. We went to football games, studied together in the main library, and went to movies and dances that both her sorority and my fraternity organized.

Glenn Miller continued to be very popular during these years, and his songs like "In the Mood" or "Old Black Magic" and "The Nightingale Sang in Berkeley Square" were often played. Needless to say, Elizabeth and I enjoyed dancing together.

Time went by fairly quickly until the Christmas holidays rolled around, and then we were apart again.

My father, meanwhile, returned from Alaska early that November and said that he had made an arrangement with another man to build a gold dredge in Alaska for the coming year. I was happy for him because I knew he had been working hard on this project and it was definitely time for it to pan out.

Chapter 27

Divorced

Our World is Completely Changed

In January of 1940, I returned to Cal in high spirits. Everything was going well and I was looking forward to the coming year. Little did I know that my happy life was about to totally change. Just three weeks later, my father went to Reno on business, and a few weeks after that he wrote a letter to my mother saying that he had started actions to get a divorce. (In the State of Nevada at that time, a person could apply for residency and get a divorce within six weeks. If you were already a resident, you could get a divorce in a week.)

My mother was crushed. She had no indication that my father was even contemplating a divorce, and I couldn't remember them having any arguments. My father had always been my hero and the fact that he would do this to my mother shattered me. My mother asked me to come to Reno with her and talk to him. We took the train and met my father in our hotel room. He was very determined about what he wanted to do; obviously he had already made up his mind.

My mother begged him not to do this to her while I sat in the room listening to both of them. When I could take it no longer, I finally said "No more Mom, let him go. We do not need him." The next day Elvira and I went back to San Francisco by train.

My mother cried the whole way home.

I was in shock. I had always been a very happy child and young man up until that time. But after that, I became much more quiet and withdrawn with my family and friends. I also turned more aggressive, and intolerant of others.

My mother told me I should write to my father before he left for Alaska, and wish him well, which of course was the last thing I wanted to do. She said I shouldn't have any animosity toward him because people do get divorced and I would have to learn to accept that. I told her I didn't want to write to him. But I did finally contact him after my mother kept urging me to do so. However, I was now much more serious and was not the carefree, happy person I had been.

Meanwhile, my relationship with Elizabeth deteriorated. She would have been sympathetic I'm sure, but I did not want to get involved in discussing my situation with her, or any one else, for that matter.

Not long after that, we went to a spring semester dance at the St. Francis Hotel that was hosted by her sorority. Another couple drove us across the Bay to the dance. But it was not a fun night for either of us. We had a long talk and Elizabeth said I was not the person she had fallen in love with, that I no longer laughed or joked and was totally withdrawn inside myself. She concluded by saying she was going to end our relationship.

I said, "Fine, if that's what you want to do." About this time the dance was over and her sorority sister and boyfriend came to our table to take us back to Berkeley. My comment was, "I'm not going back to Berkeley, I'm going to my mother's house to see how she is doing."

This was the last time Elizabeth and I ever saw or talked to each other. Mister Stubborn had no way to handle his problems and was too proud to ask Elizabeth to reconsider.

I don't recall exactly what took place after that weekend. But I was about 5'10" then in height and roughly 170 pounds, and physically strong enough to hurt people. I do remember that a couple of weeks later at the fraternity house, I had a few beers in my room, got a little more morose, which led to two more beers. It was a weekend and I felt a great need to damage something, so I punched holes in the walls of my room.

After a short while, I came to my senses and when the house manager came back, I explained what I had done. He was curious and asked why I had done it. I said "I am having a personal, emotional problem that I don't want to discuss, but I will pay all the costs and will not do this again."

Not long after, I got involved in a confrontation as I was leaving a mathematics class at Wheeler Hall. I had just turned right and started walking down the street near Sather Gate when I was hit by a bicycle from the rear. I was knocked about ten feet down the street, and the biker had not sounded any alarm of his approach. When I got up, he didn't show any concern about me whatsoever, and was getting ready to ride on down the street. I was infuriated and proceeded to knock him off of his bike, tromp on his bicycle so he couldn't use it anymore, and then polished him off.

My next problem came that spring during drill practice for ROTC. I was about to finish my two years of the required course and during one of the weekend parades, I tangled with the student behind me. Previously, while we were parading, he often pulled the butt of his rifle up instead of keeping it down as he should have. When he did this, his rifle barrel would be in my face and sometimes hit me. This time I said, "Get your god damn rifle barrel out of my face."

He made some caustic comments and I stopped marching, went over to him and punched him out right there on the

Parade Grounds. The ROTC people took the only step open to them, which was to give me a "D" for the course and told me they did not want to see me back for the balance of the semester. If they had given me an "F," I would have been required to take the last semester of ROTC all over again. Fortunately, their solution worked well for both of us.

*   *   *

From then on, world events were never far from our minds as everyone, me included, went about our everyday lives. I was also still fighting my own inner battles about the divorce, sometimes in outwardly agressive ways.

In April, Hitler invaded Norway and Denmark. By May, he continued his invasions into Netherlands, Belgium and Lux-emburg, including France by the end of the month. Churchill became the Prime Minister in England. However, as Hitler kept moving into France, the English finally had to retreat back across the Channel, as they were unable to defend France.

This was when I knew I was really in trouble as far as the war was concerned.

That June of 1940, my cousin Jack graduated from Cal Davis. He took a job as a salesperson at a large-scale ice cream company called the Creamery of America in Los Angeles, even though he knew his time there may be limited because of the draft.

As for me, when the semester was over, I signed up for summer school because I needed to take two mineralogy classes. I also opted to take a course about Russia, Germany and Italy. Russia had eliminated their Czar and installed a Com-munistic structure in their government, and Germany stopped making the reparation payments that they had agreed to after WW I. The Italians had attacked Ethiopia even though they were in the League of Nations. My courses touched on the fact that all three countries were not democratic institutions and each had set rules that made it impossible for the citizens of the country to vote in any other way except the way they were told to vote.

I also read Hitler's book, *Mein Kampf*, in which he described his earlier life, his WW I service in the Germany army and the indignation of his country having to surrender during WW I. He was emphatic that he was not going to stand for any aggressive activity from France, or England. He was confident that his country could rebuild itself and fight the Allies again. He had little competition politically. The German people accepted him, but the rest of the world hardly took him seriously. They thought his speeches and threats were outrageous. They laughed at his hair and mustache, as depicted in the movie news programs.

I felt Hitler was a very dangerous man and he turned out, of course, to be even more so than I thought. I knew that my life was going to be impacted by Hitler. I guess I studied more about Russia, Germany and Italy than about mineralogy that summer.

The rest of the fall semester went by fairly quickly. Our fraternity played a touch tackle football game where I called the plays for our team. An end on the other team wore his high school sweatshirt with the school name written on it. I wanted to see how tough he was, and called a play to run around his end. But before the ball was snapped, I took a position outside of his end and blocked him and knocked him down. He was quite angry about this, and told me that the next time I did that he would take me apart, or something like that.

About ten plays later, I called the same play and when I knocked him down again, he jumped up and started to take off his sweatshirt to come after me. I pulled his sweatshirt over his head and proceeded to punch him out while the shirt was still over his face. Even people on my own team thought I was out of line. But I didn't care, and he didn't get up easily either.

By then, I realized I shouldn't be fighting like this and made a decision to stop my aggressive reactions. I made a point of trying to get back to being a happier, and nicer person again. I struggled, but wasn't too successful.

About this time, Roosevelt and Churchill made an agreement to swap property. The United States gave the British 50 old American destroyers which they could use in submarine warfare. In exchange, we got a 99-year lease to develop American military bases on Newfoundland and various Caribbean properties that England owned. This was the first overt move on Roosevelt's part toward getting involved in the war.

Things continued to heat up in the world front. Even though I was an engineering major and engineers got to build bridges, the thought of bridge building while the Germans shot at me didn't appeal to me at all. I felt aviation was where I should be. So I took a Navy physical to become a pilot in the fall of 1940.

I had the necessary college credits and I passed their mental test, but when it came to their physical test, I did not pass. They said that my feet were flat. I protested and said that they were not flat, though I admitted I had a very small arch. I pointed out that I had no problems with my feet while playing football or basketball. But it fell on deaf ears. The Navy was very picky about whom they were choosing at that time, and I guess were only taking guys with high arches.

So I switched from the Navy and went to the Presidio to sign up for the Army's aviation program. At this particular time, there were just two separate air forces, one being part of the Navy and the other was part of the Army. Much later after WW II, a third group emerged from the Army as a separate entity which became the Air Force.

At the Presidio, I took another mental check-up and was told to go to Hamilton Field for a flight physical test. They said I had a slight eye defect and the Army would let me take the test over again in about three months. The diagnosis was that my left eye was wandering from time to time. Doing a lot of work using microscopes and levels for surveying didn't really require the use of my left eye. I was told there was a very simple exercise that I could do by myself which would cure my sight problem. I went to an optometrist – Bruce's father – in Los Angeles. He gave me some exercises to do for three months which would enable me to pass the Army's eye test.

That year my father and I had started sending letters to each other about the dredge he was building for gold mining on a small river about 70 miles north of Nome, Alaska. Finally his Alaska work was about to start up. He came to Berkeley in November from Reno, where he was living with Louise, his new wife. He asked if I wanted to work in Alaska the following year. I told him that I was a little light on money, and appreciated the offer.

While the Navy program would have appealed to me, it was not likely to happen. The Army, with my improved eyesight was a possibility after another exam, but Alaska was a sure thing and it appealed to me much more. I was still too young to be required to enlist as a draftee for one year, so I decided to take my father up on his option to start working with him for 8 months that spring, instead of going into the Army.

This would provide me with enough money to finish my schooling.

However, just about the same time I was talking to my dad and Louise, Jack also recognized the strong possibility of a war pending, and he decided to go into the military and get his year of service out of the way. So Jack "volunteered" the week before Thanksgiving in 1940, and by December 1st, he became one of the first draftees out of San Francisco. His scheduled date for release was on Monday, December 8, 1941.

However, some time later, Roosevelt changed the rules of the draft by keeping the original draftees in for another year. That meant 2 years of service for Jack. But then, after Pearl Harbor, he ended up being in the Army for a much longer time– a total of 7 years – well after the war was over. (For two of the 7 years, he managed a German fighter plane airport, near Stuttgart.)

So all in all, 1940 was quite a year, and not in a good way. It seemed that even much of the popular music that year was sad, and reminiscent of better days; Songs like "Deep Purple," "It's Only a Paper Moon," and "I'll Never Smile Again."

40 "Deep Purple" was written by pianist Peter DeRose and was his biggest hit. (He also broadcast with May Singhi as "The Sweethearts of the Air" on the radio from 1923 to 1939). Paul Whiteman played this song with his orchestra, but Larry Clinton and His Orchestra recorded the version that topped the charts in 1939.

41 "It's Only a Paper Moon" was written by Harold Arlen, with lyrics by E.Y. Harburg and Billy Rose. The Paul Whiteman Orchestra was just one of many artists who recorded it.

42 "I'll Never Smile Again" was a popular song written by Ruth Lowe in 1939, and recorded by Tommy Dorsey and his Orchestra, with vocals by Frank Sinatra.

Chapter 28

Life In Alaska

Working with my Dad

After checking out properties in Alaska for several years, by 1940, my dad reached an agreement with Barney Rolando. Together they formed a company called the American Creek Dredging Company.

The dredge that my father had already built at the site was a fair-sized dredge for mining the river. This dredge was equipped with a bucket line that used 5 cubic foot buckets for digging. This was not the same as the 14 cubic foot buckets being used in larger operations in Nome or Fairbanks, but was sufficient for the area we were going to be mining.

That year, he also built a large cooking and eating facility, an outdoor shower and lavatory, as well as five buildings with housing for the crew and owners. This was all in preparation for the operation that was scheduled to start up in early spring of 1941.

In January of 1941, I went to Reno and met Barney Rolando who was a 24-carat character. He had emigrated from Italy to Canada when he was about 20, and reached Whitehorse in 1898. While in Italy, he worked for 12 hours a day, drilling holes for blasting a tunnel in the Italian Alps. Barney worked with a single jack, a hand drill, and muscle. No motor operated equipment was involved. He left Italy because he heard of the gold find in Dawson, Canada.

When Barney got to Whitehorse, he learned that much of the Dawson gold claims were occupied and that there was little potential for him there. So instead, he started building rafts in Whitehorse for people who wanted to use the Yukon River to get to Dawson, even though they had little chance of getting a claim. About this time, he heard of the Nome gold discovery, 1600 miles to the west on the Bering Sea coast, in late 1899. He immediately deserted boat building, obtained three dogs and a sled, and made the trip to Nome. There he made some money digging for gold at the beaches, and then over time, prospected and purchased various properties in the general area of Nome.

When I met Barney, he had a house in Tacoma, Washington, where he lived during the winters. He had two sons and two daughters, all were married, although his wife had died. Barney would work the spring, summer and fall near Nome, returning to Tacoma from early November until the next April.

He told great stories about early times in Alaska, played a good game of cribbage, and possessed a unique accent. This was a mixture of Italian, English and some Swedish gathered from the large number of Swedes in the Nome area. He was going to be up at the dredge site when I got there, and we started a great friendship in Reno.

At the start of March, 1941, my father, his wife Louise, and I left from Reno by car and headed for Seattle. When we got there, the first thing my father did was check to make sure that the first freighter into Nome would be carrying his entire load of equipment, including food and diesel oil.

After a few days, we headed to Fairbanks with a stop at Whitehorse, Canada. There were 6 to 8 fighter airplanes on a landing strip there with Russian insignias, that were evidently being shipped by way of Canada to Fairbanks, on to Nome, and across the Bering Sea to Russia.

When we arrived at Fairbanks, we stayed at a three-story hotel. The first thing I noticed was that there was a rope in each room, which was their idea of a fire exit. In the event of a fire, everyone was supposed to grab his own rope and shimmy down to the next level.

When we made a drink before dinner, the whiskey was okay, but I thought the water was terrible. I tried bear meat for my first entree at dinner, but no matter how hard and long I chewed, I could only finish a few bites. Things were definitely different in Alaska.

I must admit, Fairbanks didn't impress me, but the next day when we toured the bigger dredges with 14 to 15-foot capacity buckets, I found them to be very interesting. The dredges used a hot water system that allowed them to dig down into the frozen tundra.

The following day, we took a small plane to Nome. The only planes available to and from Nome were private airplanes operated by bush pilots. When we landed in Nome, I noticed there were some more fighter planes ready to fly to Russia. They could have been from the same group that I saw in Whitehorse, but quite possibly there was a steady stream of these planes being shipped.

As I recall, the American Army pilots were not overly happy with P-39 Aircobra's as a fighter plane. The airplane was prone to get into a spin which sometimes didn't respond well to a recovery method. A particular special feature in this plane, however, was a small cannon inside the fuselage that could be fired through the housing of the propeller. The Russians liked it because it was good for shooting at German tanks.

*   *   *

Nome did not immediately impress me either. Since most of the town had been rebuilt after the fire in 1934, rather than the previous Victorians, all the buildings were basically the same drab style. There was a large area for unloading the ships, and the main street which my dad had surveyed was probably 12 or 13 blocks long. As mentioned, at one point, Nome was the largest city in Alaska, with a population of about 20,000 people. However, the 1900 Census indicates there were 12,488 people, and that one-third of all whites recorded in Alaska were living in Nome.

The businesses consisted of two bars, a newspaper, and two very large stores that sold clothing and boots. The town also had a barber shop and a YMCA located on the ocean side of Main Street. A couple of blocks away on the North side of the street, there was a hospital with a resident doctor. Farther north of town, there were two working 14-inch gold mining dredges and, of course, the airport where we landed (and where I saw the American-built fighter jets).

The town seemed to have a number of large dogs that occasionally got into fights. Usually there was a group of smaller dogs who circled the fighting dogs, waiting to see who won the current battle. There were no trees, probably due to the permafrost. However, we saw a large number of miniature plants, berries and wild flowers that were in bloom.

Along the town's shoreline, there was a beach known as Ruby Beach which extended at least 15 miles. True to its name, the fine sand was definitely red in color, due to deposits of gold. Gold was discovered in the beach sands in 1899, which was when the town was founded.

With regard to the local women, the Eskimo women, to be truthful, were not very pretty; a black tattoo of three stripes on their chin if they were married, didn't help matters.

And although there were three prostitutes in Nome, it was said that the customer demand was such that one needed to book a week in advance.

During our short time in Nome, we stayed in a small rented house for about 10 days while we waited for my father's shipload of food and oil to arrive. Our little house, like all those in Nome, had a unique aspect about it. Nome did not have a sewer system at that time, and the room with the toilet had a bucket that could be accessed from the outside of the building. Daily pickups were made to take away the contents of the bucket. I'll just say this: People were very motivated to pay their monthly bill promptly.

Every night, we had dinner at the Polar Bar and Grill. The entryway into the grill passed by a long bar. An unusual feature in this area was that there was usually about a dozen Eskimos sitting against the hallway wall. The Eskimos were not allowed to drink, but they were allowed to sit and watch others drink. If you turned around to look at them, the whole row would smile at you, so you nodded in a pleasant fashion, and returned to your drink.

When we went to dinner, there were usually several people eating in the dining room with us. However, I noticed that there was one fellow who always had a table all to himself. It was the man who drove the 'honey wagon' and picked up the toilet buckets. I never saw any companions with him, at least during the week or so that we were in Nome. I don't know whether it was his line of work, or his disposition.

Barney and I went out for breakfast early that first week in Nome with one or more of his Swedish friends. After introductions about where I was from and what I was doing in Nome, Barney would say, "Heez from California where the spaghetti trees grow."

Barney would then go on to describe the size of the trees and what the leaves looked like. He even got one Swedish friend to admit that he, too, had seen the trees one time when he was visiting California.

One morning at breakfast, Barney asked me if meeting with him so early in the morning was a problem for me. I was curious about his question, and said "No, why do you ask?" He said "Well, some of my friends tell me that you are seeing the girl drummer at the other bar across the street and you don't get away from that bar until late." I assured him that I was okay and would continue to have breakfast with him, as well as continue to have a good time with the drummer. She was a very nice looking young lady who played as part of a sister trio.

The sisters lived in Fairbanks and had been booked in Nome for a short time. They were leaving in about 10 days for another job in Fairbanks, and I wanted to make the most of our time together. I told Barney I was impressed with his 'pipeline,' however.

Shortly before we were going to fly to the camp and our dredge, I decided to get a haircut. The one barber in the shop had a couple of people before me, so I started to read a magazine while I waited. When it was my turn, I took the magazine with me, sat down and continued to read.

After a bit, the barber said, "Are you working in town?" I said, "No." He asked if I was going to work on a dredge outside of town, and I answered, "Yes," and he proceeded to cut a little deeper and a little more came off the top. I suddenly realized that not only was I getting a haircut, but he was going to make it last as long as I was going to be working. I finally got him to stop cutting, but I ended up with a haircut that lasted at least two months. My father got all my haircutting business after that.

A couple days later, the boat from Seattle arrived. After my father made sure that all of his food and supplies were assembled and would be sent to American Creek on a narrow gauge rail line, we took a small plane to the landing strip near my new home. This landing strip was about 500 feet higher than where the housing was located and about a mile away. It was situated on a knoll that permitted landings from a couple directions, and allowed for various wind conditions.

When we landed, Barney's youngest son, Babe, met us with the Caterpillar tracker and sled to take all of our baggage to the housing area. At last I got to survey the site. My father and Louise had a double cabin, and Barney had a cabin by himself. There was a married couple, named McGinnis, who stayed in a separate section of the dining room building. Sis McGinnis did the cooking and her husband was the day shift winchman. He had been a rodeo cowboy in his earlier life.

Barney's son and I shared another cabin. The other winchman was in a cabin with Andy Anderson, a Swedish fellow, about 65 years of age, who also did labor work around the camp, as well as sometimes working on the dredge. My counterpart on the dredge, who handled the same work that I did, was a half-breed Eskimo who lived in a small Eskimo village with his family, about 3 miles downstream from our camp.

When we first got there, the dredge was not fully ready. It needed a few finishing touches before we put it into the water. We caulked all the openings, started up the engine to see if it was functioning, lubricated the chain line and dug some "deadman" holes. These holes were a method of providing an anchorage for the dredge. They were dug on the bank on each side of the river.

In each hole, we placed a large log with a cable attached to it. This cable went back to the dredge and enabled the winchman to move the dredge left or right. After about 3 days of these preparations, we put the dredge into the water, using the tractor, and attached the cables from the deadman holes. From then on, it was 12 hours a day, 7 days a week with no time for church.

The dredge was placed in the center of the stream, parallel to both banks. At the rear of the dredge, there was a large vertical pole that dropped at the center of and into the bottom of the riverbed. This pole provided a pivot point so that the front of the dredge could swing back and forth while digging, and the rear of the dredge maintained its stationary center point.

The winchman would lower the bucket line intermittently as it dug until it hit the bottom of the river. When we had finished scouring the river bottom, he would then pull up the bucket-line and move the dredge forward to its next position for digging.

At the top of the dredge, there was a large 40-inch diameter steel rotating tube with holes that fed the rocks down to the flume. The tube sprayed water on the rocks at a fairly high velocity, breaking them into smaller pieces.

I operated the diesel engine and its fuel supply. I also monitored the pump, making sure that it was putting out enough water where the buckets dumped their load of rocks into the steel tubing. This provided a fluid system where the water moved the rocks down the flume, and finally dumped the unwanted rocks off the back of the dredge.

If a 10-inch or longer rock came into the flume from one of the buckets, I would personally escort it to the rear of the dredge and dump it over the side. We knew there was not going to be any gold in the larger rocks.

The flume had a series of horizontal cross pieces of wooden slats that would catch pieces of gold being washed down the flume. The larger pieces of gold were caught first and smaller pieces later. Since gold is about 19 times heavier than the water, and roughly 6 times heavier than the rocks, the gold would readily catch in the ridges of the flume.

To clean the flume and ridges, we stopped the digging and ran water down the flume from the top. The top section contained most of the gold which could easily be removed. The very fine-sized pieces of gold and rock particles were more difficult to separate and had to be subjected to a mercury extraction system.

The mercury was heated, became vaporized, and the gold and rock stopped adhering to each other. The mercury vapors next went to a containment area of cold water causing the distilled mercury to return to a liquid metal state. (The mercury was reused again later.) This fine particle recovery method was a system that had been used in mining for two hundred years or more.

There were lights on the dredge to allow for the night shift operation, but when summer arrived, we needed them less. By mid-year, one could read a newspaper at 11:00 p.m. without lights.

After I was there for about two weeks, my father said he wanted to talk to me about my work. The first thing I thought was "**Uh-oh!**" But he said, "Your work is good. I only have one suggestion." It had to do with my stamina and pace (at 20 years old I was the youngest member of the group, and in good physical condition). From time to time, I had to leave the dredge and go to the shop area to pick up supplies or a part. Whenever I did, I would run all the way down to the shop and back to the dredge.

My father felt that some of the employees, particularly the 65-year-old Swede, was not able to keep up that kind of pace.

"It would be a lot nicer if you would change your pace from running because they are trying to go too fast for their own good." I agreed, and from then on he didn't have anything to tell me, except that I was doing a very good job.

Dad had a good sense of humor and was very much a joy to be around. The fact that I did so many things with him, and even when I had my emotional problems regarding the divorce, he didn't bug me, but always tried to help me whenever he could. From the time I got to Alaska, I worked as hard as I could and he appreciated everything that I did.

When I got into a bar room fight in Nome, he didn't give me a bad time about fighting the guy. He probably knew he would have done the same thing himself. With Barney's 'pipeline,' I realized my dad probably already knew all about the fight by the time I got back to our camp. And, just like when I was a kid and got plenty of black eyes, I always got the feeling that it gave him a smile, partly at the knowledge that even with the black eye, I still came out ahead.

My dad was also not above pulling pranks to give everyone a good laugh. I remember on one occasion, it was particularly cold and I was glad my shift was over and the second crew was working. It had been a long 12-hour day and I walked back to our living area to take a shower. I was relaxing and enjoying it when all of a sudden "boom" a large bucket of snow was dumped on my head!

The American Creek area was also an unusual place in terms of nature. It was interesting to see the birds and animals go through their changes. We had a large number of ptarmigan, for instance, that were white at the beginning of the season, changed color to a grayish brown, and finally turned white again at the beginning of winter. They were unique birds with feathered feet.

There were weasels and the snowshoe hares, which also had hairy paws. They went about doing their color changes as well. Occasionally we saw ermine but didn't see any bears. There were reindeer in the area and the stream contained large numbers of fish, mostly graylings; related to trout, but with a brilliant dorsal fin.

Still, due to all the activity in the compound and with the dredge working 24 hours a day, we probably saw less wildlife than normal for this area.

Around this time, I had just about reached my full height and was gaining weight. When I arrived in Alaska I was still about 170 pounds, but within three months, I was up to 185 pounds. Work was physical and I was kept busy digging dead man holes and moving rocks quickly down the flume. Since I had to go up and down stairs to the flume area a lot, I rigged a rope that I could quickly climb by hand to get from the first floor of the dredge to the flume area.

This rope became part of my exercise course.

*   *   *

About the first of July, I got a notification by telegraph that the draft board in Nome wanted to see me for a physical. My father suggested that I take the narrow gauge train to Nome for the experience, so I started my journey somewhere around the first week of July, early in the morning.

Barney's son, Babe, had some things to pick up at the rail station so I got a ride from him on the tractor around 7:00 a.m. The 15 miles to the station went quite smoothly, but things did not happen in a rapid fashion once I got on the train. This was not a regular train. It was a narrow gauge unit on a truck body with unusual wheels. The roadbed was not stable and changes in ground temperature promoted a movement of the track. The train could compensate for this, to a great degree, by having metal wheels that were 5 inches wide on each side. These picked up the balance of some space between the wheels, but a couple of times we had to get out and move the "train" along its path by a cable. The cable would be used to pull the train ahead to where the tracks were more stable.

We had made two stops to advance the train using this cable when we experienced a large movement of ptarmigan. The birds were traveling on the ground and the size of the group was perhaps 4,000 or 5,000 birds, including a lot of young ones. We couldn't hurry them, we had to just sit there and wait while they strolled by.

All of this took a considerable amount of time, so that when I reached Nome at 4:00 in the afternoon, the lady at the reception desk at the draft board made some derogatory remarks about my "taking my time" to report. I told her I was not overly impressed with their operation either. I commented that I had spent all day getting to Nome, and I wanted her to get her paperwork finished, and the exam over with.

Shortly thereafter, the doctor took a cursory look at me – for no more than two minutes – and said, "You look OK to me." This exam basically said that I was alive, but it cost me a 70-mile trip, the loss of two day's pay and a flight back to the dredge site.

I left the draft board and booked a room at the local YMCA. The "room" was large enough to hold about 10 or 12 single cots, not exactly what would ordinarily be called a hotel room.

I next proceeded to the bar and dance hall where I had previously met the sister trio. The bartender recognized me and while having a beer, I asked him if they had any music that evening. He said "No, but there is a juke box in the dance area."

I got another beer and walked into the dining room. There was no one there. The cost of the music was 25 cents for each record (Alaska's inflated prices) and I picked about five popular records that I liked, including some of my all time favorites; "Take the 'A' Train" by Duke Ellington, "Chattanooga Choo-Choo" by Glenn Miller, and "Moonlight Becomes You" by Bing Crosby. While I was eating and listening to my music, I didn't realize that anyone else had come into the area. But two couples had arrived and were sitting at the far end of the room.

One of the newcomers came over to my table and threw two quarters down on to the table and said, "I am changing your music, my girlfriend doesn't like your songs."

I stood up and started to say, "There were only two more records to go, and I would like to have them finish," when he Sunday-punched me. I was a little late seeing the punch coming, and I caught it on the side of my face when I attempted to duck.

I now also realized that I was in a fight with someone who was bigger than me. I backed away from him after his first punch and he came toward me with another roundhouse punch, and I thought, "Thank God he is a one punch fighter."

I blocked his punch, hit him as hard I could under the rib solar plexus area, nailed him with a left hook (that brought blood), and then hit him with a right hand and knocked him down. I knew by the way he fell that he was not going to be getting up soon, as he was bleeding profusely.

The bartender ran into the room and said, "Don't fight in here." I thought to myself that it was kind of stupid to get into a bar room fight like this but I was glad I was in good condition. I went outside and waited to see if he would come out to continue his action. He never came out and obviously he was a little more hurt than I thought.

I went across the street to my sleeping accommodations, had a good night's sleep, but was very sore in the morning from where I had been hit in my jaw. I shaved, had breakfast and bought a few presents to take back to camp. Mostly I bought whiskey for Ray, Barney and the Swede, Charlie. Since Barney's son, Babe, didn't drink, I left him out. Next I booked a plane back to the camp.

The news on the shortwave that evening was something that worried me. The French had lost and surrendered to the Germans. The English retreated back across the water to their homeland and the Germans were bombing England. Norway and Denmark had been invaded as well. It was a bitter thought, and I decided not to go home but to stay with my job in Alaska until the beginning of November.

Eventually, by late September, we arrived at the point where the dredge would need to be shut down for the winter. We moved it across the stream to a sheltered place on the bank that had previously been dug out by the tractor. We basically moved the dredge up and out of the water and put it to sleep. This was the last time that I saw the dredge, as I did not return to Nome until 1991.

Remarkably, 50 years later the dredge was still there, right where we had moved it when we put it 'to bed.'

No gold mines or dredges were permitted to work during WW II due to a government law. Gold miners were out of work and owners were forced to shut down for the entire war period. Inflation during the war years was such that the gold mining industry was not able to recover. This included mines in California and other places in the West.

My father and Barney were forced to abandon their project, but the sight of the old dredge and the fact that it was still where we had left if all those years ago, was a wonderful tribute to my father's building skills and knowledge.

We spent much of October closing down the camp. In Nome, I contacted the draft board to enquire when I would be drafted. They suggested it would be close to my birthday, late in December. The last boat to leave Nome for Seattle was due to depart on November 5th, and Babe and I booked a two-bed accommodation on the boat. My father paid me off and I had a good amount of money that would last me through my final two years of college.

*   *   *

The ride down the coast from Nome to Dutch Harbor was a breeze and the food was great. But the second half of the trip was another story. The normal time for the trip from Dutch Harbor to Seattle was about 4 or 5 days. It took us 8 days. There were two people scheduled for our dining table that we only saw for the first breakfast due to the rough seas. There was one guy who had a little more staying power, but he didn't last beyond the second breakfast.

I enjoyed the trip, though, and loved being out in the open with the wind blowing and then being able to go back in the bridge area for a bit to get warm. The numerous albatross were wonderful to watch. I thought about all the great things I was going to be eating back in the States. I had been living on cold storage eggs and I could visualize how great fresh eggs would taste.

So on my first day in Seattle, I eagerly ordered breakfast at my hotel and was more than a little disappointed. Turns out I had become so accustomed to the very strong taste of the cold storage eggs that I found that fresh eggs had no taste at all!

On the second afternoon, I got on a train to San Francisco, and was soon home at 2544 Franklin Street enjoying being with my mother, grandmother, and Ginger. I was shortly reminded, however, that I had garbage duty to return to, and would I please take the garbage downstairs. I definitely had not lost my job at home.

Ginger, Nana and our cousin Barbara

Several days after I got home from Alaska, I got a telegram from the Nome draft board stating that I had to report to their Board in Nome within 4 days for induction, or report to a local draft board immediately.

This fried me. I had specifically talked to the Board before I left Nome on that last boat in early November about when I would be drafted.

There was no way to get back to Nome within 4 days in the winter time, and I had other plans with regard to their comment about "Reporting to a local draft board immediately." I had already checked on a Navy Reserve enlistment that my cousin Jack had suggested, and knew that I could enroll in the Naval Reserve. This was a much better approach than getting involved with the Army and any local draftboard.

My mother and I had many discussions over the next few days, as she was worried about the fact that I apparently wasn't getting anything done about the Nome draft board.

After several more days, my mother wanted to know what I was going to do about my problem. She assumed that the draft board would be sending soldiers to her house to pick me up.

I told my mother that the draft board would not try to pick me up on a Saturday or Sunday, and that I had a plan for them on Monday. I let her know that I would be leaving early in the morning but would see her at cocktail time.

As promised, I arrived home about 5:00 p.m., and asked my mother if any soldiers had shown up. The answer was "No." I said, "If any of them show up tomorrow, tell them that I joined the Navy today. " That was on November 27th.

I was given a rank of Fireman 2nd class based upon my background and work in Alaska, and I did not have to go to boot camp. They sent me home to wait for an assignment that would arrive by letter very shortly. While I was awaiting orders regarding where I was supposed to report, my cousin George called and told me that he would be getting leave from his Army base. He was now part of the California National Guard and he would be joining me for a little party on December 6.

After partying quite late, we eventually got home around 4:00 a.m. on the morning of December 7th. We both piled into bed and went to sleep very quickly. About 10:00 a.m. we were awakened by our Tante Emilie, who had come from her house out in the Avenues, to give us the news.

Pearl Harbor had been attacked by the Japanese.

Neither George nor I really knew where Pearl Harbor was, but our aunt explained it and also announced that the radio reports were stating that all soldiers and sailors were to report to their respective bases immediately. George looked up at her sleepily and said, "I can't win it for them today," then rolled back over and went to sleep again. I thought his approach was reasonable and also went back to sleep.

Later that day, George left with a few of his San Francisco Army buddies to go back to his base at Camp Roberts. Jack was also now embarked in his second year in the Army. On December 1, 1940, as mentioned, he'd entered the service early (prior to the war) so he could satisfy his one-year requirement and return to the job he had at the ice cream company in Los Angeles.

Unfortunately for him, his first year of service was a lost year. But it was just as well. If he had not gone into the Service early, he would have been drafted anyway in 1941.

Chapter 29

You're in the Navy Now

Mare Island

About a week later, I got notification from the Navy of when and where I was to appear. It seemed that the Navy was quite busy after December 7th. I was assigned to the Mare Island Ammunition Depot in Vallejo on December 13th.

Around noon, I took a bus from San Francisco to Vallejo and proceeded to walk down Georgia Street from the Greyhound bus station to catch a small ferry to Mare Island. Mare Island was on the western side of the Napa River and about 3/4 of a mile across the river from the town of Vallejo.

The first four blocks of Georgia Street (the main street in downtown Vallejo) were indicative of what sea-going sailors saw when they left their ship to get transportation home. Bars and restaurants were predominately on the street level, while the second floors contained a large number of brothels. Some said that many sailors who had been at sea for a long time and who planned to return home for a short visit, never made it past Georgia Street before they had to return to their ship.

The town of Vallejo was basically a Navy town. Most of the civilians who worked in the Naval yard lived in the local area, although some got to the island to work by small ferry boats coming from Antioch, Rodeo and other nearby areas. Additionally, there were some large parking areas for automobiles that accessed the top of the base by way of highways from Napa and the Upper Valley.

That day, I boarded the small ferry that took me to a Marine Guard Station where my papers were checked and then I was sent to another location that provided a full set of equipment for my stay in the Navy. This included a hammock, a small mattress, underwear, jeans, dress blues, a white hat, overcoat, work shirts, shoes and a sea bag which was designed to carry all of my Navy goodies on my back, if and when I was to be transferred.

My next stop was at the Ammunition Depot. This was an entirely separate operation from the main base with its own commandant, its own Marine guard group that provided security for this section of Mare Island, and a barracks for their Marines.

There was an area for reconditioning 14-inch and 16-inch shells used on battle ships. One of the buildings in the area housed an automatic, large circular machine which manufactured 1.1-inch anti-aircraft shells and loaded them into containers. In addition, there were several large warehouses which stored ammunition for destroyers, light cruisers and heavy duty cruisers.

The upper part of Mare Island was responsible for fabrication and building small anti-submarine vessels that were not as big as destroyers. A second area had five bays for destroyers and cruisers that were being repaired, or modified from the bombings at Pearl Harbor, as well as a series of docks where heavy cruisers were being improved. In addition, there was a final location on the main base that was used for building submarines.

Our group of sailors was assigned to Boat Patrol at the Ammunition Depot, and we were responsible for maintaining security around the eastern and southern waters of the Depot. There were two substantial piers for loading and shipping ammunition, one on the south side of the island and also one on the eastern side. The eastern pier was quite near the home location for our patrol boat. On the southern end of this pier there were several vertical pilings in the water for holding a ship's bow off the pier. Directly west of these pilings was a 50-foot floating dock used by our patrol boat and a small boat house that provided space for the crew to nap or relax.

Our manning system was to run two crews. Each crew was to operate 24 hours a day and then be relieved by the second group for its 24 hour period. Most of the activity would be at night, but there would be some miscellaneous assignments during the day such as refueling and cleaning the boat, or making sure that the fishermen were outside of the Ammunition Depot warning signs. The Marines at the Depot provided barracks, bed and food for the sailors when we were not on 24 hour duty. These barracks were located about 1-1/2 miles north from our dock and our small boat house.

The Marines also provided us with a 30-caliber WW I machine gun that was mounted on the bow of our small boat. The boat had a 4-cylinder diesel motor and was a standard boat that the Navy used to connect with other ships at sea and for transportation within a Naval base.

There was a simple communication system which consisted of bell ringing. The coxswain steered the boat from his position on the stern and gave commands to the fireman by ringing a stationary bell indicating what speed the coxswain wanted to achieve. It was basically the same as the bell system used in a gold mine shaft. The coxswain could ring one bell which would be the forward speed, two bells for neutral speed, and three bells for reverse speed. He could also increase the speeds in either forward or reverse directions by adding an additional four bells to the signal he gave.

Our direct commanding officer was Ensign Kleiser who was from San Francisco. I don't know how he got his position, but his wealthy father owned a large billboard operation in San Francisco. Ensign Kleiser also had a very well known brother who was gay and quite flamboyant, but he was not available for Navy duty. He did, however, own a large yacht that he sailed to Mare Island on several occasions. On those days, we were required to take Ensign Kleiser out to his brother's large, luxurious sailboat for drinking and partying (them, not us!) and return to pick him up later on.

Both crews for our boat consisted of five men, two sailors, a fireman, the coxswain, and a Marine who was detailed to man the machine gun. The first shift's coxswain, Al Thevenin, was an actual fisherman and a good sailor from Santa Cruz who was good with boats. Their fireman also worked on fishing boats in the Santa Cruz area. There was also one sailor who was a California State Game Warden; additionally there was a retired sailor who had rejoined the Naval Reserve. This retired sailor functioned for 2 weeks before he got a venereal disease.

After he was fit for duty again, he was given leave and when he returned, he had yet another case of venereal disease. He finally got bounced and we got another sailor for his position, who was an excellent sailor.

On my crew, I was the fireman, and unfortunately, Victor Ghio was our coxswain and the crew's direct boss. Victor did have a major ego about his capabilities, but I found out that he was not the great fisherman he expounded to be. Turns out his job in Santa Cruz had been that of a waiter in his father's fish restaurant!

He also told us that at least two of the "ladies of the evening" were in love with him. If he seriously thought that any one of us would believe that one, he was very mistaken.

We quickly came to the conclusion that we had the worst coxswain of our two crews. Victor had no understanding of the Bay tides or what the hell was going on whenever he was making a landing in rough weather. I found out right away that his signals were confusing, so I ignored most of them and throttled down or speeded up whenever I knew it was time to make a change. This gave our sailors on the boat a chance to maneuver us into the tight spot of our floating dock.

The first sailor on our crew was Wayne Phillips, who preceded me at Lowell High School by a year and a half and had also worked in Alaska in 1941 on a railroad at the same time I was in Nome. At times, he actually ran the railroad. He returned to San Francisco and got involved with the Navy, just as I had.

The other sailor was a Hopi Indian from Northern California by the name of "Happy" Gorbet. He was definately unique. Happy had been at Mare Island for only about 2 weeks when he had all the pay telephones turned into a source of income. He immediately stuffed the "return coin" section with all the paper he could find so that no coins could ever be returned. He also made a point of checking "his" phones every time he was not on duty. Happy had some other attributes that didn't fit the normal "white man" method of social behavior.

For one, he cheated in card games, and then was highly insulted when he was caught doing so.

Sometimes when he had liberty, he would go to Vallejo, drink alcohol, with which he seemed to have a problem, and then beat up on several sailors or Marines. He would come back to the base with some 'souvenirs' which might be a Marine insignia or a coxswain's arm decoration. One time he came back with a large strip of gold braid from an officer's hat.

I don't think he kept all of his souvenirs, but he may have sent them home for display.

Early on, before we really knew what was going on with Happy, Wayne and I went out to have a beer with him. Happy was talking to a Mare Island worker and the worker got up and went to the bathroom, followed very shortly by Happy.

When Happy returned soon thereafter and asked, "Why don't we get out of this place and go to another bar?" we agreed. Then, as we were walking down the street, Happy asked us if we wanted any money. We knew it was not payday, and we both said "no thank you," but that was when Wayne and I immediately realized that someone had just been rolled.

Another memorable episode with Happy occurred just after we returned from one of our patrols. All of us were equipped with a 45 automatic pistol for security. We all cleaned our own guns periodically. This particular afternoon, our boat was parked and we went to the lounging area to have a cup of coffee. Coxswain Ghio asked Happy to turn over his pistol.

"Why?" asked the Indian. "Do you think my pistol is not clean? I'll come over and show it to you."

Ghio was standing to receive the gun when Happy pointed the pistol just above Ghio's head and pulled the trigger. "Oh, my God," was all Ghio could say as he weakly dropped to the ground in shock. "You could have killed me!" Happy just put his pistol back in his holster and there was no more conversation about anyone wanting to see anyone's pistol after that.

Surprisingly, Ghio never reported Happy to any of his superiors.

*   *   *

The Marines in our barracks when we first arrived were senior and had 8, 12 or 16 years of service in the Marine Corps. They were reasonably good to us and neither of us had any Marine versus Navy issues. However, a short time later, the old-time Marines were replaced with a whole bunch of new Marines who had enlisted after Pearl Harbor. These new recruits had obviously been fed something that made them feel that they were tougher than anyone else in the world.

It took a few months and a few fights before they settled down and we didn't have any problems with them after that.

Meanwhile, the old-time Marines were shipped to a training camp for island invasions. They were the first Marines sent to Guadalcanal and fought there against a major Japanese army. When they finished their job, they were replaced by one of General MacArthur's army units to discover if any Japanese troops were still alive or trying to make a comeback.

Mare Island had a great capacity to build or repair Navy ships. They could handle any mechanical or electrical problems that existed within a ship and knew how to make changes or modifications to any of them. They were able to quickly repair cruisers, destroyers and submarines.

One thing that surprised most of us was a small submarine which had been pulled out of the water in Pearl Harbor and sent to Mare Island for reconditioning. Later, this little Japanese submarine was tidied up and finally sent on a trip around the United States to promote war bond sales.

In one case, they made a complete change-over on an American destroyer that had been sunk by a Japanese bomber in Pearl Harbor. It took the repair crews less than 5 months to recover parts from the destroyer and completely recondition the vessel. A job like this in a standard shipyard could take more than a year.

A cruiser ship was being repaired at Mare Island. My counterpart fireman on the other crew applied to go on that cruiser when it was repaired, and was accepted. He took me on a little tour of the ship, particularly of the engine room. As we went down the ladder, I looked up and saw a large, thick steel plate held in position on the ceiling wall. During combat if a bomb from an airplane, or enemy fire from a cruiser hit the deck, this panel would come down and completely shut off the room. It was a safety system to protect the engine room.

I asked him how you would get out of there if a bomb hit the ship and there was a possibility that the ship may go down. His answer wasn't a good one as far as I was concerned. Basically there *was* no escape; I reasoned that there was no way to get out because the entrance would be blocked. I recalled how many men went down inside the ships at Pearl Harbor.

I was really struck by this. I could see being nailed by a submarine and maybe that wouldn't make the ship go down, but to be trapped in the engine room did not sit well with me at all. I had always wanted to be in the Naval Aviation anyway. In an airplane I'd feel invincible; and that would be a lot different than "little to no chance" of survival in the engine room.

That was when I made up my mind to once again actively pursue the possibility of having the Navy move me over to aviation.

*   *   *

Lt. Colonel Doolittle was given the job of being the first to lead an aviation attack on Japan on April 18. Doolittle had selected pilots and trained them to be capable of flying off of an aircraft carrier. He had been an exceptional aviation pilot and was one of the most famous pilots during the inter war period. He made many of the pioneering flights in the early days, had served as a test pilot, and was a familiar figure in air-speed attempts in the New York area.

His most important contribution to aeronautical technology was the development of instrument flying; being the first pilot in 1929 to take off, fly and land an airplane using instruments alone. He was involved in the development of flying equipment, including horizontal and directional gyroscopes.[43]

After winning trophy races in the 1930s, he was transferred to the Air Corps Reserves but returned to active duty in July of 1940. Other than Lindbergh, he was probably the most respected pilot in the country.

He volunteered, and received approval to lead an attack of sixteen B-25 medium bombers from the aircraft carrier U.S.S. *Hornet*, with targets in Tokyo, Kobe, Osaka, and Nagoya.

He selected and trained his own pilots and their success in this operation lifted the spirits of the war effort for the United States. Several of these pilots lost their lives on the April 18th mission, and Doolittle himself had to bail out over China. The Chinese gorillas helped him get back to the United States.

It's interesting that although he was born in Alameda, California, he spent his youth in Nome, Alaska, and ended up the University of California at Berkeley at the School of Mines before enlisting in the Signal Corps Reserve as a flying cadet in 1917.

*   *   *

43 From http://en.wikipedia.org/wiki/Jimmy_Doolittle, (From James H. Doolittle's book, *I Could Never Be So Lucky Again*, Random House, 2009).

About three weeks after I arrived at Mare Island, everything changed. Lieutenant General DeWitt was in charge of the Western area of the United States and passed a ruling that closed down all prostitution. This included all cities, as well as Reno and other areas in Nevada. It definitely meant Vallejo.

Mare Island was under Navy control, but the whore houses were all in Vallejo. My cousin Jack's duty in Monterey was loading the "ladies of the night" onto buses to get them out of his location. He was much more efficient in this than he was in finding floating Japanese.

De Witt also removed all Japanese from the western towns and put them into "detention camps" in desert locations even though many of them were citizens. It was not until the war in Italy after Rommel had lost Sicily that young Japanese from Hawaii were inducted into the Army, but were only used for fighting in Europe.

I thought this was such a terrible injustice. I remembered playing football against the Japanese athletic club down in the Marina at age 16, and I felt they were good people. I had no indication they were any more likely to be spies than Germans and Italians, many of whom were not even citizens.

In my estimation, to say that General De Witt was a *half wit* would be too kind. I thought he was a gross individual. On the other hand, maybe Franklin Roosevelt was the one who gave the order to impound the Japanese citizens.

Whoever it was, the fervor of war must have superceded their good judgment to treat Americans of Japanese descent in such a disgraceful manner.

Chapter 30

The Brig

Didn't care for the accommodations

Early in my Naval career, I got a firsthand taste of Navy discipline. I was brought before the Captain of our group because I had not responded 'correctly' to my coxswain. Our crew had just gone through our 24 hour shift on duty, had walked the mile and a half to the Marine barracks, and was about to go to bed. The coxswain wanted me to go down to tie up the boat because the wind was coming up and he felt the boat lines should be changed. It seemed to me that this was the duty of the other crew who were already at the dock and was not my problem, and I said as much.

This caused the coxswain to report me to the Ensign who then took the issue to the Captain. For those of you who are not familiar with military pay grades, Army and Navy titles differ from each other. Army Captains are only three grades higher than a soldier, while a Navy Captain is five grades higher than a sailor and could command a ship or a base.

The latter, I found out, can also send someone to jail.

The net effect of my so-called 'crime' was that I learned quite a bit about Navy programming on court-martial cases. The coxswain got to speak his piece and I didn't get to say anything. When I attempted to speak to the Captain, in order to clarify what I thought was wrong with the situation, he replied that if I would like to apply for a *double* penalty, I could get that by opening my mouth. Otherwise, I could keep quiet and get the single penalty of five days of bread and water. I took the latter, and was sent to the brig.

The brig was not a fun situation. I thought they would let me sit on my butt and read newspapers or such while I was getting my bread and water, however, this was not so. It turned out that every hour on the hour I had to get up and stick my fingers through the door of my cell and be counted. About every three or four hours, I could go to the toilet for a short bit and then back to the cell. I got the bread and water also, but not too much of either, three times a day.

Instead of letting me lounge around, the bed was taken away from me around 7:00 a.m. and kept away until it was time to go to bed. So I had no choice but to sit on the cold floor, counting the bricks on the prison walls, wondering how in the hell the days were going to pass. But eventually they ended.

When I got back to the barracks and rejoined my group, I later found out that the coxswain Ghio now carried a large knife attached to his waist. He evidently thought I was going to attack him, which I had no thought of doing. I did come up with a much more interesting approach for revenge, but needed help from the weather. I had been making all of the boat speed changes prior to the coxswain calling for them and, in a sense, had been making all of his landings for him when conditions were tough.

Soon we had a rough tide and winds while attempting to dock. Victor started to ring bells in a rapid fashion, not realizing that the bell he called for was too much for the conditions. I gave him exactly what he asked for, even though his speed was wrong and he had not anticipated the tide correctly. When he asked for full speed ahead, I gave him full speed, and away we went. My responding to his commands – as given – made his control of the boat tenuous, to say the least.

We went in and out of the docking area in rapid fashion as well as sideways too. After about three or four times of hitting the dock forward and backwards, the two sailors on the boat were finally able to get one of our ropes onto a cleat, enabling us to come to a halt. This heavy weather procedure continued in all of the rough weather conditions thereafter. Victor did improve his landings, but only marginally.

He aged a lot during the 18 months that we were together.

After my jailbird incident, I was approached by Ensign Kleiser and a Marine Lieutenant who said that they needed to go out and review the buoy lights around the bottom of our island. The two sailors on our crew were not available, but it was not necessary for them to be on the boat, as this was just a quick trip around the buoys. The officers appeared to be in very much of a hurry and I had just gone on duty. I started my motor check-out and found that there was an oil problem, which I conveyed to them.

Ensign Kleiser told me they couldn't wait and they wanted me to start the motor "Now!" so that we could get going. Victor and I followed the commands of the officers. The coxswain got in his position to steer and I got in my position alongside the motor. We left the dock, heading out toward the buoy area, but at about 400 yards distance from the pier, the motor started to labor. It slowed down, and down some more, and shortly thereafter came to a stop.

There was dead silence in the boat. The small waves lapping at the sides of the boat were the only sounds to be heard. I said nothing for a full minute. Then I remember saying "Obviously the motor has stopped." Next I said, "There are two oars under the motor area and you will need those to row the boat back home."

They quickly got the oars out and started rowing. The coxswain steered the boat, the officers rowed, and I pointed out the directions where we should go. Nothing was said by anyone the whole return trip.

During this time, Ensign Kleiser used a bicycle to go to work in the office building of the Ammunition Depot, which was a downhill ride. When it was time to make a shift change between crews, one crew had to walk *down* to the boat area while the other crew had to walk *up* to the Marine barracks for food and sleep. We noticed that Ensign Kleiser appeared to have some difficulty returning our salutes while riding his bicycle. This opened up a whole new area for us. When we saw him coming down the hill, we would all stretch out far enough between one another, requiring him to stop and salute each one of us. For me this was great pleasure, since he was the guy who had turned me in to the Captain.

Why not have a little fun?

But the real fun was the yet to come in Reno, where my father and Louise were living.

My father had moved into Louise's house located in the southern

Playing ball while visiting my dad

part of Reno, going toward the golf course. It was quite a place. The property, approximately 2-1/2 acres, included a semi-circular gravel driveway. The building itself was a very large two-level house with a complete basement that had a workshop, big refrigerators and a social entertainment room with a bar, music system and a dance floor.

The large front porch went halfway around the house and inside the front doorway was a very large round reception area. It was like a wheel with spokes. This entry was spacious enough that you could enter each different section of the first floor, without going through another room. To one side, was the living room with a grand piano, a fireplace and tables and chairs. Next to that was Louise and my father's bedroom with a bathroom that had a "bathing pool " in the center of the room, which you could enter from either side. Additionally there was a separate shower room.

In back of the reception circle, there was a place to hang coats, and another bathroom. Continuing on around the circle, you could enter the dining room which seated at least 20 people. Next to that was a smaller area that was less formal than the living room, where a smaller group could gather. Also off that was the huge kitchen. There were steps that went down to the lower basement level.

If you went up the same stairs, you reached the area where additional bedrooms were located. The room directly over Louise and my father's bedroom was large enough for four beds and a bathroom with a large shower. On the other side, to the left of the stairway going up to this second level, was a bathroom that served three additional bedrooms. Rooms for the maids and cook were also on this second floor. It was obvious that Louise was a very wealthy lady.

The gardens in the front of the house along the drive consisted of many special irises which my father loved, cultivated and managed. There was also a gardener who watered and maintained the yards throughout the year.

There was lots of grass, trees and other flowers throughout the property, as well as a green house on the western side of the house. I also remember that after the war, I paced off the ground on the side of the house and decided that with my flying skills in biplane training, I could have landed my plane on that area, as well as taken off from there.

Anyway, Wayne and I had some real adventures in Reno because it didn't take very long for me to determine that our two boat patrol groups were not being monitored. The officers were not too smart, and I was not overly happy about the way the Navy had treated me by sending me to prison. Consequently, I found a way to take a little leeway in our regiment of working 24 hours, and resting 24 hours.

It was not difficult to go home to my mother's for Sunday dinner and come back on Tuesday. The other fireman, who had replaced the fireman from Santa Cruz (and who also lived in San Francisco), enjoyed going home for two days, as well, while I took both of our shifts.

When he came back, he would take my place for two days. Eventually everybody seemed to start using this method of getting time off, even Victor. We were able to carry out our duties, despite half of us not being there and no one was the wiser. Then I began to push the program a little longer so that people began taking three day breaks while our counterparts worked three days in a row. This allowed Wayne Phillips and me to get to Reno and have a great time at my father's place. We would hitch a ride early in the morning, and spend three days there "on vacation."

About the second or third of these Reno "vacations," Louise and my dad suggested the four of us go out to dinner at a nightclub on the west side of the Truckee River, slightly outside of the city limits. The new owners of the restaurant and lodge were a very famous pair of English singers, called the Dolly Sisters. The sisters had come to the United States from England and eventually to San Francisco where they ran a restaurant and entertainment facility before Pearl Harbor.

They had just moved to Reno, rented the lodge and were again providing dining with light entertainment. They'd play all the popular songs of the day, like "String of Pearls" and "American Patrol" by Glenn Miller, "Amapola" by Jimmy Dorsey, and Johnny Mercer's classic, "Tangerine."

When we arrived, we were greeted by one of the Dolly sisters and she introduced us to her niece, a lovely young woman named Vivian, who showed us to our table. She was very attractive. Her light brown hair was mid-length. She was somewhat shorter than myself and she had a very becoming figure. Both her smile and her blue eyes interested me as we talked on the way to our table.

Sometime near the end of our dinner, a contest was announced. It involved riding a small wooden toy horse mounted on wheels around the ballroom with a prize for the winner. Both Wayne and I volunteered to ride, as did two other older men. The four of us were accompanied by four young ladies who helped us get on our small horses. My helper was Vivian.

When the gun went off, all of the riders were having difficulty. Our legs were too long and at the first turn, all four of us had trouble balancing, and the horses fell over. We all needed help getting back on our horses. Both Wayne and I figured out on the first turn that the steering mechanism was purposely mounted backward, which made us turn to the right instead of to the left.

Our competitors did not have a clue. They were only at the halfway point when we finished. I beat Wayne by a nose. Vivian awarded me with a bottle of champagne for finishing first. I asked her if she could join us for coffee and she did. While we were talking, I asked her where she was living and if I could return in about in about a half hour to drive her home. She agreed. After taking everyone back to Louise's house, I borrowed my father's car and returned for Vivian.

The best part of our evening was still ahead, and the streets were relatively dark as we began our drive. It gave me an idea.

In those days, Reno had a very subdued gambling operation. It was a small town, about 18,000 people, and there were no huge neon signs like there are today. The clubs were small, gambling was not overpowering, and they used only modest lighting. Most of these clubs had only 4 or 5 gambling tables and maybe 10 to 15 slot machines. Some had 2 to 3 bars as they were pushing cocktails. They did not cover a whole block, nor were the doors and windows open to the street.

As opposed to the clubs, the hotels had 2 to 3 tables and some slots, but offered a place to stay. They usually had a restaurant and sometimes offered dancing. So, when you were on the streets of Reno, besides a few street lights, the only illumination was the natural light of a starry night. I asked Vivian if she would like to go out to the golf course where we could sit and talk while watching the stars. She said yes.

We passed her aunt's residence, which was about four blocks away from Louise's large home and found that the golf course was totally devoid of cars by the time we arrived. We had been talking quite a bit during the drive. I found Vivian very communicative and easy to talk to. She made me open up and I was able to tell her of my college experiences and that I would be going back to school once the war was over.

I also told her that the house my dad and Louise lived in belonged to Louise and was not my dad's. We talked about my working a year and a half after high school to earn my first year of college tuition. She was interested in the work I had done during the summers in California gold mines, and the eight months I spent on my father's Alaskan gold dredge.

I told her I would be continuing to work to finish my college education. Since we were riding in my stepmother's fancy car, I wanted her to know that I was not wealthy, and that I was paying my way through college.

We spoke freely and frankly and neither of us belittled the other in any way.

Vivian told me about her family. Her father was a machinist and her mother worked in a bakery, as she did, when she got out of high school. She was the oldest child and had a brother. She had gotten involved with a classmate when she was a senior, but by the time they graduated he was treating her very badly, and they broke up.

About that time, Vivian's aunts asked her if she would like to work for them and invited her to live with them in Reno. They were very nice to her and this gave her an opportunity to save enough money to go to secretarial school. She didn't have a boyfriend and was pleased to watch the stars with me.

The sky was unbelievably bright that night and the view of the stars was truly unreal, like a blanket of twinkling lights. It was great to watch the constellations as they made their orbit around the North Star. It was a most romantic evening for both of us!

We got to know each other fairly well that evening and obviously liked each other a lot. Later, when I took Vivian home, I promised I would be coming back within four or five days and would give her a call. I explained that I had developed a method of increasing my time off from the Navy by having my counterpart do some more of my work for me.

I also told her that occasionally the Navy required both of our crews to work together and my free easy escape to Reno might have to be postponed temporarily, but we could still continue to see each other. And we did.

Sometimes her aunts would go to work early and Vivian would call me to come to her home and we could spend several hours together there. Other times I would pick her up when she got off work and we could go out to the golf course or drive to the Moana Hot Springs to swim in the nude in one of the small natural warm pools.

Each hot spring pool was located in a private, individual room. We paid a small fee to reserve our room and they issued us towels. In our little lighted room, there were benches to sit on and hooks on the wall for our clothes. The water level was about five to six feet deep and the hot water was pumped into our small concrete pool. I remember how the warm water circulated around us as we played. We made an agreement that whoever gave up first, lost.

It was always a tie.

Vivian and I had total trust in each other, we shared a similar sense of humor and had a great love for each other. Leaving Mare Island, traveling up to Reno for three days or so made living in the Navy much more enjoyable.

When I look back on that time of my life, I think that every 22-year-old male should be involved with a lovely 20-year-old like Vivian.

Chapter 31

Delta Queen

. . . and the Forty-foot Cruiser

Sometime during the course of my traveling to Reno and back, I was suddenly presented with the sight of a large paddle wheel boat at the end of our dock. It was the *Delta Queen*. This ferry boat and its counterpart, the *Delta King*, provided overnight transportation between San Francisco and Sacramento. Both boats would load automobiles around 5:00 p.m. at opposite ends of the scheduled route, and depart at about 6:00 p.m.

Passengers would have dinner and berths on the ferry. The boats would discharge their passengers and cars at about 6:00 a.m. at either San Francisco or Sacramento. Travelers could then wait until that evening to make a return trip, or continue on north or south from that location.

The new San Francisco Bay Bridge had greatly reduced the use of the paddle wheel boats and the Navy decided to use the *Delta Queen* for living quarters for the black sailors who would be loading ammunition. Our group was moved out of the Marine barracks to staterooms on the upper deck of the *Delta Queen* and we waited a month before this new contingent of black sailors arrived. The Navy cooks that were going to provide food for the new sailors arrived a month early, also, and fed us extravagantly for the whole month. We got steaks, roasts and fish, but no alcoholic drinks. It was a totally pleasant time, but sadly, didn't last.

After the first group of black sailors arrived, their job was to load ammunition on ships. Soon more groups began to arrive. The area where the cars had been parked on the *Delta Queen* was now filled with bunks stacked four high. The noise and confusion was excessive. I started to take my three day exchange "vacations" more frequently.

The living conditions on the *Delta Queen* were not good for anyone anymore. The Navy had already started to build barracks across the channel on the south side of Vallejo. This was a much better arrangement for the black sailors. The beds were two bunks high rather than the previous four high, they had their own cooks, a Ship's Service Area and indoor/outdoor recreational areas.

There was also an office for white sailors who did clerical work for the Depot. These sailors had their own separate barracks and our group was assigned to bunk with them. Officer housing was headquartered elsewhere. Very shortly thereafter, the black sailors moved across to their new locations, commuting by bus between Vallejo and Mare Island to accomplish their three shifts.

Soon the *Delta Queen* was sent elsewhere.

The black sailors were not treated very well, but they really did goof off and didn't follow precautions about their jobs. Since there was a lack of good supervision, safety precautions were ignored, and for some reason, no one was reprimanded for this behavior. It was not a good place to be at that time. One of the most alarming things the sailors did was toss shells carelessly between themselves, rather than pass them to one another gingerly.

I recall one guy who was a sailor in this group of shell loaders said to me, "Can I talk with you?" I said, "Sure."

He said, "My brother and I are with these black sailors, but there has been a mistake. The two of us are Portuguese, not black." But they were too scared to say anything about it. I told him I would notify someone in the office, and for him to tell me his name. I reported our conversation about the fact that these men were in the wrong group to one of the officers. Two days later, the Portuguese brothers were transferred out of this crew of black sailors. [A highly significant transfer, as it turned out].

At this point, I was beginning to get upset about not receiving any information about flying with the Navy. I decided to go the 12th Naval District located in the San Francisco Ferry Building, and finally found out why I had been waiting so long. When I enlisted in the Navy, I had asked if I could quickly change over to aviation, and was told that this would be no problem. Now, after being at Mare Island for a year and a quarter, I learned from an enlisted man in the 12th Naval District that I was an enlisted man period, and could not become a cadet.

According to him, I would have to transfer into aviation as an enlisted man and learn to fly as an enlisted man. That didn't bother me, but then I was told that there would only be a very small number of enlisted men that would ever be taught to fly. Also, I was told that most all of those men had been in Naval areas that involved aviation. I realized that at the rate at which enlisted men were being chosen for this District, I probably wouldn't be flying until I was 30 years old.

Basically, I was told to "forget about it" and that I would not be able to become a Navy pilot. Needless to say, I was very disappointed.

About a week later, we were told that our patrol boat was being replaced with a 40-foot dual motor cabin cruiser which once belonged to a private person. It had either been donated, or confiscated by the Navy. Needless to say, this boat made our traveling along the "bounding main" a lot more pleasant, particularly at night or during rainy weather. I no longer had responsibility for making changes in the boat speed because the controls were totally in the hands of the coxswain.

One of my day duties was to determine whether the boat had enough gas and oil, which was provided by the Navy dispensary at the north side of the island. We could sit out at night while patrolling, and have a cocktail or two in the after cabin, using torpedo alcohol to mix into our drinks.

This was pure ethyl alcohol which was drinkable, although the Navy used it for propelling torpedoes. We could pretend that we were really wealthy, letting the coxswain handle the whole damn boat. It turned out that Victor, our marvelous coxswain, was no better making landings with the controls of the dual motor boat than he had been with the 'rudder and bell system' with a single motor. So, from time to time, I had to take over the controls and make the landings.

On one occasion, we were ferrying the commanding officer of the Ammunition Depot from Mare Island over to inspect the new living quarters across the channel. Victor was having a lot of trouble docking the boat. He made several attempts at the landing when the Captain asked, "Is **anyone** on this boat capable of making a landing?" I piped up and said I could do it. Actually, I had been getting a lot of practice every time I took the boat up and down the channel to get gas and oil.

In the meantime, Wayne and I continued our trips to Reno and back. He visited his friend, the piano player, while I visited with Vivian. She and I were both very much in love with each other, but we couldn't help feeling frustrated about the way the damn war was screwing up our lives.

About this time, our Marines were about to be transferred to where they would be training for an island invasion. Wayne and I had two Marine friends that were special to us. One was Con Dillon, who had been a gunner on our boat before he advanced to driving the Commandant's car.

The other Marine was Dick Haddad. He had talked to the Marine Commandant of the Ammunition Depot about the fact that his Marines shouldn't have to go four miles up the Island for a haircut. He told him, "You have room for a barber shop on this base and I am a barber. I can take care of their haircuts." The Major bought the ticket. Haddad got his barber shop, and did not have to patrol any Ammunition Depots in the evening or morning hours.

Wayne and I invited both of these Marines to join us on one of our Reno vacations. Two days was the maximum time they could arrange. The next problem was how to get the four of us to Reno in a reasonable amount of time. Hitchhiking worked for two of us, but finding someone to haul four of us was a little difficult.

One of the sailors on our boat had an automobile. We talked to him about our trip, and said we would supply the gasoline, which was at a premium, and he agreed to drive the four of us to Reno. We told him we would work out our own way back, so the plan was for him to take us there and return without us.

While I was taking our boat up for refueling, it occurred to me that I could fill up four 5-gallon containers to provide fuel for the trip. Next, I called my father and told him of our plan and he was in agreement saying he would have lunch for us and take us for dinner in the evening. The two Marines got a two-day leave, Wayne and I took our usual three-day sneaky "leave," and we arrived in Reno about noon.

We had a great lunch and my father started taking pictures. Haddad was Lebanese so my dad draped a towel around Dick's head to create a turban for him to wear while he presided over the rest of us. Then I called Vivian to tell her that we had arrived and had finished lunch, and that I would come down and pick her up in my father's truck, if she wanted to meet the guys. After that, I'd drive her to work a little later. She agreed, I picked her up and I dazzled my Marine friends with my girlfriend.

We all had dinner at Vivian's aunts' place and listened to catchy songs like "Kalamazoo," another Glenn Miller song, and "Praise the Lord and Pass the Ammunition" by Frank Loesser. Both Con and Dick got to ride the weird little horses that Wayne and I had tried at the restaurant on the night I first met Vivian. After dinner, we returned to my father and Louise's house, got the Marines set up in their bedroom, and I left to pick up Vivian after she finished work. In order to make sure that the two Marines were able to get back to the base (which was more controlled than our operation), we checked the bus schedule. We found out we could put them on an 8:00 a.m. bus, which would drop them off in time to meet their check schedule.

A good time was had by all. But in about two weeks, our Marines were gone. Two months later, so were we.

It was very discouraging for both Vivian and me. She was always happy being with me, but I started to seriously consider my situation, and the fact that I had no control of my life. I knew I could be sent anywhere at anytime by the Navy. The more I thought about it, the more I felt I was being unfair to her. So I knew I had to tell her what my thoughts were.

"I would love to marry you," I told her, "But I can't marry you on $37 a month as a sailor. Our situation is difficult because we are in love, but I don't have the ability to change our lives . . . by now I could have already graduated from college and would have been able to marry you."

She was upset, of course, but it was a conversation I felt we had to have. I told her that the Navy might have plans for our group and that we might end up in a much worse, more dangerous situation than we were currently in, and that I might not be able to see her. I could even end up going down with a ship if I had to take care of a boiler, for instance. Or, I might get killed in a fight with the Japanese.

I also told her, "I don't want you to sit and grieve for me. If I get transferred, you will need to find someone else."

It was very, very important to me to tell her that if I had to leave, not to live her life waiting for me to return, especially because Vivian did not have a lot of job security with her aunts. Like so many others, they were having some financial problems, even though she did not know to what extent at that point in time.

During one of our last conversations I remember telling her with considerable regret, "We are caught in a world situation, and you and I have no control over our lives. There is no way you can be with me, nor can I be with you."

Sure enough.

The Navy told us to take our 40-foot cruiser pleasure boat down to Treasure Island and turn it over to another Naval officer, and get a truck back. The next day, our group was split up and transferred from Mare Island to several other locations.

I called Vivian to tell her I was being transferred to another local base, but would try to see if I could use my Mare Island system of getting time away from the base to continue seeing her. But I think we both knew that seeing each other was not only going to be much harder to manage, but that our days together might be coming to an end.

That's exactly what happened. We never saw each other again.

*   *   *

It has always bothered me that I didn't keep in better touch with her, although we did exchange a few letters. At one point, she mentioned that she was dating an Army Air Force pilot who was stationed at an airport just outside of Reno. She felt it was a good relationship for both her and him, and thought they might have a future together.

I wished her well, of course, but I was also sad that our relationship had to end the way it did because of the war.

Chapter 32

1943 — Shoemaker

Securing the Shores and Navy Football

While serving in the military, no matter how much you miss your girlfriend or family, there's not much time left for brooding about loved ones and home. For one thing, they always keep you on the move.

My next assignment (along with the other fireman in my group, by the name of Frank, as I recall) was at the new Naval Base at Shoemaker. Located near Livermore on the north side of Highway 50, Shoemaker was a huge base and a central hub of activity.[44] Thousands of men were stationed there; either training, working, or awaiting reassignment to other ships.

Meanwhile, my former group of sailors and coxswains from Mare Island, including Wayne Phillips and Happy Gorbit, were sent to Point Hueneme for training in the small boats being used by the Marines to make island invasions. Frank and I missed our companions as we began our new duties.

My assignment was to run the boilers at the base, which was divided into three different sections. The first section of this base consisted of a large Civilian Battalion (CB), that was composed of people with a background in driving trucks, tractors and highway machinery.

[44] Today the base is no longer in existence. It has been replaced by shopping centers, a correctional institution, a string of car dealerships, and housing developments.

Their training involved learning how to build new airports on the islands that the Marines captured. The Army Air Force needed to have bigger runways so that they could bomb additional islands further out into the Pacific.

The second section of the base had a large hospital for treating wounded and recovering sailors. The third contained a very large area for housing sailors being dispatched to the Pacific, or those who were returning to be transferred to a different assignment, such as on a newly commissioned ship.

The boiler operation was part of the third section, which included the service areas. It consisted of three very large boilers that supplied the entire base with hot water and heating. There were two sailors on each eight-hour shift. I was assigned to the second shift and I soon found there was very little time allowed away from the base for me while I worked in that part of the operation.

Sadly, I could only get out for a half day. Taking a short trip to San Francisco to see family was a possibility, but a trip to Reno to see Vivian was out of the question.

Some of the other men at the base, however, had wives or girlfriends nearby, and I noticed something shortly after I arrived at Shoemaker that left a real impression on me. One day, I went to the Ship Service to get razor blades. I noticed a large bulletin board that covered information

My cousin Walt & Ginger during one of my visits

about movies that were being shown. The first thing that caught my eye, however, was the fact that there was a notice that had been addressed to **"OFFICERS AND THEIR LADIES"** on the left side of the page, and to **"ENLISTED MEN AND THEIR WOMEN"** on the right side of the page!

I was not overly impressed by the implications of this for two reasons. It bothered me that the Navy was differentiating and classifying the women in such a way. I felt it was totally disrespectful. I also got the feeling that the Navy somehow didn't give a damn about enlisted men either.

*   *   *

During Spring of that year, Mussolini was deposed and jailed. By September, he was rescued by the Germans and continued to function in government in the unoccupied sections of Italy. Although the war in Europe was beginning to change, it didn't affect our lives and activities on base at Shoemaker.

Not long after my transfer, I saw a sign in the Ship's Service Area that advertised for football players. The new base was starting a football program. I applied to the coach of this new team and went through a routine of passing, running and kicking. He told me that he already had someone who was an excellent passer and asked if I would be agreeable to playing one of the end positions on his team.

I was overjoyed!

Here I was, someone who had never played football in high school or college, and now I was trying out for the Navy team. By the time we played our first game, I had secured a place on the first team as a right end.

For most people who may watch today's version of football on television, the game we played in the 1940s was totally different. There were rules that made ours a much tougher game. If you were on the first team, or substituted for a first team player, you played both offense and defense. A player could be replaced, but he was not allowed to return to the game until the next quarter. No punters or field-goal kickers were allowed to come in and kick the ball and then leave, like they do today.

This meant the people playing the game did everything. The players, generally the quarterback, called the plays, and the coaches were not allowed to make calls from the bench. While there were some large players, no one weighed 300 or 350 pounds because football was a game that required endurance. Fat players could not have lasted a quarter.

When I started working out for the football team, I was moved from the boiler operation to taking charge of two large barracks for incoming and outgoing sailors. In this position, I monitored the barracks at night with some assistance from two subordinates, one in each barrack. This also made it too difficult to get back to Reno.

But my new position was a vast improvement from being a boiler operator.

We started practicing in late July when the temperature in the Livermore Valley was 100 – 102 degrees for much of the time. The Commanding Officer for the base was previously a football player at Annapolis, and from time to time would come out to the practice sessions and talk with us, either as a group or individually.

One time, he asked me what I wanted to do in the Navy. I explained the whole story to him that when I had enlisted, I had been assured it would be possible to move into aviation. I told him about the 12th Naval District's explanation that my request to transfer into aviation as an enlisted man would never happen.

I also told him — which was not too smart either — that I'd checked out officers on this base and they didn't impress me, although they were a *slight* bit better than the last group that

I had been involved with at Mare Island. I also expressed my view that University of California was a better university than most, including Annapolis. If I had not been a sailor, I would have had enough college education to automatically apply as a cadet. But since I was an enlisted man, even with the amount of my education, I could not apply now.

He and I also discussed the fact that I had talked to an Army recruiting person. He informed me that if I could get my Commanding Officer to approve my taking the Army test, and I passed it, the Army would then send my Commanding Officer a letter requesting a discharge. He indicated that he was willing to help me try to do that.

I received my Captain's permission, passed the Army's physical and mental tests, and the Army requested my discharge through the Captain. A week or so later, he told me that someone in the upper levels of the Navy would not approve my discharge. I was disappointed, but playing football wasn't all that bad, and I thought maybe later I could get on his Navy basketball team in the spring.

*   *   *

The new football team consisted of several people with college football experience. The fullback later joined a startup professional team that was situated in Brooklyn, New York, at the end of the war. Our quarterback went to a NFL team in Philadelphia at the conclusion of his service and the other end played professional baseball for the St. Louis Browns, also after the war, as their center fielder. (Yes, St. Louis did have an American League baseball team that moved from Philadelphia to St. Louis. Later they moved again to Oakland.)

Because we were late getting our team together, we played only four games, occasionally skipping a week or two between games. Our first game was played at Kezar Stadium against the University of San Francisco. Everything that I read in the *San Francisco Chronicle* stated that the University of San Francisco's star backfield player was a great punt returner. We all looked forward to seeing this "wonder" play.

We received USF's kick-off, and after one or two first down plays we were required to punt. Our kicker punted to the left side of our field where the "wonder boy" caught the ball. He ran towards my side while looking over his shoulder at the other end who was gaining on him.

Unfortunately for the USF runner, looking over his shoulder was a bad habit. I had a clean shot and undressed him from the football.

We got the ball, and he couldn't play any more that day. We scored two touchdowns and towards the end of the game, I got past my defensive man when our passer threw the ball to me. I went up for the ball, came down with the ball, but was not able to run because I also came down with two major cramps. My replacement finished the game which ended very shortly, but sadly, no touchdown for Root that day.

Our second game, two weeks later, was against St. Mary's Pre-Flight. This game was different because they were an experienced opponent. They had four All Americans, a couple of professional players and a battery of football players who were instructors in the athletic program at the pre-flight school. We got the ball first and after the kick return, the next play was around my end. I hit the defensive tackle, moving him towards the center very quickly. We made about five yards and when I returned to the huddle, I told the quarterback to come my way wherever he needed to gain yardage. Little did I realize that their tackle had plenty of experience and he beat me up for the rest of the game. We lost by three touchdowns.

Our third game was against the College of the Pacific, today known as the University of the Pacific in Stockton, California. Their excellent coach, Alonzo Stage, had previously been coach at the University of Chicago when that college was in the Big Ten.

The President of the University decided to drop football because he didn't feel that the game was a 'college activity.' (Hard to believe, isn't it?) Alonzo's open-game style made a difficult game for us, and we had a tough time beating them.

The fourth and last game was played near Monterey, where the Navy had a pre-flight school. This team also had an all professional line and a backfield composed of four All

Americans. Surprisingly we were ahead by a touchdown as we started the second half of the game. They ran the ball back after our kick-off. Their coach started yelling at them and delivered a sterling speech which was a distinct threat to his entire ball club.

He said "If you lose this football game, you will all know what a fleet post office number is." This meant that they were going to lose their football jobs and would be assigned to the fleet rather than playing football for his team. His 'pep talk' brought an immediate response and they beat us by about four touchdowns in the second half of the game.

Shortly after our football season was over, my Naval Captain told me that I had been chosen to enter the Navy flight program as a cadet, not as an enlisted man. Soon I would be receiving information of where to report. I thanked the Captain for his help, but he told me it was not his activity that promoted the change. I thanked him anyway.

About this time, in November of 1943, the Mare Island Marines attacked Tarawa.

We learned later that many of the Marines' landing craft were sunk by the Japanese before they hit the beach. These island beaches had long stretches of shallow areas which kept the boats from coming directly into the shore, and a lot of the Marines had to walk through the water with their rifles over their heads. Wayne Phillip's landing craft was demolished by the Japanese; shelling him and causing him to float in the shallow waters until another landing craft picked him up.

Happy Gorbit, however, was able to release his Marines and make two more landings on his assigned beaches. Con Dillon made his trip to the beach and proceeded to crawl over fallen palm trees that had been knocked down by shell fire. He went over one tree and discovered he was within gun site of a Japanese soldier who was defending a small area of the beach. When Con threw himself backwards, the Japanese soldier shot him in the fanny. Con returned the compliment by killing him. Dick Haddad, however, survived the beach landing without any injuries.

Near the first of December, I reported to the Ferry Building in San Francisco and joined the some 320 other aviation cadets who had been similarly chosen. To my surprise, we were all enlisted men. Some had been in aviation capacities such as rear gunners on dive bombers, or as Marines that survived island invasions like Guadalcanal.

All of the new aviation cadets were about my age and it turned out that we would become the only group of enlisted men to enter into the cadet Naval aviation program. The Navy proceeded to take enlisted men into aviation, but not with the potential of becoming officers, and thus they remained enlisted men.

We left San Francisco by passenger train, which was parked in front of the Ferry Building, and journeyed down the coast to the college at San Luis Obispo, which the Navy was using for housing and training aviation cadets. Everyone had a good time on the way down, but we didn't get much sleep. When we arrived at our destination, we were greeted by a group of young cadets who had been in the Navy only two or three months.

They started giving orders in a manner that they had become accustomed to in their entry into the cadet program. The situation basically was that all of us had already been in the service for quite some time and we were not going to take any crap from teenagers.

The noise level from the new recruits was quick and profane. There were cries of "screw you" and other equally important statements. The cadets proceeded to march us toward California Poly and our barracks, but it was not an orderly march on our part. The more the cadets tried to manage our group, the louder we became. I am sure they were very happy to turn us over to some officers, who had us line up by name and assigned us to our barracks.

We went to school, we drilled, got involved in athletics and went to classes. Our room had four bunk beds and we marched to breakfast, lunch and dinner. The school taught basic physics, mathematics, as well as information on aircraft motors, and weather forecasting. At the end of our three month term, the group of enlisted men was divided into smaller groups to be trained at small airports in the West.

Shortly before we were to leave San Luis Obispo for these smaller airports, some non-thinking officer told us to clean up the brush outside the perimeter of the University grounds. I knew at once this was a very bad idea, especially right before we were deployed.

I explained to the officer that having people cut this brush, carry it to a burn site and destroying it, would create a problem for the cadets who had been given the detail. He was entirely uninterested in my concern, even when I asked him if he had ever heard of poison oak.

"No," he said and didn't want to hear anything about it. I told him that it wasn't a problem for me because I didn't get poison oak, but there would be a lot of people who would get it.

The following morning, sure enough, there were a whole variety of poison oak cases from marginal to really serious.

We were held over for three days more and then finally shipped to our respective small airports.

About a week after I got to Prescott, I had a delayed reaction. I ended up with a doctor who gave me some medicine that corrected my problem. But after that I became susceptible to poison oak for the rest of my life.

I felt some sympathy for the younger class in front of us. They took a lot of hazing from the class before them, but anytime they tried to do something to us, our group of enlisted men would tell them to forget about it.

Several in our group were awarded medals during the time we were in San Luis Obispo, and everyone had to attend the presentations. One fellow seemed to constantly be in trouble with the officers for not obeying dress rules or failing to properly make his bed.

However, when he was awarded his Navy Cross, the only higher award being the Medal of Honor, they finally stopped bugging him about his lack of bed making skills!

Chapter 33

Prescott, Arizona

. . . and news of the loss of a friend

After graduating from San Luis Obispo, the cadets in my squad were split up into groups of about 24 guys, then sent to flying schools in the west, mostly in Arizona and California. My squad was sent to Prescott, Arizona. There were two additional classes of young cadets that preceded our arrival. Every day we were transported to the airport, about five miles away, for aviation classes and flying instruction.

For roughly three months, our training consisted of ground courses, athletics and flying five days a week. The elevation of the airport was 5,045 feet, and our runways were fairly long. Our days off were a half day on Saturdays with a full day on Sundays. We flew and soloed in Piper Cubs for the first two months and during the third month we moved into biplanes, the Waco D-7. This multipurpose military plane, with a 420 hp Wright R-975 engine, was similar to the biplanes we were going to be flying in Norman, Oklahoma, later in our primary training.

Our barracks were located in the Arizona National Guard building, but we ate breakfast, lunch and dinner at the airport. During the day, we studied with teachers who were not Navy personnel, but all had an aviation background. The classrooms were in Quonset huts at the airport.

Most of our activities at the Prescott base were in competition with the other cadet teams in athletics and marching drills. Friday night was the time for our marching drill competition. The prize was an extra half day of free time on Saturdays, which meant two full days of leisure time on the weekend.

Our team had marched in drills at San Luis Obispo, all of the Marines and sailors had boot camp experience, and I had gotten my fill of drill in two years in Cal's ROTC. But I was the team captain and I wanted the time off, so I made sure we won the drill contest every week that we were in Prescott. However, it wasn't always easy to keep some of the cadets in line. One of our members, Bob Shillo, for example, was a very unusual individual.

He was a Marine and had been a paratrooper, although none of the rest of us knew that the Marines even had a paratrooper group. He was sent to Guadalcanal to defend the airport. The Japanese were making frequent excursions to create problems for the airfield. Bob had been wounded in one of the battles and after he recovered, he found himself a member of our group.

Shillo had an extreme interest in mathematics. He was always trying to solve mathematical problems of weird shapes such as parabolas, ellipses, hyperbolas and other unique mathematical equations. For some reason he started to ask me how I would solve these kinds of things, and I would tell him I would just pick up a book that contained information on how to solve three-dimensional problems and go from there.

But I came to find out that what he was actually interested in was the thought process a person used to solve it, such as coming up with a formula that would handle a parabola or hyperbola. He had written down a whole series of mathematical analyses that he had been working on and sent them back home in a box for safekeeping.

He had another unique habit of thinking about his mathematics while we were doing drills. Since I was our drill leader for our Friday night competitive drills with the other cadet classes, and I gave the commands for the marching drills, *he* became my unique problem.

Our group was in a formation of three groups. Shillo was in the back group. When I called for a left or right march, Shillo would often be dreaming about his next problem and didn't hear the command. So now we had Shillo going off in one direction and everyone else – 22 guys – off in another.

I had to get the main group to stop while I yelled at Shillo to get into the proper place, all without having it look like a mistake. When I finally got his attention, he realized he had wandered off. But I still had to find a method to get him about-faced and marched to where I had the other cadets marching in place, awaiting his arrival.

Luckily for me, this was successfully done so that every-one thought it was just a special routine. He didn't do this every time, but Shillo could be mentally somewhere else – completely oblivious of everything and everyone around him – often enough to make it difficult for me. Nonetheless, we still man-aged to win those marching competitions.

One of the better parts of the reward for winning was enjoying the great wide open western town of Prescott. People there were involved in mining, ranching, and some forestry. Originally designed to be the capital of Arizona, the downtown streets were extra wide. Even a large wagon team of horses could make a "U" turn in the middle of one of these streets. The bars were available to us because we were older than other cadets.

There were no military bases in Prescott during our time. The aviation cadets that preceded our class were 18 years old and, therefore, they were not allowed into the bars. When we got our first leave, we headed for one of the bars and found that several soldiers, who came from outlying areas, were a little bit uptight when we first arrived on the scene. Previously they had very little competition for the women and they started making critical comments about our being there. It took one short fight in that bar with four or five soldiers being thrown out into the street to make them understand that we were there to stay.

Many of the bars had booths and dance floors which made it easy to meet young ladies and have an enjoyable evening. We listen to songs like "Juke Box Saturday Night" by Vaughn Monroe, "What a Difference a Day Makes" by Charlie Barnet, and "In the Blue of the Evening" by Jimmy Dorsey. It took about two weeks before I met someone, who conveniently lived across the street from our barracks and our drill field. She lived with her sister and they both had husbands away in the Service. She could look out her window and see how our marching competition was going on Friday nights.

I explored the opportunity of making some Mare Island type of evening excursions after hours. I found out that our local control was very similar to that I had experienced at Mare Island, nobody was watching us after we went to bed. Our bunks in the National Guard building were on the upper deck of the basketball court and it was very easy to go down the steps, out the back door and walk over to her house. Later Bill Schaumburg joined me visiting her sister.

We would play cards, and sleep there until 4:00 in the morning. At that time, we would go back up to the Armory, take a shower, make our beds and take the bus that transported us to the airport for breakfast and aviation activities. We were never stopped and had a great time with the sisters, but I did lose about 15 pounds because of my nocturnal activities.

It was an experience not to be missed on how to have fun in the Service.

We also had spirited athletic contests with the other cadets at the airport. We played soccer, touch tackle football and softball, without losing any games. Again, I was chosen to be captain of our teams, which I enjoyed. I also experienced an exceptionally sore toe while I was playing soccer. I had intercepted a ball while another cadet was trying to kick it, and ended up with a dislocated right toe. This was at the end of the game so I stayed on the field for the next few minutes until it was over.

My toe was hurting and when I carefully peeled the shoe and sock off, I knew I had a major problem. Our physical education instructor told me to grab the top of the locker door while he pulled and turned the toe backwards to where it should be. **Ouch!**

This helped me, but the toe remained swollen and made flying more difficult, especially on landings. The biplane I was flying at that time had a tendency to veer to the left during landings. This was correctable by applying some brake pressure on the rudder with the right foot. For a while, I couldn't use my right foot to apply any pressure, so I crossed my left foot over to the right rudder to keep the plane flying in the correct direction.

Flying the biplanes was a lot more fun than flying the small trainer planes. We read books about flying acrobatics and practiced these skills to some degree. It was important to understand these maneuvers, but not a good idea to let anyone see you making a loop.

There were several hills around the airport that could be used as a shield. I must admit, this is where I did my first

Prescott, Arizona - In front of a bi-wing
Me (in the middle) and fellow pilots, including my friends Bill Schaumburg from Chicago
(far left) and Al Steele, who played 2nd base for Oakland (next to me, 2nd from right)

solo loop and it came out exceptionally well, as I am still here today.

In Spring of 1944, we finally graduated from Prescott and had five days to get to St. Mary's Pre-Flight in Moraga, California. Al Steele, who lived in Oakland, and I decided that I we could hitchhike to San Francisco.

Our first ride was good because we met someone who was willing to take us to the valley below us. However, this left us standing in Wickenburg at 10:00 a.m. with very few cars heading westward. We started to peel off our dark Navy uniforms as the temperature increased. About 2-1/2 hours later, a kind gentleman who was going to Los Angeles stopped and offered us a ride. He started his car, bringing the speed up to 45 miles hour, which was the maximum speed allowed by the government in order to conserve gas during the war.

Our host drove at this speed for about an hour when he became tired and asked if one of us would like to drive, and I volunteered. He hopped in the back seat and went to sleep. For some reason, after a short bit, the speed started to approach a higher level. The automobile was traveling quite well, so there was a joint decision between Al and myself to push it a little faster. The gentleman woke up later and scolded us a little for the higher speed. He returned to the front seat and drove the rest of the way at 45 miles an hour.

When we arrived in Los Angeles, we decided to take a train to San Francisco. Our cadet uniforms had a single star on each arm and people didn't know what rank we held. One elderly lady addressed us as Admirals and complemented us on our fighting the war. We tried to explain that we were not Admirals, but she wouldn't buy it.

There were several other incidents like this. Once we arrived at the San Francisco station, however, we were approached by an older man who asked, "What time does the next train leave for Los Angeles?"

Army/Navy vigilance - my cousin George and I watching the sky, even when we're off-duty

I guess he thought our uniforms made us look like conductors. Al went to Oakland and I went to Franklin Street to spend the balance of the days remaining of our leave.

However, upon arriving home, I had a real shock.

I was having breakfast one morning and picked up the *San Francisco Chronicle*. There on the front page was a half page spread that showed an American pilot on his knees in the sand, about to be beheaded by a Japanese officer.

The gruesome picture showed his face clearly as he was looking down to the sand. The caption in the headlines revealed the young man's name – Bill Newton – a fraternity brother and friend of mine.

I was sick to my stomach.

Bill's family lived in Berkeley. I felt the fact that the *Chronicle* made headlines of the incident was very, very improper. To see your son and brother about to be murdered by the Japanese was beyond cruel. Having the Army or Navy privately notify the family of his death was the accepted practice of the time.

I often thought about his sister, Elizabeth Newton, a very pretty girl who was engaged to another of my fraternity brothers. I wondered about the grief she and her family must have felt about the death of her brother, compounded by the shock of having to see it so graphically and insensitively portrayed in the morning newspaper. I went on to St. Mary's Pre-Flight greatly saddened by the news.

Shortly thereafter, on June 6th, the Normandy Invasion began. I knew that I would most likely be involved in the war in the Pacific Theater.

Chapter 34

St. Mary's Pre-Flight

Swimmers Unite

Before we left Prescott for our leave, someone in our squad said he had a plan on how we could stay together at St. Mary's Pre-Flight. He said that he had been told that we would be given a swimming test and that 'poor swimmers' or 'non-swimmers' would be kept together. Once we got to St. Mary's Pre-Flight, all of a sudden, we had a lot of both types in our group. You might say, we dog paddled and splashed our way into staying together at St. Mary's Pre-Flight.

Swimming was one of the major athletic items in our list of competitive sports. As non-swimmers, we were given swimming lessons for the first two weeks and became quite proficient. There was some talk about how our non-swimming group could beat the other cadets in our meets after such a short instruction period. I'm sure the swimming officers knew that something was up, but no one said anything about it, maybe because we were enlisted men.

In addition to swimming, we had gymnastics, wrestling, boxing, basketball and touch tackle football. We played two athletic sports each day for a week and rotated them throughout the full time we were at St. Mary's Pre-Flight. Our schooling consisted of learning Morse code, weather forecasting, navigation and Naval officer customs and procedures.

When we got into wrestling, I found that our instructor was John Woudenberg. He had been an All American in football at Colorado as well as the college heavyweight wrestling champion. He was also the same football tackle I played against while I was at the Shoemaker base.

He said "hello," and then singled me out to be the person who would help him demonstrate holds. This meant turning me around, dumping me onto the floor and holding me down. Some of my 'good' friends would say, "Would you do that again, coach? We didn't see exactly how you did it."

Meanwhile, I tried to see who was asking the questions so I could bounce him around later.

In gym class, I set a record for rope climbing. From the starting position of sitting on the floor, at the sound of the whistle and using only my arms during the climb, I could hit the bell 15 feet above the floor faster than anyone else. This was second nature to me, after doing a lot of rope climbing during the time I was working on the dredge in Alaska.

Boxing gave us a chance to have a great time hitting other people around. We had head protection which was a good idea. Al Steele and I selected each other and had a great time sparring with each other. As mentioned, he was Oakland's minor league's best second baseman before the war and he had a good right hand. I had a pretty good left hand. He got a few extra shots from me because my left hook was a little closer to his nose than his right hand was to my nose.

When we started touch football, the coach for this sport also turned out to be the football coach for the St. Mary's Pre-Flight team. He had us throwing balls at one another for a short bit and then made us start passing to runners. He finally asked me to start throwing passes by myself while he called out where the receiver was supposed to go. After a bit of this, he asked me if I would like to come out for the St. Mary's Pre-Flight football team. I agreed to this, but was concerned that I would not be fulfilling my programmed school activities. He said after I completed my schooling, and if I was still on the base, he wanted me to practice for the football team.

I told him I would like to do that.

We took courses that required star navigation. As we got involved in making star fixes, we were given some stars and had to figure out where they were during the time we could see them. This was designed to indicate that you had enough knowledge to accomplish this in a very short amount of time. We had two minutes for each of the stars, and needed to have a measurement of each star as to where it was in relationship to us.

But Shillo – who of anyone in the group should have been stellar at this task – got himself involved in not listening to what the teachers wanted, but instead in the development of a whole system as how would be best to analyze the situation. He would come up with some very lengthy analysis which was not what anybody wanted. Once again, he would do his own mental problem solving to determine what the star's height was, and why it was that height and then relate the same situation for the other stars. Meanwhile the rest of us would be using a book that told us what the star's position already was!

He did a great job at everything . . . except what the instructors wanted.

I came to the conclusion that he was just too bright. For example, sometimes several of us would go to the movies. He, however, was not interested in the movie, but instead figuring out the best place to sit in relationship to the size of the theater, relative to the size of the screen, and the correct projection angles. That was Shillo.

He said one time that he joined the Marines right when the war started, and yet it was a month and a half before he found out that the Marines were a part of the Navy. Eventually he flunked out because he tried to turn everything into a unique problem and at the same time solve that problem. He was the kind of guy who was compelled to over-think everything and see the world in his own, very individual way.

An event I'll always remember occurred during our training one evening in July when we were just about to go to bed in our large barracks. There was an extremely bright light from the north that flashed and quickly disappeared. The combat Marines in our barracks yelled **"Hit the deck"** which we all did. Shortly thereafter we heard a very loud noise and felt a concussion powerful enough to damage windows and doors at St. Mary's Pre-Flight.

When I heard there had been an explosion at the new Ammunition Depot at Port Chicago, I immediately remembered how uneasy I had felt, along with some of my fellow sailors a year or so ago, about the way explosives were handled there. Port Chicago, as I mentioned, was on the south shore of the channel across from my unit at Mare Island, but closer to Martinez. It was equipped to handle several ships at one time for transporting ammunition to the Pacific Front.

Both Wayne Phillips and I had been convinced that something was going to happen eventually, and we made a point of staying as far from the depot as possible.

We felt the training was minimal, and poor, and that the officers were not good both because of the lack of discipline, and because they did not require the black sailors stationed there to take necessary precautions regarding how they handled ammunition. We had seen how quickly they had gotten into the habit of tossing shells back and forth among themselves.

Obviously the Navy did not release much information concerning the incident– I guess because it was war time – but people in the area knew there had to have been tremendous casualties among the men working there, as well as to the ships and equipment. However, nobody knew then the actual extent of the damage.

It turned out that more than 10,000 **tons** of explosives were set off by the blast. In fact, it was   the worst home-front disaster of WW II.

Much later, after the war, information surfaced that indicated that virtually everyone working there at the time was killed instantly– 320 sailors on duty, as well as civilians – plus 400 more were wounded. Two-thirds of those killed were black sailors. (At that time, nearly all of the sailors assigned to that dangerous duty were.)

According to reports, the seismic shock wave was felt as far away as Boulder City, Nevada, and the explosion was so powerful that the largest remaining pieces of a 7,200-ton ship were the size of a suitcase. (See Appendix for sources for more information about this disaster).

While the damage in San Francisco was minimal since it was 45 miles away, and we suffered only minor damages to windows and doors at St. Mary's Pre-Flight (20 miles away), the explosion damaged or destroyed every rail car, building and structure in Port Chicago. Two ships were sunk. Every-thing above the waterline was torn to pieces. The Coast Guard rescue vessels were also eliminated.

Tensions quickly began to build among the men who had to work on the pier, and 258 refused to work on the ammu-nition depot. Of these, 208 were court-marshalled on bad con-duct charges, and lost three months pay for disobeying orders.

Another 50 sailors, were charged with mutiny, which could have led to death sentences. However, they received 8 to 15 years of hard labor instead . . . and after the war, they were given clemency.

*   *   *

Our Naval Aviation had severely damaged the Japanese Navy's air force and ships. It now appeared there was no longer the same need for the number of new pilots that the Navy had originally anticipated. They had determined that half of us would be sent for a three month aviation training program in Norman, Oklahoma, and the balance of the cadets would be transferred and trained for positions as Ensigns on ships.

Very shortly, a list of all the cadets in our group was posted on the wall breaking out those who were going on to Norman, and those being eliminated from the cadet program. Each cadet was rated on scholastics, athletics, flying, officer potential, leadership and physiological tests for the ability to be a pilot. This evaluation had started from the beginning of our training at San Luis Obispo, and continued throughout Prescott and other preliminary flight schools, including at St. Mary's Pre-Flight.

I spotted my name on the list and found that I had the best ranking (with the lowest score), of anyone on the list. It turned out, I was the only cadet to get a #1 score in all 30 categories, and nobody got a 31. There were only three people who got scores of 33, and the rest of the numbers went up from there.

The Navy used this type of evaluation to classify the top third of a class, middle of a class, or the bottom of a class. Those of us who had the lowest scores were accepted for Norman. Unfortunately, some of my best friends were eliminated from the aviation program. Al Steele didn't make it, nor did Bill Schaumburg, and several others.

Since there was a delay in our being sent to Norman, I was able to continue football practice and play on the Navy football team. I only got to play four games that season, however, because I was going to be transferred.

During this time, all of us had a week's vacation and I went to Reno to visit my dad. Of course being there made me think of Vivian. My father had sent me a letter a while back telling me that she had gotten married, and also that her aunts had developed financial difficulties (just as Vivian had feared).

I would have liked to see her, however, I thought the wisest course was to mind my own business and not bother her (if she even still lived in Reno).

I did, however, get to see Ginger and my family in San Francisco.

After my week's leave, my first game was against my previous team from Shoemaker, which now had monster - sized players.

Ginger in her pearls, me in my uniform

This included one Chicago All Pro tackle, Joe Stydahar, who had been selected as a League All Star for six years in a row.

He weighed in at 270 pounds. Another player was an All American guard from Georgia who weighed 240 pounds. Shoemaker brought in some of the football players from the Monterey Pre-Flght School, which had been shut down earlier.

By now, the Shoemaker base had installed a football stadium for viewing games. The locker rooms were separate, but the showers and lavatories were shared by both teams. I have funny memories of sharing these facilities with some of the bigger players. Everything about them seemed bigger. I will leave most of this to your imagination.

I was now a running back, a second string left half back, operating on a single wing formation. When I got into the game against my old team, the left side of my offensive line was not able to control these two huge players. After I got the ball, all I could see were two very large people coming right at me.

I didn't get smashed, but I threw the ball very quickly and not always at a person.

On the St. Mary's Pre-Flight team, our center called all the plays. His name was Gomer Jones, and he was an All American from Ohio State. He kept calling dinky little passes that were just around his position, and most of these were dumb decisions. It was also a dumb decision for him to call any of the plays at all, just as it was dumb for the coach to let him do so. As a result, things did not work out too well, and St. Mary's lost the game.

We played College of Pacific at night and finally did win that game. Next we played UCLA in the Coliseum in Los Angeles. We were glad to have Bob Tichenal playing on our team as a right end. Previously he had played for USC, when he was younger. At that time, both UCLA and USC played their games in the Coliseum.

Jane Russell's husband, Bob Waterfield, was the passer and a runner for UCLA. Both were stars in Los Angeles at the same time, Jane being a movie star and her husband was a first rate football player.

Waterfield was having a tough time getting his team to make any yardage. He opted to use a play that theoretically was designed to fool everyone by faking a hand-off to someone else. He started around the right end, while our tackle caught him as he went by, grabbed him by his shoulder pads and dumped him on the turf. John Woudenberg was the tackler, and Waterfield didn't play much after that.

We beat UCLA by three touchdowns, as I recall.

Woudenberg was not only strong, but he was fast and had an unbelievable amount of energy. In practice, he could catch me when I attempted to run around his location. He couldn't beat me in a 50-yard race, but he was exceptionally quick for short periods of time. Later, after the war, both Bob Tichenal and John played for the original San Francisco 49ers.

My last game was played at Kezar Sadium in San Francisco and my mother and Tante Elena were there to see us play. By that time, I had received word that our group was to be sent to Norman, Oklahoma, on Sunday right after we finished our game.

This game was against the Army who had a young black soldier from Ohio State who would eventually become an All American after the war. He was exceptionally fast and hard to catch. Meanwhile, Gomer was still calling passes within three yards of his position and driving me nuts. I had been put into the game to do the passing and obviously the other team had scouted Gomer and found out that he would just pass around his own position.

I made some comment about "Why don't you let me move out and pass on the run for 25 or 30 yards?" Gomer, however, didn't appreciate my comment. He wouldn't budge and we lost to the Army.

After the game, the Navy flew another cadet and me to Fresno to pick up our train carrying the other cadets who were going to Norman, and at last I was on my way to Oklahoma. We had a good time on that train traveling south to Las Vegas, and then east to Norman.

Our base was approximately 18 miles south of Oklahoma City and was just across the highway from Oklahoma University. Our field was on the west side and had two main landing pads, a host of small external landing sites situated away from the main base, and best of all . . . about 400 biplanes!

I liked the look of this place already.

Chapter 35

Norman, Oklahoma

Night flying and going solo

The Norman base was for pilot primary flight training. We were also involved in plane and ship recognition and
more weather forecasting. Cadets were to take code instruction,
navigation, plus a lot more swimming. One swimming exercise started after we got into the pool. We swam to the center,
climbed about 12 feet up a rope that the Navy had hanging over
the pool, dove off the rope into the pool, and then swam under-
water to the end of the pool.

We also trained in hand-to-hand combat, which we
called "how to kill people." The Navy called it something fan-
cier. One of our instructors in this program was Len Eshmont.
Len was a very competent instructor but had to cope with a
particular Texan whenever he tried to demonstrate a hold. The
Texan had made All American in football a couple of years prior
to getting into the flight program. He was larger than Eshmont
and proceeded to try to make each exercise into a combat issue
between himself and Eshmont.

After a little of this, Eshmont became quite angry and
both of them began to start a battle in the middle of the floor.
Len had the guy down on his stomach and in a position where
he couldn't get up. As he applied pressure, Len asked, "Do you
give up?" The Texan kept saying, "No."

The only thing I could think was that he was too damn
dumb to know when he should give up. This went on for at

least 10 minutes more with Len working the Texan over, but he would still not give up. Eshmont finally freed him from the hold, his opponent remained on the floor. He didn't try it again.

Len Eshmont went on to become one of the original players (a running back and defensive back) for the San Francisco 49ers, but died in 1957 at the early age of 39. The Len Eshmont Award – the Niner's most prestigious award – was created in his honor, and is given each year to the player who most exemplifies Len's "inspirational and courageous play." He was quite a man, and well-liked among the cadets.

Our flight training consisted of three months in a biplane which was the Navy's version of the Stearman.

STEARMAN-N25

Length:	25 ft.	Max Speed:	125 mph
Height:	9ft.4in.	Ceiling:	13,400 ft.
Wingspan:	32 ft.2 in.	Range:	525miles
Gross Weight:	2,712 lbs.	Crew:	2
	Engine - Radial: 220 hp		

This was a super plane for me. I enjoyed flying in an open cockpit and doing acrobatics. Our instructors were good, and taught us how to fly using the Navy's approach for landings on an aircraft carrier. The method used the throttle for speed control, while slowly dropping the tail onto the deck, instead of the Army's system of flying a long approach straight to the landing strip.

After three weeks with instructors and finally soloing, we received a check-ride. Unfortunately, after my ride my instructor was not satisfied with my test, and he gave me a "down-check." I was devastated.

Two days later, I was set up for a second check by the head instructor. I started out well, following his requests for handling some procedures, such as a spin, a snap roll and an Immelmann. I recall him saying, "Take it easy for a few minutes and then I'll give it back to you." I took my feet off the rudders to relax and he started into a slow roll, and when the plane was upside down, he said "Emergency, it's your plane!"

I rolled out and took a look to see where an open field was located and said, "I'm landing over there." We kept going for a short time towards the landing site when he said, "That's enough," and we headed for home. When we landed, he said, "There is nothing wrong with your flying, and you have an up-check."

After that, there was a whole series of maneuvers that we went through for training. One was learning how to handle landings on the small dirt fields which were at various distances around the airport. The instructor dictated the one to land on, meaning you had to determine where the wind was, and how to play that wind so you could land on the first third of the field with a slip.

Once you were on the field, you were expected to have enough speed to take off, turn back towards the field, and make a cross direction landing. This sometimes resulted in a need to go underneath telephone wires, but the instructors were good, and understood what had to be done to get cadets to cope with a cross direction landing. But occasionally a mishap would occur.

One time I remember a plane flipping on its landing and turning upside down onto the ground. The instructor evidently told the cadet to be careful to not hurt himself getting out of the plane since they were upside down. The student did what he was told, but when the instructor released his own seat belt, he immediately banged his head as he hit the ground!

We also received instruction on night flying. Roughly 40 cadets took their planes to one of two elevations above the field. The cadets at the lower elevation were to make three "touch and go" landings while the other group circled the field at the higher elevation. The landing area was lit only with flares. After the first group completed their "landings," they changed places with the second group proceeding to the top elevation, and the second group came down to go through their "touch and go's."

However, the people in the tower did not notify us that there had been a wind change. I was with the group at the higher elevation and when I came down to make my three landings, I quickly discovered there was not enough field for me to touch down in the flare area. The wind had changed so much that our downwind approach had to be drastically changed to compensate.

Everyone in my group gave up on the first try and came around again for the second attempt, this time with a lot more distance on the downwind leg to accommodate a longer approach for the landing.

When I was on my second downwind leg, some of those flying at the higher elevation started to come down too early and joined our group. I glanced 90° to my left, and saw a plane's red/green wing tip lights were in the wrong sequence and were coming directly at me. Obviously the pilot had gotten out of position and we were on a collision course.

I dropped the nose of my plane just as the other plane went over me. I looked up and even in that dim light I could see oil spillage on his fuselage. After he passed me, I pulled up and proceeded to make my landing. I quickly rolled off the landing strip and parked my plane in its proper section of the tarmac. By then, I had enough of this "practice" and had plenty of anxiety about the tower people who were running this operation.

I dropped my flight gear in its appropriate area and watched the rest of the proceedings. Other pilots were making strange landings all over the place. Something went wrong with the whole evening's affair, but nothing was ever said about the fact that I had made only one landing and no one ever quizzed me about why.

We did a lot of acrobatic and three-plane formation flying in our biplanes. Sometimes we did these acrobatics individually. Other times we would have three pilots in formation doing standard echelons. The lead plane signaled one of the outside wing planes to shift across to the opposite side of the formation, so that we were in an echelon position instead of a 'V.'

It just so happened that we were somewhere near an Army Air Force base where their cadets were flying a stepped down version of standard pursuit ships. They were using P-45's which were good fighter planes at the start of WW II, but not competitive with later versions. They were evidently beginners in their pursuit training. Every now and then one of the Army pilots would make a pass at us and pretend that he was going to shoot us down.

After a few tries of this type, we decided to combat him. When we saw someone coming, we immediately changed our direction as he would slice by either on our right side, or our left side. The moment he was past, we picked the spot where we assumed he would be coming back after us. He would suddenly have three planes coming down on him from his rear because our bi-wing planes could maneuver within a tighter radius than he could. Generally the Army pilot would break off and head for home, leaving us to wait for next time.

One evening about half way through our training at Norman, we were advised that a movie called *The Fighting Lady* would be shown after dinner. We were also told that the

Navy's top flying Ace at that time would be discussing his background in fighting the Japanese. The movie was in color and was surprisingly great viewing. The pilots were shooting up airplanes throughout the program. When it was over, Commander David McCampbell rose to discuss his activities.

The cadets had been given questions to ask the Commander that were quite dull, until finally one of the cadets asked a question about our training program, which really got our attention. He wanted to know if the airplane and ship recognition class we were taking was really viable. McCampbell, who had probably had a few belts in the Officer's Quarters while we were watching the movie, answered, "I'm not too good at recognizing the type of plane I am shooting down. My wingman, Roy, has a good eye for that and he tells me what they were after the fight is over."

This prompted other questions. One was about the heavy emphasis on navigational instruction. The Commander said, "Well, I was leading a fight to knock out a small island and instead of approaching it from the front, I found myself on the other side of the island and had to come back in the wrong direction. It was the most successful aviation strike I made."

By this time, he was starting to get a lot of questions about our training, which must have infuriated our instructors. The question period was stopped and we were all told that this was the end of the meeting. Most of us thought that McCampbell's description of what was going on was really great.

A few days later, when I was talking with another cadet about where he had put in his time prior to joining our group, he mentioned that he'd been a sailor in one of the Navy's training areas. Eventually our conversation got around to where Harry Leib's name came up. Harry had chosen to take the four year commitment in ROTC at Cal where I met him in my fraternity. He had become a Navy pilot and instructor for the Navy flight program.

Sadly, however, his life was cut short far too soon.

He had been killed in an accident with another plane in mid-air. Harry was trying to get the student out of the back seat of the plane, while he was on the wing pulling the canopy off the student. Leib was unable to get the student out and he stayed just a little too long himself. By the time he jumped and got his parachute open, he was too close to the ground for it to open completely and he died.

There were quite a few people from our fraternity who were killed. One had been in a submarine that was sunk. Second Lieutenant Brocaw was unfortunate enough to be stationed in the Philippines when the Japanese attacked.

He had to go through the Death March used on the prisoners they captured. He survived the march and remained in prison in the Philippines until just before MacArthur attacked. About this time, the Japanese began to ship these American officers to Japan in unmarked ships. The Americans were eliminating anything coming off the Philippine Islands – a strategy of which the Japanese were well aware – and a U.S. submarine sunk my friend's ship, killing everyone aboard.

Bruce's brother, a pilot on a bomber, was shot down over Austria, and put into a concentration camp. However, he did survive, and was finally rescued after the war was over.

Occasionally, I heard about other fraternity brothers who died. It was not an easy thing for people who were my age to hear, particularly for those who had been involved in Cal's four year ROTC program.

*   *   *

Christmas time rolled around in Norman, Oklahoma. We were listening to Bing Crosby's "White Christmas" and "Coming in on a Wing and a Prayor" by Jimmy Mc Hugh, and people were receiving boxes of cookies and other goodies from home. I received one from my father which was a well protect- ed box containing six pints of bourbon whiskey. I had told him we had a problem getting drinks. There were a lot of clubs that would welcome us in, but we had to bring our own bottle, as Oklahoma was a "dry state." We never seemed to get enough time to get to a store that sold alcohol, so we just drank cokes.

Everyone wanted to know what my father sent, so I told them what it was. I had to store the bottles under the barracks because I couldn't be caught with them in my living quarters. My father had removed the bottle caps adding enough booze to fill the bottle to the top so you couldn't hear that the bottle contained liquid. I told my friends that we would share them the next time we could go to town, on the next weekend.

There were four of us and we went to get our train to town, but suddenly, as I was walking along with two pints un- der my clothing, I felt a "pop" and knew that this was not a good thing. My friends immediately understood, one ran into the "Ship's Service" and bought a glass jar of peanuts that would hold a pint while the other two helped me very gingerly walk to the restroom so I could take my pants off and dislodge the leaking bottle without injuring myself. The activity was consummated expeditiously and we all had drinks at the club that evening.

Our final training event was a cross country flight from Norman to Ponca City, Oklahoma, and back. It was about an hour and a half flight directly north to where we landed and got fuel. The weather had been changing from something reasonable to something less than that during the first part of the trip. It was a major problem for the other cadets later that day.

When I took off from Ponca City, I plotted a path which I felt would be reasonable on the basis of the wind conditions and fence lines. I flew low enough so I could use the fences to keep me at the correct angle. I was about two thirds of the way back to Norman when another biplane joined me. He was the only other airplane that I saw during my return trip. He waved and I waved back at him. Not long after that, I could see the Norman air field; it was pretty much in the midst of a winter storm. I landed my plane and my companion came in right after me.

When we got out of our respective planes, he said, "I'm sure glad you knew where you were going, because I certainly didn't." I thought I had lucked out, but didn't say it. Out of approximately 25 planes that were sent out on this cross country trip, 20 didn't make it home. They landed in fields all over Oklahoma. Fortunately, no one was hurt and in a couple of weeks we were on our way to Pensacola, Florida and the big time.

By February, the Allies and Russians were putting some heavy pressure on German infantry. At the Yalta Conference, President Roosevelt, Churchill, and Stalin planned the defeat and occupation of Germany, and they proposed the first meeting of the United Nations in San Francisco.

That same month, on February 19th, the Marines attacked Iwo Jima. I realized things were really heating up and I was reminded, once again, that I may be getting much closer to the war than I wanted to be.

Chapter 36

Pensacola, Florida

Flying High

Our trip from Norman to Pensacola, Florida was on a very, very old train that may have seen duty in the Civil War. There was a coal burning heater in the center of each car, but luckily, even though it was February, it was warm enough that we didn't have to use it. This relic took us east to Memphis, turned south down to Jackson, Mississippi, then rolled into Mobile, Alabama on the way to Florida.

At our midday stop in Jackson, we didn't see a single white person at the train station. We did see signs for drinking water that said "Black" or "White," so theoretically both races used this station. The areas we traveled through were very poor. Along the way, we also saw deteriorating remains of old mansions and plantations.

We finally arrived in Pensacola in the western part of Florida panhandle around mid-day on the second day.

After two days of indoctrination at the main base at Pensacola, we were transported to the primary training center at one of the first of several nearby outlying fields. This one was called Whiting Field. Here we no longer trained with biplanes, but had graduated into SNVs, low single wing airplanes with fixed wheels.

SNV - I			
Manufacturer:	Vultee	Max Speed:	166 mph
Length:	28 ft. 8 in.	Ceiling:	21,000 ft.
Height:	9 ft.	Range:	1,050 mi.
Wingspan:	42 ft. 2 in.	Crew:	2
Empty Weight:	2,976 lbs.	Pratt & Whitney:	R-985
Gross Weight:	4,360 lbs.		

These planes had two seats, one for the cadet and another for the instructor, one behind the other. They were, however, crappy planes to fly. It had me wishing for my old Navy biplane at Norman.

Each of us became familiar with the SNV doing a lot of flying time with an instructor, until we finally soloed. We next flew in formations as a group of three planes. Cadets would take off in unison with the two wing planes gaining a small amount of altitude before the lead plane left the ground.

Every morning we checked the bulletin board to see what our pairing was. Supposedly all three pilots were to be changed, but for some reason only one other pilot rotated into our group. If he was from our original group, we ran things straight, but if not, we played games with our new cadet.

If he was the lead pilot, the chosen formation put one of us on each side of him. When the lead pilot gave the signal to take-off, he was supposed to allow the two wing pilots to gain a little more altitude than he had. We purposely kept our altitude lower than normal so that the new cadet, as lead pilot, was faced with having to make his take-off longer than usual. This caused him some concern about whether he would have enough runway left to make his take-off successfully.

This was great for me and my companion, as we were still learning and gaining the ability to move our planes from a "V" formation to an echelon and back again. If one of us was the lead pilot, once we got in the air and adjusted to our surroundings, we would test the other fellow by calling for an echelon formation. He would do this by moving across the back of the formation at a slightly higher elevation using a little extra speed and take a position farther out on either the left or right wing.

While he was making his move, my compatriot or I would make a slight turn in the other direction. He soon found out he was way out of position. This made him increase his speed even more to catch us. We did this stunt two or three times to the new man and when we finally landed, he would either tell us he had something wrong with his plane or that he was going to have to improve his cross-overs. Generally we explained that he was flying okay, and we were just having fun.

We also flew evening flights in formation. We started out with five planes, the fifth being piloted by an instructor. He would monitor the flight and contact us by radio as to what we should be doing. If someone was having trouble staying in the formation, he would be challenged to catch up with the rest of the group. Eventually we got good enough so we could go solo without an instructor.

We didn't have any major problems, but there was one situation when one of our planes was lined up for a night take-off and one cadet chewed up the tail section of the plane in front of him. Obviously, the cadet who lost his tail was not overly happy.

There was another incident during an evening flight where a cadet needed to bail out of his airplane over the water. There were boats, however, to pick him up as soon as he made his water landing. Here again, our instruction was always very good.

There were substantial lightning storms from time to time. One morning about one minute after reveille, a very large lightning bolt struck outside of our barracks. When we looked outside, we saw that the sidewalk had been totally torn up for a full block by that lightning strike. Until that time, some of us were a little lax and not getting up immediately at the sound of the bugle. That morning and the following week, reveille prompted us to get out of bed quickly as we associated it with the lightning bolt.

Within two months, we moved from Whiting Field to another base for our next step: Ellyson Field. This new base was devoted to instrument training and here we had an exceptionally good airplane to fly.

SNJ			
Manufacturer:	North American Aviation	Max Speed:	250 mph
Length:	29 ft. 6 in.	Ceiling:	21,500 ft.
Height:	16 ft. 8 in.	Range:	750 miles
Wing Span:	42 ft.	Crew:	2
Empty Weight:	4,158 lbs.	Pratt & Whitney	
Gross Weight:	5,300 lbs.	Redial:	550 hp

The plane had retractable landing gear and was fully equipped with instruments for blind flying and a better radio. We flew with our head under a canopy much of the time to fully utilize these instruments. The "hood" or canopy was designed so that the pilot could not see the ground or the sky but could see only the instruments that were in front of him. The instructor could see everything from the ground up.

Early on, I got vertigo and the instructor popped open the canopy so I could see that I was flying straight with the instruments. Something in my head told me I was making a turn and that made me lean my body into the direction of that turn. This was a weird sensation. The idea was to fly the instruments, totally believing in them, and not to depend on your inner self to know where you were. The more you practiced, the better you adjusted to trusting the instruments, not your inner ear equilibrium. After a time you didn't pay attention to your ears.

One of the instructors on this base was a Marine by the name of Ted Williams. He trained to be a Marine pilot shortly after setting his baseball batting average record of .404 in 1942. From time to time, he played a little baseball for the base team where we were training. He was generally batting against some college or Minor League pitcher and the other team adjusted and moved their outfield back about 500 feet when he got up to hit the ball.

If we did well with our flying, our instructors would sometimes let us relax by giving us a chance to take over the plane, do slow rolls, or other acrobatic maneuvers. We also flew solo using ground instruments to direct ourselves through a two-hour flight path back to our home base.

Another unforgettable event took place when a new cadet was soloing. He took off and quickly tried to retract his wheels, but did not have enough speed or clearance to do so. There was a loud noise as the plane's landing gear and propeller contacted the field. This was a grand lesson on how to screw up a take-off in this great airplane.

After we completed our instrument training instruction, we were transferred back to the main base at Pensacola. By this time we were starting – not fully but somewhat – to be treated like officers. Two cadets shared a room, our closets had lights to keep our clothes from mildewing, and there was a recreation area where we could go to have a beer or two after flight time was over.

As cadets, we had been separated by what type of plane we would be flying in advanced training. The members of our original group, primarily based upon age, went into sea- planes. Younger cadets were selected for fighter planes or dive bombers and sent to other bases such as Corpus Christi, or similar locations.

The newspapers and radio were full of news about the invasion of Okinawa on April 1. Shortly thereafter, on April 12, President Roosevelt died and Harry Truman became President. But none of this really affected me directly and I started my final aviation courses in PBY's.

PBY's

Manufacturer: Consolidated		Max Speed:	189 mph
Length:	63 ft. 10 in.	Cruising Speed:	110 mph
Height:	18 ft.	Range:	2,860 miles
Wing Span:	104 ft.	Crew:	3 officers; 4 crewmen
Empty Weight: 17,526 lbs.		Engines:	2 variable speed
Gross weight:	33,369 lbs.	Pratt & Whitney Redial:	1,200 hp
Inertia Starter		Machine guns:	2; 30-caliper; 1; 50-caliper

Our group moved to another location on the western side of the Pensacola base for training in sea-planes. The PBY was one of the types of sea-planes that was being used in combat. The English, Canadians and Australians, as well as the Americans, had great success with this plane.

The German battleship Graf Spee, had sunk two English battleships and was heading home to its harbor when an English Air Force PBY spotted it. In ensuing battles with the English fleet, the Graf Spee sank before it reached its destination.

The PBYs were instrumental in spotting Japanese battle ships at the Battle of Midway. The American Navy was able to capitalize and totally change the Japanese-American relationship after the beating at Midway, as the Japanese were now the people being pursued.

*   *   *

April was a busy month for the war in Europe. On April 21st, the Russians reached Berlin, and the on the 28th of April, Mussolini was captured and executed. He had tried unsuccessfully to escape from the German part of Italy (with his girl friend) by fleeing into Switzerland. The next day, April 29th, the German Armies surrendered unconditionally in Italy; and finally on April 30th, Hitler committed suicide at the Reich Chancellery in Berlin.

We knew VE-Day had arrived with the war in Europe ending on May 8th. As I mentioned, however, my training continued as we were still at war with the Japanese.

The long sandy beaches on the western side of Pensacola were good for launching or beaching the planes. The seaplane section also faced the Pensacola Bay, a large bay where we had plenty of room to make water take-offs and landings.

My roommate was Bill Price, an ex-Marine from northern California. He was a weapons instructor while he was in the Marines Corp. He and I flew in the same plane with two other cadets, Alan Sparks, an ex-sailor from Kentucky who had been involved in Naval aviation during the war, and another sailor from Texas. The four of us would fly the same sea-plane about four hours a day, each cadet flying one hour with our instructor, while the rest of us took life easy in the back of the plane.

Due to my early experience around gold mine stamp mills, I had developed a capacity for sleeping soundly. This talent came in handy while the other cadets were making landings in our PBY. The reason for flying four hours a day in this manner was that once our plane was fueled and on the Pensacola Bay, it would have been inefficient to return to base each time to rotate the pilots.

We had a lot to learn on a PBY. It had two motors, an electrical starter system and a backup inertia starter, in case we had an electrical battery problem.

The PBY had two wing floats that could be used for landing and taxiing on the sea. There were two blister-type side bubbles for picking up or discharging people and a wing-walk area for accessing either wing tip. The pilot could use one or the other wing tip for maneuvering in the water. After landing and reducing the speed, the pilot could send one man out on the left or right wing to make the wing lower in the water. By using the wing tip, tail and motors, the pilot was able to manuver the plane fairly easily.

We got our first instructions at wing-walking and inertia starting early in our career. The inertia starter was a manually operated device that was used only if the airplane's electrical system didn't work. The manual starter was a major grunt and was located slightly in back of the cockpit. You cranked slowly, meanwhile sweating profusely. You cranked and cranked until all of a sudden you reached a speed where the engine could be started. Unfortunately, when we first began to understand how to crank and how to time the speed, the pilot might not have his act together. Then it would be necessary to start hand cranking the starter all over again.

In order to get out to the end of the wing tip, a person had to leave the bubble blister area, travel along the fuselage, and climb up on top of the wing, while walking very carefully. The next move was to turn left or right toward the correct motor, being careful not to get blown backward before reaching the wing tip. Life jackets were a must, as was the need for a calm pilot who didn't gun his motor as you were moving past the propellers. He could blow you right off the wing. When the plane was finally positioned for take-off, it was necessary to move back past the motor, get back into the blister, and to be sure to close it properly.

We were involved with take-offs and landings in both smooth and windy weather. When landing on a slick surface, there was a distinct vision problem. It was difficult to determine how high you were and exactly when the landing would take place. Once you touched the water, there was a major tendency for the nose of the airplane to dive down below the water surface. It was very important to pull back on the stick and hold the nose level constantly. If the water was rough, it was much easier to read the conditions and know how high you were from the surface.

We did a variety of things to increase our knowledge of navigation. Any pilot is required to understand his location at all times. However, when flying sea-planes, our only navigational tools were using the sun or stars to determine where we were since there were obviously very few fixed land indicators in the ocean.

We started out at the beginning, making star shots at the home base by computing where two or three stars intersected. That would give us an indication of where we were.

The star chart gave us the elevation and location of a star at a particular time day or night. A timed shot of the star was possible by holding the transit's viewer on the star for a full minute, which would give us an average reading of that star's position and height at that specific time. That was the first component of the shot. Next we would pick a second star and go through the same reading and recording. This was compounded by having to adjust for the plane's travel during the shots. It was not simple.

Once we became acquainted with our instruments, we were introduced to a large silo, which among other things, contained a mock-up of a cockpit with instruments that would record speed, altitude and other miscellaneous items. This silo was located on the base. The next procedure, while seated in the simulator, was to taxi out to the water for a take-off, climb to a specific height and direction, and watch the daylight change until it finally got dark. We could change the speed of the plane in the simulator from time to time and the clock in the silo would read the change and adjust to it.

The silo also contained a large map that could rotate in any direction, while displaying stars at different time periods allowing a pilot to make a simulated trip from our base, out over the ocean and back to our base; all the while standing on land. It was necessary to make several star shots and plot them on our own individual map over a period of three hours.

Using this map as we approached the airport at Pensacola, theoretically the sun would come up and we could recognize if we were approaching the base on course or possibly were off course during our "flying trip."

We also had a certain amount of life raft training utilizing an airplane cockpit that was positioned about 15 feet above the waterline of the base swimming pool. The unit consisted of a short 10 foot section of a cockpit with no prop, wings or tail. A cadet got into the unit wearing a life jacket, a parachute and floatation gear which was a collapsed portable life boat. Next he fastened the seat belt harness. The cockpit would be shot down a steep incline of track, hit the water, turn upside down and start to sink. The cadet had to release his seat belt harness, swim down and away from the cockpit, and rise to the top of the water before opening his life jacket.

The next step was to pull a CO_2 cartridge ring, which inflated the portable boat, and crawl into it. If you had not checked your equipment before getting into the cockpit, once you were in the water you might discover that the Navy had removed the cartridge ring and you had to blow up the raft by mouth. A great procedure, but I'm glad I never had to do it in a crash.

We had lots of flying in rough weather conditions. Thunder storms came through the Pensacola area on a frequent basis in early June and throughout July. The Pensacola base radio broadcast information about these storms as to whether or not they might possibly come over our landing areas. If so, we would make an early landing in order to wait out the storm's passage. As soon as it was determined that the storm had passed, we received radio clearance for starting our flight again. We could have three or four of these storms blow through in a four hour period.

Our group made two survival training trips to a deserted island south of Pensacola. After a search of all the cadets to find out if anyone was bringing apples, oranges, or candy bars, our commanding officer gave us some minor fishing equipment to catch fish so that we could eat whatever we caught. Another important lesson was how to find water on a small island. We soon realized that there was some water between one to two feet below the surface of the island. By the second trip, we were

much more knowledgeable about how to handle the small crit-
ters – from bugs to crabs to small fish. We also had a net to toss
for catching the smaller fish.

We did a fair amount of flying over and landing on the
water at night. These landings were done using flares for light
and they could be difficult as the wind was often variable or
changeable and these conditions were more than a little dangerous. It was certainly not as much fun as landing in daylight.
Again, like in Norman, Oklahoma, we ran into a condition
where someone didn't understand that the wind had drastically shifted. After recognizing the problem and extending
our downwind approach, we were able to compensate for the
change in speed and crosswinds.

When we were flying solo, one cadet would be pilot-in-
command for a certain length of time, while another member of
our group would be the co-pilot. As the last pilot in charge had
completed his time allotment, we would make a landing and
the four of us would discuss the flying we had just finished,
critiquing any errors we had made. In essence we were making
a check-ride between ourselves every time the four of us flew.

Each of us from time to time would make an error at
an approach or whatever. By evaluating each other about what
we had done or how we should have done the task, we became
fairly good at knowing what errors needed correcting. The four
of us thought we had trained well and all would pass the final
PBY check-ride since we were of equal ability.

Our final check-ride was scheduled for August 5th.
Soon we discovered the check pilot we had drawn for our
ride had given twelve down-checks in a row before our test.
When we introduced ourselves to him, he was very curt. Our
group got into our plane, took off and each cadet proceeded to
go through his check-ride, again rotating as each man finished

before our final landing. The only words the check pilot spoke during each of our individual rides were commands for the next required maneuver.

At the end of the session, we taxied back to the beach and got out of the plane but the officer had still not said a word about our flights. As he started to walk away, I said, "Pardon me sir, you haven't graded us yet." He replied "four up-checks" and strode off. We knew then that all four of us had qualified as Naval Aviators.

A little later, the four of us discussed what had gone on during the entire check-ride. In retrospect, we felt that our check pilot was trying to make things difficult for us, that he couldn't fault us for any mistakes and was ticked-off because he didn't like enlisted men becoming officers.

At 8:15 a.m. the next day, August 6th, Japan refused to surrender and Harry Truman commanded the *Enola Gay* to drop the first atomic bomb on Hiroshima. Seventy-five thousand people were killed. When the Japanese still did not respond, he finally dropped the second atom bomb on Naga-saki, three days later on the August 9th.

Meanwhile for us at the base, over the course of the next week we were kept busy getting fitted for our uniforms, dress whites, officer's hats, carry bags and other miscellaneous materials related to graduating. Our graduation ceremony, which included getting our Navy wings and commissions, took place at 8:00 a.m. on August 14th, 1945.

Two hours later, after the Japanese discovered we were the Ace flying group that had been commissioned at Pensacola, they knew it was all over.

They immediately surrendered . . . unconditionally.

Chapter 37

Corpus Christi

Stuck in a holding pattern

Even though the war was over, our military service was not, as I soon came to realize. My last military lesson had nothing to do with flying, but rather with just how **slowly** "military wheels" turned. After two more long days at Pensacola, we were finally released, and given two weeks leave before we had to check in at our next base – Corpus Christi, Texas.

Getting back to California was difficult because of all the confusion related to the war having ended. However, I was able to get a flight into Los Angeles on a Navy plane, and see my sister and her new husband, Jack Sullivan there. He had been in the Army and was shot down while on a flight over Germany. After parachuting out, near Belgium, he was captured and imprisoned for at least a year and a half.

He was released from his German prison camp after Germany surrendered on May 7th, 1945, and he married my sister in June. Once discharged from the Army, he started working for the American Can Company in downtown Los Angeles.

Although it was a quick visit, more of a 'stop and go,' it was good to see them, and I was pleased to get a chance to meet Ginger's husband. The next day, I took a train to San Francisco, and spent time with my aunts, my mother and grandmother before flying to Reno to see my father.

Far too soon, I had to report back to Corpus Christi, Texas.

My initial training in Corpus Christi was in PBM's, a larger and more advanced sea-plane than the PBY. I spent about three weeks flying the PBM, doing take-offs, landings and other maneuvers, when I was given a decision to make. They asked me if I wanted to stay in the Navy, or get a discharge. (It turned out my time in the Service qualified me for an early release.)

On the form they gave me to complete, I checked off the box indicating that I wanted to be released – As Soon As Possible. The Navy immediately stopped training me in PBM's. Other than that, nothing else happened in a timely fashion at all.

For about a month, I earned my flight pay as a co-pilot by towing targets for cadet fighter pilots in a PBY. Aviators got flight pay for flying an airplane during any given month, but if you did not fly, you received only the standard rate for an officer of your grade, which was about 30% less.

Most of the time towing was not too bad. All of our Navy pilots understood what the procedures were. They flew a pursuit curve, zeroing in on the target which we were towing, and released their rounds at the target. Unfortunately, we had one relatively unskilled Chilean pilot who was taking instructions at Corpus Christi, along with several of his Chilean Navy companions.

He blew his approach by not locking on to the pursuit curve, and he was late shooting at the target. By the time he started firing, both our plane and the target were directly in his line of fire. Our PBY caught a couple of bullets before we could cut the target loose and leave the area.

Meanwhile, I was getting increasingly upset because the Navy wouldn't release me.

The only high point during this period of time was when I got to do some real flying. Since the Navy was moving equipment, such as airplanes, to resale operations, I volunteered to fly planes to the West Coast. They checked me out and gave me a SNJ to fly to San Diego. I took off in the afternoon and they directed me to the San Antonio Air Base for an overnight, and then I was to fly to San Diego the next day.

I arrived in San Antonio, parked my plane, and then found out that they didn't have a room for me as a Navy Ensign. They told me they could, however, sneak me into a traveling General's quarters for the night, for which I thanked them profusely.

These quarters were more than just a sleeping arrangement. I had a huge bedroom with a king sized bed, a radio and a very sophisticated record player, plus a second large room with nice furniture, carpeting, a bar, and another radio. I could have camped out there for a week. Generals were certainly well treated!

Unfortunately, I had to leave the next morning right after breakfast. I took my SNJ and flew on to San Diego, delivered my plane to the Navy there, and caught a Navy transport plane back to Corpus Christi that same afternoon. I made this Corpus Christi to San Diego run two more times . . . but without the special General's living quarters.

During my last four days in Texas before they released me, I spent all my time engaged in a ridiculously tedious regiment just to divorce myself from the Navy. They had me running from one end of the base to another to physical testing facilities, to mental testing areas, and to obtain what seemed to be a never-ending list of signatures. This involved going to over 30 places across the Corpus Christi base. Most frustrating of all, was having to go back and forth to the *same* places to get a particular signature from each individual facility.

They routed me around in circles since the signatures had to be obtained **in a specific order.** This left me with no option but to follow their sequence. I'd no sooner walk to Station A and stand in line for a half hour, than I'd have to head 3/4 of a mile over to Station B, before heading right back to where I'd started.

Of course, this meant standing in long lines at each location for at least a half hour in order to get what I needed before I could proceed to the next station. Talk about a run-around! I was very upset, to say the least.

Then after I had finished this daunting task, I had to use my own money to fly back to San Francisco to attend another two days of **B.S.** On the first day, the officers who were processing my paperwork took their own sweet time; every-thing I did was devoted to all things Navy.

Worst of all, on the second day, I found out that I was not actually being discharged at all! Instead, I was going to be tied to them for another 10 years in the Reserves.

I would be required to take a physical exam at least once every year, or so, at their specific locations. Several of these spots were in areas that were not necessarily easy to get to. This meant my college classes, my jobs – and my life – would continue to be interrupted to satisfy the Navy for the next decade.

One of my discharge projects on the second day was to write down "my thoughts" of my life in the Navy. By this time, I'd definitely had it with their "all their Procedures," and I asked for four sheets of paper to allow me adequate space to define exactly what I thought of them.

I'm sure they threw my pages in the 'round file'– also known as the waste basket – but it made me feel happier to unload.

For one thing, I was still royally pissed off about their throwing me in the jug when I was at Mare Island, just for standing up for myself and stating an obvious, simple truth.

It was, after all, my final chance during my military career to tell it like it really was . . . versus telling them what they wanted to hear.

Chapter 38

Disengaged

. . . and Freedom

I finally got out of the Navy on November 4th, 1945, and took a nice long vacation at 2544 Franklin with my mother, grandmother and Basque relatives. They eagerly welcomed me back, but they did let me know that even though I was disengaged from the Navy, my chores and garbage duty at home were immediately reinstated upon my return.

Then I went to Reno to visit with my dad and Louise. While there, I applied to the University of Nevada at Reno to request a transer to UNR from Cal Berkeley before returning to the Bay Area. The university accepted me for the coming semester. I was glad about this because UNR had a much better mining engineering course than Berkeley since they specialized in underground mines. Cal, at that time, was beginning to concentrate almost solely on the recovery of oil.

The opportunity to spend that Christmas at the conclusion of the war with my family in San Francisco was very meaningful to me. During my years in the military, even with the occasional visits, I really missed spending time with them.

The next day, December 26th, 1945, was the end of my 25th year, otherwise known as my First Quarter Century, which brings me nearly to the end of my story, but not quite. I have just a couple final thoughts to reveal, and they are these:

Our immediate family was lucky during the war years. Jack took a long "vacation" in Germany, sampling German wine; George got to "visit" some of the Army's finest hospitals because of an ear problem. So in reality, I was the only one who was actually "shot at," even though it was at the hands of an inept Chilean pilot, which I was none too thrilled about.

After all, whatever the circumstances, a bullet is a bullet.

While I did have many good, interesting, even memorable experiences with some of the dedicated officers, coaches, and especially my friends and fellow pilots in the military, I feel compelled to state for the record that it was a not always a pleasant experience . . . not by a long shot.

Although there were a number of great instructors in the Navy, there was also a group of not-so-entertaining officers who I learned to dislike with a passion. I daresay those who served in the military will know exactly the kind of men and untold stories to which I refer.

I'm just telling it like it was, something I've done all my life, in all aspects of my life.

So in the end, I will say this about my years in the Navy.

At least I learned how to fly!

Lloyd Root

Published: December, 2009, on the occasion of my 90th birthday

A Final Note

With a birth date of 1919, I was born closer to the end of the Civil War than to today. Three of my grandparents were born either before, or during the Civil War, and my parents were born less than 30 years after the end of the Civil War. Consequently, my ancestors and other role models had values more in tune with the late 1800s than the early 20th Century.

As a child and young man, I was raised under a distinct ethnic influence – a strong Basque upbringing by my family – as well as exposure to diverse multi-cultural influences in my neighborhood. Then, too, I lived during the era when the major industries in the raw, open and majestic State of California were mining, ranching, farming and fishing. People worked physically hard, and cared deeply about their family, and their country.

What an interesting quarter century to have been alive. I have lived a good life with friends and family who I have treasured. I want all of them—wherever they are now—to know how much I appreciate them.

Even though they say "You only live once," I've proved them wrong. After writing this book, I feel like I've actually lived it a couple times. And what an adventure it's been!

Afterword

I hope you enjoyed reading this book about the first part of my life. My writing experience has been especially meaningful and gratifying to me because a few years ago I had a health challenge. As a result, I was unable to speak clearly and had problems with recognizing words. Using a dictionary was a killer. For a homework project, a professional suggested that I should try to write about my early life and recollections as a method of restoring my speech.

Now, 5 years later, I can finally say I've finished my homework, and have successfully completed my assignment!

Acknowledgements

I want to thank Chloe Rounsley, the writer, book editor and designer who helped bring my story to life. Her guidance, enthusiasm, and expertise helped make this book a reality.

*   *   *

Without my wife Diane, I wouldn't have completed this book. She took my dictation, corrected my mistakes, and endured stories of old girlfriends.

We have enjoyed life together continuously for over 35 years and the love just grows and grows. Diane is a beautiful woman in more ways than one. She is a keeper!

Telling it Like it Was

Appendix

Chapter 1
California Gold Rush
   http://en.wikipedia.org/wiki/California_Gold_Rush
John Greenwood, Greenwood, (North Central) California
   http://www.usneighbor.org/Greenwood2.htm
 El Dorado County, California history
   http://www.westernlivingcenter.com/history/history-greenwood.
   htm
   History of Placer and Nevada Counties, California (historical volume)
Hollister Free Lance Newspaper articles, including May 19, 1903 issue
Ranch of the Three John's
   Home Away from Home by Jeronima Echeverria, University of Nevada
   Press, 1999
Census reports, including 1900, 1910
Various historical family documents

Chapter 2
San Francisco
   City of San Francisco and it's Vicinities - 1852 map from a
   Trigenmetrical Survey
San Francisco earthquake and fire
   Elvira Root's personal account of the earthquake, handwritten at the
   request of her son, the author (when she was 90 years old)
   http//earthquake.usgs.gov/regional/nca/1906/18april/index/
   http://earthquake.usgs.gov/regional/nca/1906/18april/index/
   casualties.php
The Great 1906 San Francisco Earthquake -The worst natural
disaster in U.S. history (by Chris Frantz)
   http://www.infoplease.com/spot/sanfran1906earthquake.html
The Great Shake:San Francisco, 1906; article by Ellen Klages
   www.exploratorium.edu/faultline/great/1906/1906_7.html
The California Earthquake of April 18, 1906 (introduction from
the Carnegie Report, reprinted in 1969)
   http://www.eas.slu.edu/Earthquake_Center/1906EQ/

http://en.wikipedia.org/wiki/1906_San_Francisco_earthquake
A Seismogram of the 1906 Earthquake
  http://earthquake.usgs.gov/regional/nca/1906/18april/
  seismogram.php
Timeline of the San Francisco Earthquake, April 18-23, 1906
  Excerpted online from *Chronology of The Great Earthquake,*
  and the 1906-1907 Graft Investigations, by Gladys Hansen
  http://www.sfmuseum.org/hist10/06timeline.html
Photographs of: huge crowds on Market Street watching fire,
  damaged buildings at Third and Market, damage along the
  water front near the Ferry buildings , buildings destroyed
  around Union square, and many more historic photographs at:
The Virtual Museum of the City of San Francisco
  http://www.sfmuseum.org/1906/photos/html
The Bancroft Library, A State of Emergency: Martial Law
Proclamation by the Mayor E.E. Schmitz, April 18, 1906
  http:bancroft.berkeley, edu/collections/earthquakeandfire/
  exhibit/room03_item04.html
E.H. Harriman
From *Mr. Swan's Big Idea* by David Alan Vasquez, SoPo Press, 2009.
(from *The Life and Legend of E.H. Harriman* by Maury Klein, University
of North Carolina Press, 2000).

Chapter 3
Stanford University
  http://www.stanford.edu/about/history/
Leland Stanford, Stanford University
  http://en.wikipedia.org/wiki/Stanford_University
William Randolph Hearst
  http://www.zpub.com/sf/history/willh.html
  http://en.wikipedia.org/wiki/William_Randolph_Hearst
  http://www.hearstcastle.org/history/william_r_hearst.asp
George Hearst
  http://en.wikipedia.org/wiki/George_Hearst
Charles Adrian Baum, "Spider Baum"
  http://www.spiderbaum.com

'Spider's Family' by Mark Morris (information about Spider's career Mark Morris also provided family photos of Adrienne Baum and George Washington Root from the Morris Family Collection)

Robert LeRoy Ripley

http:en-wikipedia.org/wiki/Robert_Ripley

Elihu Root, United States Senator from New York

http://www.britannica.com/nobel/micro/510_1.html

http://en.wikipedia.org/wiki/Elihu_Root

http://nobelprize.org/nobel_prizes/peace/laureate/1912/root-bio.html

http://college.hmco.com/history/readerscomp/gahff/html/ff_157900_rootelihu.thm

Chapter 4

1915 World's Fair; Panama-Pacific International Exposition

http://www.moah.org/exhibits/archives/1915/

http://en.wikipedia.org/wiki/Panama-Pacific_International_Exposition

http://www.nps.gov/goga/planyourvisit/upload/PPIE_1915_0304.pdf

Lincoln Beachey, Aviator

http://en-wikipedia.org/wiki/Lincoln_J._Beachey

http://www.centennialofflight.gov/essay/Explorers_Record_Setters_and_Daredevils/early_exhibition/EX7.htm

Chapter 5

Mapa de la Republica de Mexico

Durango, Mexico

http://en.wikipedia.org/wiki/Durango

Pancho Villa

http://historicaltextarchives.com/

http://en.wikipedia.org/wiki/Panch_Villa

http://www.mexconnect.com/articles/1305-francisco- pancho-villa

http://www.popsubculture.com/pop/bio_project/pancho_villa.thm

Chapter 6

Prohibition, the 18th Amendment, the Volstead Act
  http://history1900s.about.com/od/1920s/p/prohibition.htm
  http://en-wikipedia.org/wiki/Prohibition_in_the_United_States
Wine making in California
  http://en-wikipedia.org/wiki/History_of_California_wine
  http://en-wikipedia.org.wiki/California_wine
Joseph Strauss, Chief Engineer, the Golden Gate Bridge
  http://www.pbs.org/wgbh/amex/goldengate/peopleevents/p_
  strauss.html
  http://en.wikipedia.org/wiki/Joseph_Strauss/(engineer)
The Virtual Museum of the City of San Francisco
  http://www.sfmuseum.org/hist10/ggbridgeing.html
  http://en.wikipedia.org/wiki/Golden_Gate_Bridge

Chapter 11

Charles Lindbergh
  http://www.acepilots.com/lindbergh.html
  http://www.charleslindbergh.com/history/index.asp
The U.S.S. Akron and the U.S.S. Macon
  http://www.montereybaynoaa.gov/research/macon/macon.html
Nevada County Gold
  http://www.ncgold.com/History/EmpireMine/hisotry.html
William Bourn, Filoli Estate, Empire Gold Mine
(now Empire Gold Mine State Park)
http://www.ghosttownexplorers.org/California/empire/em-
piremine.htm
Historic photographs of ore carts, men going down into the mines
on skips, mules at work, and Pelton wheel:
  http://www.778.com/sights/empire
To view one of the garden pools at Filoli: http://en-wikipedia.org/
wiki/Filoli

Chapter 12
Lyman Gilmore, Grass Valley miner, engineer & pioneering aviator
  http://Sierranevadavirtualmuseum.com/docs/specialex/
  biographies/gilmorel. htm
Lyman Gilmore - Aviation Pioneer
  http://www.ncngrrmuseum.org

Chapter 13
The Red Baron, Manfred von Richthofen
   http:www.acepilots.com/wwi/ger_richthofen.thml
Max Immelmann
  http://en.wikipedia.org/wiki/Max_Immelmann
  http://www.acepilots.com/wiwi/ger_immelmann.html
Stanford March "Come Join the Band" (official fight song)
  lyrics by screen-writer Aurania Ellerbeck Rouverol (a Stanford stu
  dent at that time); set to Robert Browne Hall's New Colonial March.
  http:/en-wikipedia.org/wiki/Come_Join_The_Band

Chapter 14
Wall Street Stock Market Crash
  www. http://en.wikipedia.org/wiki/Wall_Street_Crash_of_1929
what is a dollar worth
http://www.minneapolisfed.org/Research/data/us/calc The
Great Depression
  http://en.wikipedia.org/wiki/Great_Depression
the Price of gold in 1933
  http://www.finfacts.com/Private/curency/goldmarket
  price.htm (note: they spell currency with just one 'r')
The Bonus Army
  http://www.eyewitnesstohistory.com/pfsnprelief4/htm
The Lindbergh kidnapping
  http://en-wikipedia.org/wiki/Lindbergh_kidnapping
  San Francisco Chronicle, From the Archives, May 13, 1932
Lindbergh's Baby found dead (May 13, 2009 edition) Archived

Chapter 15
Amelia Earhart
  http://news.nationalgeographic.com/news/2003/12/1215_
  031215_ameliaearhart.html
  http://en.wikipedia.org/wiki/Amelia_Earhart
Lawrence Tibbett
  http://en-wikipedia.org/wiki/Lawrence_Tibbett

Chapter 18
Adolf Hitler
  http://en-wikipedia.org/wiki/Adolf_Hitler

Chapter 20
Golden Gate Bridge
  http://en-wikipedia.org/wiki-Golden_Gate_Bridge
Bay Bridge
  http://www.dot.ca.gov/hq/esc/tollbridge/SFOBB/Sfobbfacts
  html
  http://en.wikipedia.org/wiki/San_Francisco_-_Oakland_Bay_
  bridge
Harry Bridges, union leader, waterfront riots, Bloody Thursday
  http://www.sfmuseum.org/hist/thursday.html
  http://en.wikipedia.org/wiki/Harry_Bridges

Chapter 21
Nome, Alaska
  http://en-wikipedia.org/wiki/Nome,_Alaska
  http://www.nmoealaska.org/
Plot Map (Lloyd Root, Sr., surveyed Nome after the 1934 fire)
  http?/www.tomsnome.com/nomephot.html

Chapter 25
http://www.lib.berkeley..edu.CHEM/Hilde.thml

Chapter 29
Lt. Col. Doolittle
  http://en.wikipedia.org/wiki/Jimmy_Doolittle
  (from *I Could Never Be So Lucky Again*, by James Doolittle Random
  House, 2009)

LaVergne, TN USA
04 February 2010
172015LV00001B/2/P